2-16-62

2-16-62

FOUNDATIONS
FOR A
PHILOSOPHY
OF
CHRISTIAN EDUCATION

LAWRENCE C. LITTLE

FOUNDATIONS

FOR A

PHILOSOPHY OF

CHRISTIAN EDUCATION

NEW YORK   ABINGDON PRESS   NASHVILLE

FOUNDATIONS FOR A PHILOSOPHY OF CHRISTIAN EDUCATION

Copyright © 1962 by Abingdon Press

Library of Congress Catalog Card Number: 62-7440

SET UP, PRINTED, AND BOUND BY THE
PARTHENON   PRESS,   AT   NASHVILLE,
TENNESSEE, UNITED STATES OF AMERICA

DEDICATED

to my wife

KATHERINE McKENZIE LITTLE

without whose constant encouragement
and assistance
this book could never have been completed.

Foreword

This book has grown out of the experience of a lifetime devoted largely to teaching courses in the theory of character education, the philosophy of religious education, and closely related fields, first in a church-related college of liberal arts and later in the department of religious education in a university.

Students enrolled in these courses have represented two groups whose background and interests have been sometimes widely divergent. First there have been those whose special training has been confined largely to psychology, the social sciences, and general education, and whose contacts with theology and religious education have been marginal and often quite superficial. A second group has consisted of clergymen, directors of religious education, and students who were preparing for professional leadership in the field of religion. Many of these have been graduates of theological seminaries but they have had only a smattering of knowledge of psychology and education.

As these groups have studied together, they have found an increasing bond of common interest and the gaps between their former areas of specialization have been progressively overcome. This experience has convinced the writer that the development of an adequate philosophy of Christian education has been impeded by the lack of communication between specialists in the behavioral sciences and theology and that an acceptable philosophy must rest upon foundations that combine in proper balance the legitimate insights that come from both fields. This book seeks to point in the direction of the needed synthesis.

Although intended primarily as a textbook in the philosophy of Christian education in theological seminaries and in college and university departments of religious education, the book should prove of interest and value to pastors, directors of religious education, church-school officers and teachers, and the general reader who seeks to find the basis for a better understanding of human nature and its capacities for moral and spiritual growth.

It should be pointed out, however, that the book is not presented as an *adequate* statement of the philosophy of Christian education. No such statement exists at the present time, and its formulation remains one of the tasks for the future. An effort is made instead to indicate the *foundations* upon which an adequate philosophy must rest and to whet the appetite for further reading and study. If the book accomplishes these results, it will have served its intended purpose.

LAWRENCE C. LITTLE

Contents

Part Three

RELIGIOUS
AND THEOLOGICAL FOUNDATIONS

Part Four

HOW FIRM A FOUNDATION?

PART ONE

Toward New Dimensions in the
Philosophy of Christian Education

I. THE NEED FOR
A MORE ADEQUATE
PHILOSOPHY OF
CHRISTIAN EDUCATION

One of the most crucial needs of the church today is a more adequate philosophy of Christian education. A careful observer of American life will be impressed by the extensive educational effort of the churches. More than half of the children and youth connected with Protestant churches are enrolled in Sunday schools. A majority of their parents depend upon these schools as the principal avenue of religious instruction. Hundreds of thousands of adults devote their time and energy to church-school administration and teaching. Huge investments are involved in denominational publishing houses, and millions of pieces of curriculum materials pour from their presses every week. The church schools are the chief instruments for recruiting and training the future membership of the church. Christian education is undoubtedly the largest single phase of the total work of the churches. It would be difficult to find a church leader who doubts its importance.

It is not at all clear that those who are engaged in these far-flung efforts understand the real nature of their work and the full significance of what they are attempting to do. Many of them pursue their course with a nonchalance that belies any genuine seriousness of purpose. Since they have no definite conception of aim, they are uncertain as to the proper form and content of instruction. And since they have no certain knowledge of results, they cannot see how improvement can be made so that the outcomes could be more productive in terms of the ends sought. Probably most of them do not realize how much depends upon the effectiveness of their work. These understandings depend in large part upon a coherent and valid theory of Christian education.

Among the minimum essentials of an adequate philosophy of Christian education would seem to be dependable knowledge and reasoned conclusions regarding the needs and capacities of human beings, the ways of growth and learning, the nature of Christian faith and its relation to other aspects of life, the mission of the church and its responsibility for Christian nurture, the goals of Christian education, and methods for guiding experience so that the goals may be achieved. The typical church-school teacher has only the haziest notions of what is involved in each of these areas.

The Present Ferment in Educational Philosophy

Christian education is not alone in its need of a more adequate philosophy. The entire field of educational philosophy is in ferment today as perhaps never before in the entire history of education. Catastrophic changes in American society and in the whole world situation are making new demands upon education. The geometric acceleration of physical power in recent years through advances in science and technology has shown the pitiful inadequacy of social controls. The schools are often made the scapegoat for an obvious breakdown in character and morality.

Rapidly accumulating bodies of data bearing upon the nature of personality and the conditions that affect its development suggest the poverty of previous conceptions of human nature. Research in the motivations of human beings has revealed how subtle are the effects of pressures which are not at all a part of formal schooling. Recent discoveries in nuclear physics, the immanent possibility of intercontinental warfare, and the ineptitude of international politics have raised the most serious questions about the future of civilization unless we can find something in which to place our hopes that is more dependable than "other-directed" individuals and "organization men."

In educational circles everywhere there is increasing recognition that we need to re-examine our fundamental presuppositions regarding man and his place in the universe, reassess our values, determine with greater clarity our educational aims and objectives, and make a better use of our resources and procedures in the light of our accepted purposes. Public education has given increasing attention to such consideration in recent years. The more thoughtful leaders in Christian education, likewise, are rethinking the theoretical basis upon which their work should proceed.

Some Occasions for Confusion

That confusion should reign in the area of educational philosophy should not be surprising, for the same applies in the field of philosophy as a whole. One factor that has occasioned confusion is undoubtedly the rapidity of change that has characterized nearly every aspect of life during the last few decades. It is trite to say that the culture of America and of the entire world is passing through the most cataclysmic period of transition in the entire history of mankind.

I recall that, in my boyhood, my father greeted a neighbor with the query, "How is the world this morning?" Whereupon the neighbor replied, "I don't know. I haven't seen the morning paper." This was considered a joke then, but neither of the men could possibly have realized how very appropriate such a remark would be just a generation hence. Sometimes the morning paper is already out of date, and people sit glued to their radios or television sets eager for news that may have far-reaching effects upon their lives and is happening so fast that no newspaper could possibly provide adequate coverage. In times of epoch-making transitions, it is only natural that there should be uncertainty regarding the nature and ends of education.

Another factor contributing to the general confusion has been the vast accumulation of specialized knowledge in practically every field of human interest and the sheer inability of any individual or even group of individuals to piece it all together into a consistent and unified whole. When those of us who are older learned science in secondary school and college, we achieved a smattering of knowledge in most of the fields of science then recognized. This knowledge was presented in neatly organized textbooks, and we were likely to feel that we knew science fairly well if we mastered the content of the textbooks. We found no great difficulty in putting the several parts together into a total view of man and the world that seemed to serve our purposes quite satisfactorily.

The relative simplicity of the science of those days has been enormously complicated by vast discoveries which make necessary the task of rethinking the entire basis upon which our conceptions of the physical universe proceeded. Only one illustration must suffice here. The textbooks in chemistry and physics only a generation ago contained no mention of uranium. But the discovery of nuclear energy

17

has so completely revolutionized our understanding of matter that most of us have had to unlearn much of the natural science we studied in high school and college.

The extension of the more and more highly specialized fields of knowledge has grown so rapidly in recent years that no one can properly claim a complete mastery of even one field, much less of all, and the true expert must admit that preoccupation with his specialty precludes anything more than the most general acquaintanceship with other fields. An adequate philosophy must somehow take into account the dependable findings in all relevant areas of investigation. In fact, sometimes the assumed certainties of one field are almost completely upset by accumulating knowledge in some other specialized area. With the growing need for a comprehensive view come the mounting difficulties of achieving an effective synthesis.

The problem of co-ordinating the results of several branches of inquiry is complicated by the fact that differing assumptions often actuate study and research in the various disciplines. For example, the strictly mechanistic principles that have produced such dramatic results in physics and chemistry are thought by some to be all that are needed in biology, psychology and the social sciences. Moreover, many investigators insist upon the validity of their own presuppositions and conduct their researches without much consideration of the findings of specialists in other fields. Some good examples of the types of conflict that may be occasioned by divergence in fundamental assumptions are the historic controversies between mechanists and vitalists in biology, between behaviorist and hormic psychologists, and between traditional theology and evolutionism.

All of these factors in combination make the problem of formulating an adequate philosophy of education exceedingly complex. Such a philosophy can be based only upon understanding of the needs and capacities of human beings, the nature of culture and its effects upon attitudes and behavior, the values that are sought through education, the purposes and results of instruction, and the ways by which experience may be guided so that the aims may be realized. It is obvious that common agreement is lacking with respect to each of these elements. And none of them remains fixed in our rapidly changing culture.

One of the obvious facts about education is that knowledge gained by formal schooling tends to become obsolescent at an alarming rate. In the confused and complex world in which we find ourselves, one can understand the feelings expressed by the King of Siam in the play, *The King and I*, as he considered the problems involved in ruling a modern nation. He complained that when he was a boy, "What was so was so, what was not was not." But now that he is a man, he says, "Some things were *nearly* so, others nearly not." And in his head were many facts of which he wished he were more certain he was sure! [1] The person who is truly educated today must be able to distinguish between the things that are so and those that are not, and he must revise his views constantly as he discovers that what he once regarded as in the first class really belong in the second. Hence there is increasing emphasis upon the relatively greater importance of implanting the love and pursuit of learning over the content of learning itself.

But many teachers continue to teach innumerable things that are no longer so and they develop in their students the disposition to accept these things as so without critical examination and evaluation. The history of education is replete with illustrations. The old Greek conception of the four elements—earth, air, fire, and water—persisted for centuries after it became clear that reality could not possibly be that simple. Even before the beginning of the Christian Era astronomers had concluded that the earth was spherical in form. Strabo, who was born about 63 B.C., wrote his famous *Geography* on the basis of acceptance of this view. But it was only after Columbus sailed to America, fifteen hundred years later, that the universities stopped teaching that the earth was flat. Unfortunately, we do not have to go back that far to find examples. Much "education" in the recent past has been based upon conceptions of human nature and of learning that cannot stand in the light of modern knowledge.

Formulating a philosophy of education may have seemed fairly simple in other times—when society was stable, for example; when education was regarded as the discipline of a nature that is inherently evil as a result of original sin; when there was general agreement over standards of right and wrong; when instruction was intended chiefly to impart knowledge. But these simple conditions no longer obtain. Today the problem is much more complex, and disagreement over many of the issues makes it even more difficult.

This is not the time nor place to consider the chief philosophies of

[1] Richard Rogers and Oscar Hammerstein II, *The King and I*, in *Six Plays by Rogers and Hammerstein* (New York: Random House, 1951), p. 387.

education that compete for acceptance in our contemporary world. In fact, it is literally impossible to treat within a brief compass all the schemes of classification and all the views that are currently bidding for recognition. Attempts have been made to systematize the study of philosophy of education by organizing it around such time-honored terms in general philosophy as naturalism, idealism, realism, and pragmatism.[2] The main outlines of study have also been subsumed under such terms as progressivism, essentialism, perennialism, and reconstructionism.[3] Some authors have approached the problem by considering the basic issues in contemporary education in the light of certain variant positions with respect to them.[4] While others have focussed attention upon concrete practices in education and have sought to lead to an understanding of these through combining an analysis of historical trends with an examination of the fundamental questions of the nature of man, society, and the learning process.[5] Mere mention of these selected types of approach illustrates the difficulty of exact definition and the lack of a generally accepted philosophy of education.

Contrasting Philosophies of Christian Education

The lack of consensus in the general philosophy of education is paralleled by existing variant philosophies of Christian education. These range all the way from viewpoints that hold to the exclusive authority of the church or the Bible, relegating to a minor place if not actually disparaging the value of other sources, to those that build directly upon the findings of modern science, making whatever concessions may seem necessary to the Bible and to ecclesiastical tradition. Only a few examples of these contrasting philosophies can be cited here. These are given primarily for the purpose of illustrating the fact and the nature of the diversity. The list is by no means exhaustive. At attempt will be made to state each of the approaches sharply in order to show the contrasts, and hence the differences may be somewhat exaggerated. No effort will be made to deal with many points of

---

[2] J. Donald Butler, *Four Philosophies and Their Practice in Education and Religion.* NOTE. Publication data are omitted in all footnotes referring to books listed in the bibliography, pp. 203-32.

[3] Theodore Brameld, *Philosophies of Education in Cultural Perspective* and *Toward a Reconstructed Philosophy of Education.*

[4] John S. Brubacher, *Modern Philosophies of Education* and *Eclectic Philosophy of Education;* Philip H. Phenix, *Philosophy of Education.*

[5] Kenneth H. Hansen, *Philosophy for American Education.*

refinement held by individuals within the general positions outlined.

AUTHORITY OF THE CHURCH. One type of philosophy of Christian education revolves around the concept of an infallible church and is best exemplified perhaps by the one promulgated by Roman Catholic writers. The outlines of this are contained in the decrees of church councils and in papal encyclicals and its elaboration is kept within prescribed limits by the requirement of an imprimatur of some recognized church official in any publication intended for general use.

According to this view, man belongs to two orders, the natural and the supernatural. He is born into a family and depends for his temporal welfare upon the state, both of which are natural orders. He is created by God for the purpose of serving him on earth and attaining eternal salvation, possible only through membership in the church which belongs to the supernatural order and mediates the divine life of grace by means of her sacraments. God has conferred upon the church the right to teach and has granted her infallibility in matters of faith and morals. Her title in the supernatural order gives her a right to education that is absolutely superior to any title in the natural order. The church is therefore the only adequate educational agency. The norms of the Catholic philosophy of education are firmly laid down in the traditions of the church, and all variant philosophies are labelled as false.

The task of Catholic education is to transmit church tradition, to enable pupils to define church doctrines and usages with exactness and to distinguish these from errors and defend them against objections, and to help them to understand and accept the duties imposed by church discipline. There is no need to attempt to accommodate statements of educational philosophy to the findings of empirical science, since the validity of these findings is judged on the basis of their consistency with church doctrines.

The doctrine of an infallible church and its consequent implications for the philosophy of Christian education, although most clearly defined and stoutly defended by the Roman Catholic Church, is by no means confined to this branch of Christendom. The Eastern Orthodox churches are about as firm in their insistence upon the final authority of their ecclesiastical systems, doctrines, and practices.

Protestantism as a movement broke with Catholicism over the claim of the latter that it alone constitutes the true church and substituted the authority of the Bible for the authority of the church. In

21

theory at least, Protestants claim the right of the individual to private interpretation of the Bible. As a matter of fact, however, there have grown up within Protestantism certain systems of biblical interpretation that have become almost as rigid as the system against which the original Protestants rebelled. This problem will be considered later in the discussion of theology as the basis for a philosophy of Christian education.

AUTHORITY OF THE BIBLE. The philosophy of Christian education that is characteristic of Protestant fundamentalism grows out of the idea of an infallible Bible. According to this view, there is a sharp dichotomy between the natural and the supernatural. The Bible, as the Word of God, belongs to the supernatural realm and contains concepts of God and of man that could never have been the products of human experience and reason but the direct revelation of God himself. The Bible alone contains an adequate description of man's nature and needs, depicts his condition of alienation from God, and outlines the means and methods of his redemption and salvation.

Although not all fundamentalists agree upon what the Bible teaches about human nature, most of them agree that all human beings are born in a state of natural depravity and that they are therefore incapable of being saved except by regeneration, a miracle of divine grace. The aim of education is to provide knowledge and guidance so that sinners may be led to repentance and, after their regeneration, to provide for their nurture as Christians. They cannot grow into a regenerated state by natural processes and must avail themselves of the grace of God. The true church is composed only of persons who accept the Bible as the infallible Word of God and who have been supernaturally regenerated. And only the true church can provide Christian education. Education under other auspices may be useful to the natural man; but, since the Bible is the only book that deals adequately with man's supernatural needs, it is basic and constitutes the textbook of Christian education. The content of Christian teaching must at all points be in harmony with the Bible as the authoritative rule and guide for faith and life. The results of scientific investigation are always to be accepted or rejected in accordance with their agreement or disagreement with the Bible.

FAITH IN THE SCIENTIFIC METHOD. At the opposite extreme from philosophies of education that are based upon belief in the supernatural origin and final authority of an infallible church or an infallible Bible are those that stem from implicit faith in the scientific method. Infallible science is perhaps too strong a designation, since proponents of this approach constantly stress the inevitable tentativeness of human knowledge and are likely to be suspicious of any claim to "ultimate truth."

In contrast to the view that final truth can be revealed to man by some source outside himself and that it can be contained in any set of dogmas or in any single collection of writings, holders of this viewpoint stress the importance of a continuing human quest for knowledge through the patient and persistent use of experience, intelligence, and reason. Such terms as "modernism," "liberalism," and "naturalism" are often used to designate the basic position of those who take this approach.

Its proponents are usually wary of any notion of a sharp dichotomy between the natural and the supernatural such as is maintained by those who insist upon the infallibility of either church or Bible. They are unable to accept the validity of the claim of any group of churchmen—*qua* churchmen—that they have a corner on truth through the possession of a body of doctrine; and they point to the wide variety of interpretations that have issued from those who make this claim. They have a firmer confidence in the validity of human experience and reason than do the proponents of an infallible church or an infallible Bible. They stress the changing views regarding the origin and nature of the Bible that have resulted from the use of scientific methods in biblical research. They insist that an understanding of human nature can come from personal experience and observation and from the findings of the behavioral sciences, and they are more likely to turn for this understanding to such fields as psychology and psychiatry than to either church tradition or the Bible. Moreover, they believe that they better understand the nature of the church and of the Bible as a result of anthropological, sociological, and historical studies than do those who assume that these have emanated from supernatural sources and are not proper subjects for scientific investigation. They find no basis in the results of scientific studies for the claim to infallibility for either church or Bible.

Perhaps it should be pointed out that persons who hold such views are not all outside the churches nor are they unacquainted with the Bible. They are not all "secularists" in the sense in which this term is often used. Many have been active churchmen and students of the Bible all of their lives, though their fields of special interest and responsibility have been outside professional theological and ecclesiastical circles.

As previously stated, these contrasting positions have been stated sharply in order that they may be clearly distinguished. There have been many modifications of these basic viewpoints in Christian education literature. It is possible that none of these as stated would be defended *in toto* even by those who identify themselves with one or another approach.

Few leaders of Catholic education would openly dispute any of the points outlined in the paragraphs describing their philosophy, but nevertheless many of them carry on their work and discuss their approaches to education without taking them too seriously. Particularly at the point of insights that come from use of the scientific method, not many would deny that their understandings have been enriched from sources outside ecclesiastical tradition and official pronouncements by the hierarchy.

The main stream of Protestantism, too, has veered away from rigorous insistence upon the literal inerrancy of the Bible in matters of history and the explanation of natural phenomena. Although the term "fundamentalism" still carries a connotation that can be applied appropriately to some Christians, most of the orthodox leaders prefer to be known as "conservatives" rather than as fundamentalists. And most of these have relaxed their rigid insistence upon the absolute authority of the Scriptures at points where the accumulating evidence of science seems to challenge the adequacy of explanations based upon literal interpretations of the Bible. And scientists, at least those familiar with the Christian tradition, are much more sympathetic to the claims of biblical scholars, theologians, and professional church leaders now than they were a generation ago. So the differentiation between those who hold to the pre-eminence of church doctrine, or the Bible, or the scientific method in determining the major orientation of Christian education theory is not as sharp as it used to be.

SECTARIAN THEOLOGY. Reference has been made to the divergent systems of biblical interpretation that have grown up within historic Protestantism. In spite of common allegiance to the Bible, in actual fact partisan systems of theology have become more definitive for many than the text of the Bible. Even within orthodox Protestantism it can hardly be said that there is only one system of doctrine. The "fundamentals" of Christian theology are stated differently by different groups, though each group believes that its own statement is closest to the truths contained in the Bible. Protestantism has split into many sects holding a variety of beliefs and practices. There is no external authority to curb the proliferation of variant theologies, no pope who can become a final arbiter at points of difference. Dissenters cannot be kept in line by a refusal of the *nihil obstat* of an official censor. Hence there have grown up within Protestantism diverse systems of biblical interpretation. And, though most Protestants decry the evils of division and the gaps between the main groupings have been somewhat narrowed by experience in the ecumenical movement, there still exists the specter of sectarianism which is more characteristic of Protestantism than is orthodoxy.

Progress toward any generally accepted philosophy of Christian education has been impeded because of the determination of the various branches to see that their own theologies, their particular understandings of the Bible, of the church, and of Christian education are regulative. Presbyterians have tended to judge statements of educational philosophy on the basis of their consistency with Reformed theology. Baptists have judged them in terms of their own traditional concepts. So also have Episcopalians, Lutherans, Methodists, and all the others.

In the past, the chief sources of theology have been the Bible, the pronouncements of church councils, and the writings of leading theologians of the various sectarian groups. Of these, perhaps the most powerful has been the last named. The writings of Calvin have been regarded as normative for Calvinists, of Luther for Lutherans, of Wesley for Methodists, and so on. These men addressed themselves to the problems of their own generation and they thought of education in terms of the conditions that obtained in their own times. Many of the problems of modern education never came within the compass of their thought. It was but natural that the theologians of succeeding generations, who followed the patterns established by their forefathers, should overlook the nature and prime importance of education.

On the other hand, there have been great advances in understanding of the nature of personality and of learning through the results of study and research in the behavioral sciences and through experimentation in general education. Because church-school leaders have been faced with the necessity of moving ahead in their educational tasks, many of them have turned for insight to these new sources, sometimes to the serious neglect of the Bible and theology. The most widely influential statements of the philosophy of Christian education in the recent past have been dominated by concepts arising out of the behavioral sciences and secular education.

This has resulted in an unfortunate dichotomy between theology and Christian education. Theologians typically have reacted to this situation by charging that Christian education has become "humanistic" or "naturalistic," and that therefore it is no longer a fitting instrument for fulfilling the mission of the church. Educators have countered with the charge that theology is so abstract that it is practically irrelevant in educational operations. This lack of communication between theology and education has resulted in the impoverishment of both fields of endeavor. And it has undoubtedly retarded the development of an adequate philosophy of Christian education. It is imperative that the breach be healed if the churches are to meet their full responsibilities in the difficult days that lie ahead.

II. SOME PROMISING
CURRENT TENDENCIES

The previous chapter was concerned with the need for a more adequate philosophy of Christian education and with some of the factors that have made progress toward its achievement difficult. It seems proper to turn now to a consideration of some recent trends and current tendencies that show greater promise for the future.

Improved Status of Christian Education

Christian education has moved from the position of an orphan in the household of faith to that of an honored member of the church family. The older professional leaders in religious education may recall the struggles that went on three or four decades ago to gain recognition for education as one of the essential ministries of the church. At a time when most denominations were expanding their programs and enlarging their staffs in such departments as evangelism, missions, and stewardship, only grudging support was accorded to Christian education. Little notice was given to education in the typical theological seminary, in which future church leaders were being trained. As a consequence, thousands of pastors took charge of local parishes with little knowledge of the learning process and with practically no understanding of the fundamental principles of education. They were thus poorly equipped to give assistance and guidance to their church-school workers. These followed traditional patterns of instruction with little attempt at improvement. Rare indeed was the church that employed a trained director of religious education. It is little wonder someone felt that the Sunday school is "the most wasted hour of the week." And it was the common assumption that Christian education happens only during this hour—all the other activities of the church were considered something else.

All of this has changed radically in the last decade or so. Practically every denomination now has a well-staffed department of Christian education, its leaders comparably equipped with those in other departments. Theological seminaries generally have raised religious education from a subordinate position, usually in the department of "practical theology," and have given it a place of its own, with the same status in most instances as departments of biblical history and literature, church history, and systematic theology. Graduates of theological seminaries now rarely complete their seminary studies without at least some introduction to the psychology and sociology of religion, educational psychology, and Christian education. Their training often includes practice and supervision in church-school work. A number of leading universities have established departments of religious education in which hundreds of theological seminary graduates are continuing their study.

More churches are seeking directors of religious education than can find qualified persons to fill the positions. In an increasing number of churches where directors are employed, they are given the title of "minister of education," and they enjoy equal rank with colleagues whose energies are devoted primarily to preaching and the "pastoral" ministry. Efforts are constantly being made to improve the quality of church-school teaching through leadership education. Although the time devoted to religious instruction is much too limited, the time that is so utilized is far from wasted. And there is a growing realization that Christian education is much more than Bible study once a week—that it is indeed the functional aspect of all the activities of the church and therefore requires the co-ordinated effort and support of all the members, organizations, and agencies of the church. It is but natural that a field so well established should seek a better rationale for its work.

The Growth of Protestant Co-operation

One of the phenomenal aspects of Christian education in recent years has been the increasing measure of participation in co-operative activities by the educational boards and agencies within the various denominations of Protestantism. The World Council of Christian Education has become an important agency of Protestant co-operation throughout the world. The Division of Christian Education of the National Council of Churches (formerly the International Council of Religious Education) is one of the strongest divisions of this interdenominational body. Practically every state in the union has its State Council of Christian Education, and there are thousands of district and city councils in which leaders of a wide variety of ecclesiastical and theological orientations are able to move together toward the improvement of their educational ministries.[1]

The principal emphasis in the work of these agencies has been upon service rather than ideology, but attention has been called again and again to the importance of "educational and theological foundations" for their work. As early as 1940, the International Council published a statement of basic philosophy [2] which enjoyed wide popularity. In 1944, the council established a study committee to inquire into the present status of Christian education; and this committee was specifically directed to take account of the necessary adjustments in the program of Christian education to meet the requirements of the changing world situation and the need for a considered statement regarding "the place of theological *and other concepts* in Christian education." [3]

In presenting its report, the study committee stated:

The foundations of Christian education are to be found in the nature and condition of man who is to be educated, in the faith which the church professes, and in the principles of education which define how learning takes place. These may be examined separately, but the findings from such study will be intimately interrelated in the resulting Christian education.[4]

The chapter on "The Foundations of Christian Education" contains sections on the nature of man, the faith of the church, principles of educational procedure, and implications for educational practice.[5] Thus the need for combining the theological and educational approaches in an adequate philosophy of Christian education was recognized and clearly stated. The report of the committee marks a notable advance in the effort to provide the statement of such a philosophy.

During the fifteen years that have intervened since the publication of this report, however, many changes have taken place in theological thought and in concepts of education. It would seem

[1] William C. Bower and Percy R. Hayward, *Protestantism Faces Its Educational Task Together.*
[2] *Christian Education Today.*
[3] Paul H. Vieth (ed.), *The Church and Christian Education*, p. 7. Italics supplied.
[4] *Ibid.*, p. 52.
[5] *Ibid.*, chapter II.

therefore that the "foundations" should be periodically reconsidered in the light of these changes. Although the study committee rendered an outstanding service at a time when there was little recognition of the importance of combining theology and education, the question may now be raised whether or not it was entirely successful because of the difficulty of the task and whether its report can be regarded as definitive for our present time.

A careful reading of the report will reveal that its phraseology is dominated by theological terms prevalent at that time; and that education, as such, played a much less important part in the considerations of the committee than did theology. The report is undoubtedly weighted on the side of theological as contrasted with educational concepts. This was perhaps inevitable under the circumstances and because of the constitution of the membership of the committee, which was made up for the most part of leaders whose backgrounds were primarily theological. Anthropologists, psychologists, sociologists, and specialists in the practices and philosophy of general education were notable by their absence. If a philosophy of Christian education is really to combine the valid insights of theology regarding the nature of the Christian faith with a proper understanding of human nature and of learning, it can hardly neglect the contributions that specialists in these fields have made. If the original intention of the study committee is to be fully realized, its work must be continued and the results frequently re-examined and evaluated.

Since the publication of the report of the study committee, cooperative Protestantism has shown an increasing willingness to establish and maintain communication with specialists in fields other than theology. For example, the programs of the annual meetings of the Division of Christian Education of the National Council of Churches include each year many addresses and papers presented by specialists in other disciplines. A recent meeting of the Professors and Research Section was devoted largely to problems of communication between theology and the behavioral sciences. Such facts speak well for the future development of the philosophy of Christian education.

Constructive Contributions of Individual Leaders

When I began teaching a course in the principles of character and religious education thirty years ago, there were few good books dealing with this subject. As compared with the resources available to my colleagues in the department of philosophy, my own were so meager that I tended always to be apologetic. About the only usable text-books were Bushnell's *Christian Nurture* (1847) and Coe's *A Social Theory of Religious Education* (1917).

There began in the 1930's an increasing stream of constructive and relevant materials. Giants like William Clayton Bower, Ernest J. Chave, George A. Coe, Harrison S. Elliott, Hugh Hartshorne, Herman H. Horne, Lewis J. Sherill, Theodore Soares and Luther A. Weigle looked at religious education from the joint standpoint of their experience as churchmen and their knowledge of general education and they provided individual statements of educational philosophy that still stand as monuments to their genius and insight in spite of the corroding effects of time and change.[6] Younger leaders like Frank Gaebelein, Ernest Ligon, Harry Munro, Randolph Miller, Paul Vieth, Campbell Wyckoff—and many others—have contributed their share. Journals like *The Christian Century, The International Journal of Religious Education, Religious Education,* and *Religion in Life,* and a host of denominational publications have added to the store. So there is now a sizable body of theoretical and philosophical literature as grist for the mill of those who seek to develop a more adequate philosophy. Perhaps each reader should be on his guard against premature partisanship, else he will miss some of the insights that each writer has contributed. But no longer need one feel apologetic about his resources if he attempts to guide study in the philosophy of Christian education.

Research and Experimentation in
Character and Religious Education

Another of the promising current tendencies in Christian education is the willingness of leaders to make wider use of the results of research and experimentation in efforts to extend knowledge and increase understanding of the nature of personality, the learning process, character development and religious education. They are no longer content with the meager treatment of these problems in traditional sources and are turning for pertinent data to research journals and other current scholarly publications.

The National Council of Churches has a well-established Department of Research and Survey which makes a continuing and valuable contribution to available knowledge in many fields related to religious

---

[6] The publications of these authors which are pertinent to the present study are listed in the bibliography.

education. Its biweekly publication, *Information Service,* is almost a "must" for those who seek to keep informed about current developments in religion. Several of the denominational boards and state councils have organized departments of research. The recently established Religious Research Association is designed to provide a channel of communication between religious leaders and scientists in related fields.

Because space here is necessarily limited, and because reference to research findings will be made many times throughout the remainder of this book, no further discussion of this area is attempted here. But the range of the available resources may be suggested by stating that in a recent compilation of the titles of relevant doctoral dissertations completed in America universities, a total of more than six thousand was found to deal with problems of character and religious education.[7] This does not include, of course, the thousands of masters' theses and journal articles that are quite pertinent.

Some Current Trends in Theology

The previous chapter referred to the former rigidity of sectarian systems of theology and held that the assumption of finality on the part of the proponents of the various systems had impeded the growth of an adequate philosophy of Christian education. There are some current tendencies in Christian theology, however, that show promise of reversing the negative trend and of making possible more constructive contributions toward the development of a theory of Christian education.

TOWARD AN ECUMENICAL THEOLOGY. One of these tendencies has been a growing interest among theologians in finding areas of agreement in their conceptual systems and a diminishing zeal for defending differences. The ecumenical movement has provided a framework of common experience and fellowship in which particularities are being lost in a growing unity, an atmosphere in which it seems increasingly possible to blend historic forms of interpretation into understandings which include but transcend them all. Participation in the ecumenical movement has enabled many theologians to recognize the limitations of their own particular systems. Statements of the Christian faith that have been worked out through the collabo-

---

[7] Lawrence C. Little (compiler), *Bibliography of Doctoral Dissertations in Character and Religious Education* (Pittsburgh: The Department of Religious Education, University of Pittsburgh, 1960).

ration of devoted men of various sectarian persuasions seem richer and broader in application than those that smack too much of narrow exclusivism. This does not mean that they are trying to find a least common denominator nor denying the fact of differences, but they are determined in their efforts to respect one another and to move together toward deeper understandings. In this new climate, there has been a "return to theology" throughout Protestantism, in which laymen as well as clergymen have shared, and this movement has profoundly affected thinking about Christian education. One leading Christian educator has held that theology is the "clue" to Christian education and he makes it the basis for his philosophy of Christian education.[8]

BIBLICAL THEOLOGY. Another trend in recent theology has been a growing interest in biblical theology, which takes into account new understandings of the origins and nature of the Bible that have grown out of the results of modern historical and critical scholarship. Studies in this field have enabled theologians to distinguish between the permanent truth contained in the biblical revelation and the mythological elements embodied in the account of the revelation. This has saved them from the necessity of defending a literal biblicism in order to maintain the authority of the Bible and to appropriate its meaning for men and women today.

The proponents of biblical theology hold that the essentials of the Gospel are applicable to the people of every age, to men of modern science as well as to the ancients who were creatures of a very different cultural situation. Moreover, these essentials are distinguishable from expositions of theologians of the past, conditioned as they were by the thought patterns of their day. As these studies have proceeded, the relation between revelation and knowledge gained through scientific investigation is seen more clearly, and the gap between theology and science seems less abrupt.

Biblical theology is still in a very fluid condition and statements made by scholars in this field vary widely.[9] Some of the current outlines seem overly simplified and others are strangely reminiscent of schema provided by expositors in the past. But there seems increasing

---

[8] Randolph C. Miller, *The Clue to Christian Education.*

[9] Among the outlines of biblical theology that should be of interest to Christian educators are: Miller Burrows, *An Outline of Biblical Theology;* Randolph C. Miller, *Biblical Theology and Christian Education;* Stephen Neill, *Christian Faith Today;* and G. Ernest Wright, *God Who Acts: Biblical Theology as Recital.*

agreement that the "abiding truths" contained in the Bible may be distinguished from the "changing categories" in which these truths are expressed. This insight should furnish new incentives to Bible study and should enable Christian education to use the Bible more effectively.

THEOLOGY IN COMMUNICATION WITH OTHER DISCIPLINES. The content of theology has been improved through a better understanding of the principles of effective communication. The nature of the physical universe is better understood by theologians as they become familiar with the findings of the natural sciences. Human behavior is less of an enigma because of the contributions of the behavioral sciences. Understanding of the Bible has been enlarged through the work of historians, philologists and archaeologists. Truths from all fields are increasingly recognized as parts of one truth, God's truth. Dogmatic assertions of finality on the part of either a theologian or a scientist appear today as inept and inexcusable. Increased comprehension of the whole of reality through interdisciplinary communication and co-operative study should be of great benefit to Christian education.

Some Counter Tendencies

It would be untrue, of course, and quite unrealistic to suggest that these tendencies are universal and that there are no counter tendencies. There are many churches whose programs of Christian education are so archaic that they are about as suited to our times as Noah's ark would be for modern navigation. There are so-called directors of religious education who are little more than flunkies for their pastors. There are pastors with whom competent directors find it very difficult to work. The status of many directors is hardly one of equality. There are still a few theological seminaries whose intellectual diets are sadly lacking in most of the vitamins that can be supplied by contemporary knowledge.

Not all denominations take responsible parts in the ecumenical movement. Some agencies, in fact, seem to find their *raison d'être* in actively opposing the National Council and the World Council of Churches. Some theologians talk as though they were God, and with whom scientists find it difficult if not impossible to carry on effective dialogue. There are also scientists who are so enmeshed in their own specialities that they cannot talk to those in other disciplines. Some of them have gone to church so seldom that they simply do not know what has been going on in religion. The existence of all of these must be taken into account in assessing the present status of Christian education and the possibility of developing an adequate philosophy. But the tendencies described in the foregoing sections of this chapter are not illusory. They are real, and they portend greater hope for the future.

Toward a Wider Perspective   1177957

One of the hopeful signs in the current situation is the fact that the leaders of Christian education are increasingly aware of their weaknesses and are beginning to seek knowledge and understanding from whatever sources seem to be relevant. They recognize that proper consideration should be given to both historic formulations and current trends in theology. But they also understand the inherent limitations of theology. One of the points at which there is demand for a more inclusive view is human nature with its complex needs and potentialities. Another is the type of education that is suited to these needs and capacities. Theology cannot furnish all the data required for an understanding of human beings, their motivations, the impact of cultural forces, and the changes in behavior that come about through growth and maturation. Theology has practically nothing to say about the actual processes of human development nor the ways in which the curriculum can be adapted to varying needs and capabilities. It cannot help much in determining the immediate goals of the educational process. These and other requisite insights must come from other disciplines. Anthropology, biology, psychology, sociology, general education and other fields that might be mentioned provide data that supplement the picture of man that comes from theology.

Thoughtful leaders of Christian education are aware of the complexities of the work in which they are engaged and to which they are committed. They welcome understandings from whatever sources they may come. One of the requirements of an adequate philosophy of Christian education for today is a synthesis of the knowledge about human beings and the ways they learn that comes from "secular" sources and that which comes specifically from the Christian heritage. And this synthesis must be stated in a way that can be understood and appropriated by the workers who are engaged in the actual processes of Christian education from day to day.

III. COMPONENTS OF
A PHILOSOPHY OF
CHRISTIAN EDUCATION

Several elements are necessary in an adequate philosophy of Christian education and these must be blended together in such a way as to make a coherent whole. Many current statements are faulty in that they either omit important components or they patch these together in a sort of hotchpotch that aids very little in an understanding of the total process.

It is not my purpose to attempt a complete philosophy, but merely to discuss some of the foundations upon which such should rest. It may be helpful at the beginning, however, to suggest some of the many facets of the total problem, so that these may be seen in proper perspective, even though detailed consideration may be given to only a few. Because of the complexity of the problem it seems unlikely that any one individual could frame a satisfactory statement of a total philosophy of Christian education at the present time. Some reasons for this difficulty were pointed out in the preceding chapter. Others will be suggested as this study proceeds.

Christian education is a two-sided term and implies that there are at least two points of reference that should be kept in mind and brought into proper relationship to each other.

It is *education* and therefore it involves the elements that are naturally included in a consideration of the persons who are being educated and what happens to them in the educational process. It is *Christian* and this fact gives it a special orientation and a new dimension. A certain body of experience and set of values, a particular way of looking at persons and at the aims of education are necessarily in-

36

volved in Christian education and these must be taken into account. At many points Christian education differs very little from good education of any kind. But at certain points it is distinctive. There can be no adequate understanding of Christian education unless the elements common to all education are recognized and the characteristics that distinguish Christian education are identified.

Theory of Personality ("Image of Man")

Since Christian education is a ministry to persons, like all other education it must rest upon some understanding of the nature of personality. Education of whatever kind is aimed at human beings and it can accomplish its purposes only to the degree that it is related significantly to their interests, needs and capabilities.

One of the reasons why the general philosophy of education is so confused at the present time is the fact that writers in this field have not been able to keep abreast of the rapidly accumulating data on personality and its development that have been assembled in recent years by investigators in the behavioral sciences. Current philosophies of education are limited either by the fact that they have been derived deductively from the general philosophical positions of the writers, without too much consideration of empirical data, or that they are based too largely upon findings from a specialized area of investigation to the neglect of relevant data from other areas. The philosophy of Christian education is similarly lacking because it has been based largely upon church tradition and theological considerations to the comparative neglect of data from general education and from anthropology, psychology, and sociology.

A satisfactory theory of personality must include a dependable account of the biological and constitutional factors that enter into "original" human nature, the effects of maturation and of interactions with the environment, the innate and acquired "drives" that motivate the behavior of the individual, and the effects upon behavior of the manner in which individuals are able to achieve their goals in the midst of the circumstances in which they find themselves. It must take into account the wide differences that result from varying combinations of the several elements which enter into the making of a given personality. Data that may aid in reaching these understandings come from a variety of sources and await an effective synthesis. This problem is one of the central concerns of this book.

Theory of Learning and of Human Development

Christian education is posited upon the assumption that change and growth are possible and desirable and, like all other education, it requires some understanding of the processes of human development. It is easy to find illustrations of church-school practices that grow out of faulty conceptions of how growth takes place. Children are sometimes treated as if they were adults, with little consideration of their changing needs and capabilities from birth to maturity. They are sometimes taught as if the mere accumulation of factual knowledge about the Bible and of church doctrines were all that is needed in Christian growth. Frequently the members of a group are all treated alike, with little concern for the differing problems of individuals that arise out of the varying circumstances under which they live. Sometimes education is used as a means of discipline, under the apparent conviction that bad children are thereby made good. A better understanding of the principles of growth might help to obviate such blunders.

An adequate approach to the problems of human development must be based upon an understanding of the learning process. Great advances have been made toward this understanding by scientific studies of human learning during the last half century, carried on primarily by psychologists but increasingly recognized by professional educators as having important bearings upon their work. Educational psychology is now generally recognized as a foundation science upon which to base educational practice.

The accumulation of data bearing upon the learning process has been so rapid and extensive that so far it has proved impossible to piece it all together into one fully satisfactory theory of learning. It now appears that the formulation of such a theory may remain as an uncompleted task for a long time. There are a number of current theories that compete for acceptance, and these must be subjected to further critical study and experimental verification. In the meantime the fullest possible use should be made of the insights that have emerged from efforts to understand learning and the conditions that affect it.

Learning involves more than the mere acquisition of factual information. Indeed, the learning of facts may be impeded by physiological and psychological conditions unrelated to the subject matter presented. The whole child, not just his mind as an isolated fragment of his total being, undergoes change in every successive experience.

38

Hence our concept of learning must be broad enough to include such seemingly diversified aspects as control over the emotions, the development of motor skills, the perceptive functions, the processes of conceptualization and of comprehension, the ability to solve problems, and the acquisition of attitudes and ideals. These overlap and interpenetrate. Over-simplication will inevitably result in misleading interpretations of the learning process.

It is important to consider the stages or phases in the developmental process. Growth does not occur in a uniform fashion but dominant features during certain periods may differ from those in others. There are "developmental tasks" [1] associated with childhood that are markedly different from those characteristic of adolescence or adulthood. Not only so, but individuals within the various age ranges differ considerably in the achievement of the developmental tasks generally associated with their respective age groups. An adequate concept of development must take these differences into account.

Certain external conditions and types of relationships are more conducive to wholesome personal development than others. Many forms of abnormal conduct are now recognized as being the results of undesirable environmental situations that can be remedied through better understanding of the effects of such conditions, through removal of the hindrances to proper growth, and through the reconstruction of relations between the persons who compose the interacting groups. Experimentation and observation may add considerably to present knowledge in this field. A philosophy of Christian education should take these findings into account.

Understanding of Social and Cultural Foundations

Education takes place in a social matrix, in a complex web of human relationships and of institutional arrangements that affects profoundly the habit patterns and value systems of the individual. The outcomes of education in the case of any human being depend in large measure upon his family, peer groups, type of community, and the general cultural situation of which all these are parts. These outcomes are not realized through formal instruction so much as through actual participation in the ongoing life of the community. Children learn as much through observation of their elders' actions and perception of their attitudes as through what they read in textbooks and hear from

[1] Robert J. Havighurst, *Human Development and Education.*

teachers. Hence an understanding of the social order and of modern culture is an essential element in a philosophy of education.

To reach an understanding of modern culture is an exceedingly difficult task. American society is very complex. Its communities vary greatly in size, availability of natural resources, heterogeneity of population, forms of occupation, provisions for orderly government and for education, levels of cultural development, and in many other ways. Even within a given community there may be groups representing a number of national, racial, and religious backgrounds. There surely will be groups of differing socioeconomic status. These variations will be reflected in differing manners, customs, attitudes, and outlooks on life.

The type of community exerts a powerful influence upon the development of the individual, whether urban, suburban, exurban, or rural. The particular area within the total community—commercial, slum, manufacturing, or residential—is equally important. Social stratification has tended to bring about differing social, moral, and ethical standards among the various groups. The value systems of the several groups must be considered by anyone who attempts to frame a philosophy of education. The greatest possible use of the knowledge provided by research in cultural anthropology, social psychology, and sociology should be made by those who seek to understand the impact of culture upon personal development.

Awareness of the Function of Education

Education has a twofold function with reference to social values. One of its essential functions is to preserve the social gains embodied in the culture. Civilization can be maintained only if it is re-created anew in each generation. Education is a means of conserving the values of the cultural heritage and of transmitting these to the rising generation. Unless this function is performed, all the gains accumulated through centuries of human effort will be lost.

But transmission of the cultural heritage is not enough. Exclusive attention to conservation leads to rigidity and stagnation. An additional function of education is social reconstruction through the evaluation and modification of tradition coupled with imaginative and creative search for more inclusive values.

Attention was called in an earlier chapter to the revolutionary changes that are taking place in American society and in the total world situation, and it was suggested that educational philosophy is in ferment because of inability to cope adequately with these changes. One of the persistent problems in education is the "cultural lag," the tendency on the part of society to be backward looking with respect to its values. Education, if it is to serve its full function in modern society, must not only make us vividly aware of our past and of the values in our present social order. It must enable us to see that loyalty to the best we know and true devotion to our heritage require us to search for means of social and cultural improvement.

Any philosophy of education, Christian or otherwise, must be concerned with the nature of personality, the processes of human development, the social and cultural setting in which personal growth takes place, and the function of education with respect to individual growth and cultural evolution. Christian education shares these concerns with education of whatever sort. But it differs from other kinds in that it approaches these problems as well as many others from a certain perspective and from a distinctive point of view. It is necessary to turn now to some of the distinguishing marks of Christian education.

Concept of the Church

Every type of education is influenced by the nature of the agency that sponsors it and by the basic presuppositions of those who carry on the work. Christian education is no exception. It is an enterprise of the Christian church and therefore is conditioned by the understanding the church may have of its nature and mission.

The Christian church today is the outgrowth of a long historical process. It had its origins in Judaism whose exact beginnings stretch back into the prehistoric past. The ancient Hebrews, through a series of dramatic and unforgettable experiences, moved from a primitive polytheism to belief in the existence of one God with whom they were believed to have a special covenant relationship. Their understanding of the nature of God and of his requirements for his "chosen people" was deepened and enriched through the vicissitudes of their history over a period of several centuries and through the cumulative insights of a succession of great prophets. They came to think of God as a God of justice, righteousness, and mercy, who makes certain moral and ethical demands which are inescapable. They felt that their national misfortunes were due to their disobedience to God's law. The record of their pilgrimage from a primitive and barbarous tribalism to a sense of nationhood and of direct obligation to the ethical de-

41

mands of Almighty God constitutes a superb chronicle of moral and religious advance.

Jesus of Nazareth, who took the higher claims of the Jewish faith with the greatest seriousness, gave to the religion of his people a new turn through his vital and complete commitment in daily living and through creative adaptation to the needs and conditions of his own time. He gathered around him a group of devoted disciples whom he taught through both precept and example the new way of life he had adopted and which he felt was demanded of loyal children of God. His disciples never completely understood him; the leaders of his nation rejected him; and he was put to death, accused of blasphemy and treason.

His followers were temporarily scattered as a result of this tragedy but they soon came together again, inspired by stories of mystic experiences which led them to believe in his resurrection and his continuing presence among them. They began the effort to interpret their experiences of fellowship with him, to practice in their own daily lives the principles he had enunciated, and to proclaim the gospel he had expounded. They came to accept him as the supreme revelation of God, the Messiah whom the Jews had long expected. Out of these experiences and efforts arose the Christian church.

The church at first was little more than a sect of Judaism, and much of its theology was wrought out in the struggle to gain acceptance of its faith by the Jews. But it soon spread to non-Jewish peoples and won converts in ever-widening circles. It has continued to extend its influence through the centuries and is today the most powerful religious movement in the world.

In the course of its history, Christianity has come into contact with cultures of the greatest possible variety. It has influenced these cultures as it has in turn been influenced by them. The necessary accommodations to varying cultures have resulted in the adoption of many forms of organization, worship, service, and doctrinal expression. But it has retained the permanent core of its faith, implicit trust in Jesus as the supreme revelation of God and in his teachings, attitudes, and manner of life as norms for human living.

Christians differ in their interpretations of the nature of the church and in their conceptions of its mission. These differences have come about through the continuing influence of previous group experiences and cultural associations and because of human inability to state in final and concise form a complete explanation of the imponderable mystery of the nature of God and man's proper relationship to him. They have been the cause of many divisions and controversies among Christians, all of whom claim supreme allegiance to Christ. In recent years the differences have been a matter of growing concern and the occasion for renewed efforts to discover the true nature of the church and its mission. As Christian groups have worked together at this task, their particular sectarian expressions are increasingly recognized as incomplete in themselves but as possibly containing elements that may be included in the total truth. Thus the way seems open for a more complete understanding as the proponents of differing traditions pursue their common quest.

For purposes of the present discussion, it may be suggested that the Christian church is a fellowship of those who regard themselves as the people of God, who try to fulfill the obligations implied in the acceptance of this relationship, and who seek to express in their own living the attitudes and way of life exemplified by Jesus. It is composed of individuals of varying degrees of maturity, bound together in continuing community, all endeavoring to deepen their understanding of the meaning and possibilities of human life and to find ways of realizing its highest potentialities as seen in the perspective from which Jesus viewed it. The mission of the church is to witness to the good news of what God can do for human beings when they let him have his way and to extend to others the privilege of joining in the fellowship of those who seek to do his work.

A philosophy of Christian education must be more than a restatement of Jesus' teachings in their original form. We must take him seriously but not literally. Across the centuries the followers of Jesus have attempted to interpret his message in the light of their own understanding of its meaning and with reference to the conditions and needs of their own times. It is necessary for Christians to make such efforts today. A philosophy of Christian education, then, must somehow combine the basic outlook of Jesus with the best knowledge and understanding of Christians of the present day.

The chief source of information about Jesus is the Bible which consists of two parts, distinctive but clearly related. The Old Testament is a collection of writings embodying the best of ancient Jewish thought and tradition. Without a knowledge of the Old Testament, it is impossible to understand many of the allusions in Jesus' teachings. The New Testament depicts his reactions to the Judaism of his day and the impact of his personality and thought upon his contemporaries.

It is difficult for us to understand the Bible today because it deals with a world quite different from our own. Its writers held views of nature and of the forces that actuate human behavior which seem very strange to us. So the "quest for the historical Jesus" is not enough. To recover the historical Jesus, we must understand the world in which he lived. Modern scholarship has aided enormously here. With confidence we can now make distinctions between historical facts and their interpretations by people who saw them through eyes different from our own. We can understand what Jesus' basic beliefs and convictions were and so can associate them with our own conceptions of the physical world and of human nature. But we can learn still more as the results of biblical research are better co-ordinated with the findings of history, archeology, and anthropology.

Jesus did not set forth any systematic philosophy of life or of education, nor did he outline a concise theory of personality. He did not establish formal rules for the conduct of life, nor provide a blueprint for church organization and program. He lived life spontaneously and creatively, and he met the problems of living as he faced them from day to day. Hence his basic outlook on life must be inferred from the story of his career and the outline of his teachings as these have come down to us in the Bible. They have been made the object of study by countless numbers of Christian scholars across the generations, whose writings are invaluable resources for us today.

But a knowledge of these resources cannot be made a substitute for our own thought and our continuing efforts to gain an understanding that will serve our needs in the changing world of today. We cannot gain the requisite understanding by simply repeating the thought patterns of the past. God gave us minds and we must use them to the full extent of our ability, albeit with a full recognition of their inherent limitations. Else we can have no philosophy of Christian education adequate for our times.

IV. CONTRASTING APPROACHES
TO HUMAN NATURE

One of the essentials in any valid statement of a philosophy of Christian education is an understandable concept of the nature of personality. The query of the ancient Psalmist plagues us still: *What is man?* Unfortunately, until only recently this problem was hardly recognized by the typical religious educator. He assembled his pupils, studied his materials, proceeded with the task of teaching, often assured himself of varying degrees of successful achievement, without bothering his head about the essential nature of the pupils he taught or the ways by which changes in their behavior are effected. A responsible teacher today must ponder this question.

The Chasm Between Theology and Psychology

The thoughtful individual who faces the problem soon becomes aware that two principal approaches to human nature that are relevant to Christian education have often been divergent: the theological and the psychological. One who reads widely in the two fields will recognize that there exists a wide semantic chasm between them which has hindered effective communication between specialists in the two areas.

On the one hand, theologians typically have assumed that they have the final answer already revealed in some person, institution or body of sacred literature; and all they need to do is to make explicit what is contained in the divine revelation. The tools of empirical research are not regarded as essential. By some, they may even be thought an impediment in a proper assessment of the truth about man. Theologians are aware that there are widely divergent interpretations of what is contained in revelation. But their energies have often been expended in arguments among themselves and in efforts to gain acceptance for their particular views by forensic methods. Little appeal has been made to direct observation or experiment.

Psychologists on the other hand, in an effort to make their discipline "scientific," have gone about their task as if little wisdom is contained in ancient documents, sacred or otherwise, and as if valid knowledge depends solely upon experimental efforts in the laboratory. Working as each individual or group is forced to do within restricted limits, psychologists have also tended to become sectarian. As experimentation has added new insights regarding limited aspects of the whole of human nature, the proponents of the several "schools" have tended to blow up their generalizations into philosophies, disregarding or even denouncing the findings of their colleagues who are dealing with other aspects or working with different tools.

In the fairly intense struggle among the various *systems* of theology and the many *schools* of psychology, there has been little time or opportunity for communication across the chasm that exists between the two disciplines. In general, psychologists have paid little attention to theological discussion; and, conversely, theologians have not been greatly concerned with the results of psychological investigation. But, since both psychology and theology are concerned with human beings, presumably the fields of their activity might be expected to overlap; and psychologists and theologians should be able to learn from one another. But that they have made little effort to establish effective communication must be apparent to any thoughtful reader who examines the literature.

In many of the current books in psychology there is no reference in the index to either religion or theology. It would seem that if such ideas as redemption, justification, and atonement, which are basic concepts in theology, have any relation to the truth about human nature, they would not have entirely escaped the attention of psychologists. Similarly, many of the great theological treatises of our time pay little attention to the problems which are the chief concerns of psychologists, educators, social workers, and others who are dealing with the experience and problems of real people.

It is not difficult to demonstrate the extent and depth of this chasm. Victor Murray has called attention to it in his discussion of the contrasting viewpoints of McDougall and Barth and has considered some of its unfortunate consequences in current conceptions of human nature.[1] Striking illustrations may be found in comparative studies of the writings of leading psychologists and theologians in America.

Few can deny that Gardner Murphy and Reinhold Niebuhr are among the most eminent American scholars in their respective fields. Yet an examination of their views on the nature of personality leads to the conclusion that both have little acquaintance with the field of specialization in which the other is a recognized authority.

In an attempt to formulate a theory of personality through a synthesis of modern research findings, Murphy published in 1947 a monumental volume of a thousand pages.[2] In this he listed a total of 749 books, papers and research reports. But his index includes only seven references to religion. The inference is clear: either Murphy felt that theologians have contributed little to knowledge about personality or he was unaware of the extent of the contributions they had made.

One of the well-known outlines of a theological approach to human nature is that by Reinhold Niebuhr.[3] In his *Human Nature*, Niebuhr contrasted what he called the "Christian" view of man with the "classical" and "modern" views. But the contents of his book indicate clearly that, at the time of writing, he was unfamiliar with a vast amount of material on the nature of personality and the manner of its development which was available to students of these problems. His references to contemporary anthropological, psychological, and sociological research findings were meager indeed. One conversant with this literature will doubtless conclude that Niebuhr was too ready to identify the "modern" view with that expressed by only a limited selection of authors.

In a subsequent publication, Niebuhr twice referred to Murphy's book and, in both instances, he apparently misunderstood or overlooked the main points of Murphy's discussion.[4] He found "confusion" in the mind of Murphy in spite of the fact that, in the very paragraph to which he referred, Murphy had pointed out some of the limitations of psychology and had suggested the spirit in which he thought these limitations should be faced. Murphy gave as one ex-

[1] A. Victor Murray, *Natural Religion and Christian Theology*, pp. 2-4.
[2] Gardner Murphy, *Personality: A Biosocial Approach to Origins and Structure*.
[3] Reinhold Niebuhr, "Human Nature," *The Nature and Destiny of Man: A Christian Interpretation*, Vol. 1.
[4] Reinhold Niebuhr, *The Self and the Dramas of History*, pp. 32, 129-30.

ample of shortcoming the fact that psychology had been unable to resolve the fundamental paradox between the view that human nature is incapable of effective functioning except under conditions of individual fulfillment and the apparently opposite fact that a man may so lose himself in serving others that he seems to care little about the enhancement of self. He stated that this paradox had not been resolved in any of the current explanations, including that of Christianity which extols both ideals and thus "leaves us in confusion." [5]

Murphy thought that the paradox between individual fulfillment and self-forgetfulness could be resolved only when a deeper exploration of personality is made than had been made up to that time by psychology. He felt that the difficulty is not with research or with the definition of personality but with "plain fogginess as to the nature of man." He was confident that the use of the scientific method is legitimate and that, although not yet ready, it would eventually be able "to integrate the older insights of an intuitive or poetic sort, which, though pointing the way, will reach effectively into the unknown only when supported by the methods of a future science." In the meantime, he felt that it would be "sheer impertinence" to predict what the larger integration would find. [6]

The conclusion seems inescapable: Murphy, a psychologist, and Niebuhr, a theologian, were dealing with the same problem; but they lived in entirely different worlds. Their grasp of the total problem was too limited because of restricted vision. The competence of both men in their respective fields of inquiry placed them in an excellent position, through collaboration, to assist greatly in the formulation of a more adequate theory of man. Though they lived in the same city for many years, however, their composite contribution was practically nil because the lines of communication between their thought worlds had not been firmly established.

The Dangers of Partisanship

It is possible, of course, to make an arbitrary choice between the scientific and the theological approaches to personality. It is not difficult to see that many psychologists and many theologians of the present day are taking this easy way out of the dilemma. In the example of divergence just cited, one may look to Murphy or to Niebuhr as his authority and disregard what the other has had to say. It is fairly

[5] Gardner Murphy, *op. cit.*, p. 924.
[6] *Ibid.*, p. 925.

evident that much of the controversy that has gone on in recent years over the relation of theology to Christian education has come about because of commitment, however unconscious this often is, between a basically scientific or a predominantly theological orientation.

History should teach us, however, that the easy way is not always the best way. There are surely insights in the theological tradition which are permanently valid. There are just as surely recent scientific findings which must be taken into account if we are to attempt the formulation of a theory of personality that has reasonable promise of enduring significance. We shall be immeasurably impoverished if we blindly bypass or stubbornly reject the values in either approach.

There is ample precedent for the view that premature partisanship is likely to aggravate our difficulties. When the Sadducees arrested the apostles in ancient Jerusalem and the Council sought to put them to death for their nonconformity, Gamaliel argued that to do so might be quite disastrous. Better let them go, he counseled, "for if this plan or this undertaking is of men, it will fail; but if it is of God, you will not be able to overthrow them. You might even be found opposing God!" (Acts 5:38-39 R.S.V.). Paul argued that no one should say, "I am one of Paul's converts," nor another, "I am one of Apollos'," for to do so was being plainly "unspiritual" (I Cor. 3:4 Phillips). He rather exhorted the early Christians, "By all means use your judgment, and hold on to whatever is really good" (I Thess. 5:21 Phillips).

Basis for the Contrasting Approaches

In contrasting the scientific and the theological approaches to personality, it seems desirable to indicate the meaning which I attach to these terms. It should be remembered that there can be no final and strict demarcation, except possibly with reference to the starting point and the methodology of the two fields of inquiry. A scientist, as scientist, begins by marking off some designated area of nature or experience and he tries to confine his investigations within the limits of the field selected. Hence scientists are usually physicists, chemists, biologists, psychologists, and so on. A scientist expects to become an "expert" only in his limited field. But he soon discovers that he cannot always stay within these narrow limits. So, some chemists become biochemists, and some psychologists take a biosocial approach to human behavior. Many scientists go beyond the boundaries of their specialization and try to combine the outcomes of their own observations and experimental efforts with those of others into an inclusive view of nature, and thus they become philosophers in effect. Many theologians seek to be as "scientific" as they can be but, as theologians, they limit themselves to the special field of religious phenomena.

For purposes of the present discussion, the rather simple definitions of science and theology contained in Webster's dictionary may be sufficient to distinguish the two approaches to human nature. *Science* is defined as "accumulated knowledge systematized and formulated with reference to the discovery of general truths or the operation of general laws. Especially such *knowledge when it relates to the physical world.*" *Theology* is defined as *"knowledge of God and the supernatural.* . . . The critical, historical, and psychological study of religion and religious ideas." [7]

By the *scientific approach* is meant a method by which the phenomena of the "natural world" and the experience of human beings are observed, analyzed, classified, and explained by the observer, without recourse to external and superhuman authority. A scientist collects data in the area of his special interest, arranges these in categories which he sets up for purposes of classification, forms hypotheses by which he can predict and control the effects of manipulation of the data, tests these hypotheses by experimental methods, observes the results of his experimentation, and states his conclusions with the expectation that these may need revision in the future as new data throw light on the validity of previous generalizations. As a scientist, he is more interested in discovering the facts and of explaining them than in maintaining an orthodox position, either with respect to past systems of explanation or with the viewpoints of his colleagues. His only authority is "natural" experience and reason, though he may utilize the results of the work of other scientists. He is a "naturalist" in the sense in which this term is ordinarily used, in contrast with supernaturalism.

Few scientists can remain "pure" scientists. They find that they need to know what their colleagues in different fields have discovered, and they seek to piece together the results of scientific investigation into some kind of ordered totality so that the whole of nature may be understood. In the attempt to achieve knowledge of the whole, a scientist must leave his special field and become something of a philosopher.

[7] *Webster's New Collegiate Dictionary* (Springfield, Mass.: G. & C. Merriam Company, 1953). Italics supplied.

A philosopher need not differ from a scientist in attitude and method. But he deals with a much larger body of data. He cannot expect to become an expert in all the specialized fields in which his scientist friends are engaged. But he must be close enough to the experts to grasp the significance of the general conclusions that scientists have reached in their several fields. As he seeks to view reality *sub specie aeternitatis*, in its essential or universal form, he must have the assistance of scientists who are dealing with the factual data. In co-ordinating the results of science, he finds that scientists differ in their basic assumptions and that these differences in fundamental orientation tend to bias the judgment of scientists working in different fields. He seeks to reconcile these differences by the use of logic and reason. In so far as possible, a philosopher utilizes the dependable results of science. But there are contradictions in the reports of scientists, and there are gaps between the fields covered by the several sciences. At these points he must take recourse in speculation and conjecture. But in it all, he tries to be both inclusive and consistent in his view of reality.

Theology has something in common with both science and philosophy. Like science, it observes, classifies, and interprets the data of religious experience (its special field of responsibility); and, like philosophy, it seeks to relate the findings in its own field to reality as a whole. But theology operates under special difficulty because it is con-concerned with the "supernatural," and by definition this realm cannot be reduced to exact analysis and explanation. If theology restricted itself to observable and measurable data, and to human experience in terms of "natural" explanations, it would have no quarrel with either science or philosophy. But usually theology starts with certain assumptions that cannot be verified by the ordinary methods of science and philosophy. Belief in God is a *faith* and not a verifiable hypothesis. Unless theology assumes the validity of this belief, beyond the possibility of final demonstration by science as we know it today, it is nothing more than a form of philosophy.

Since theology admittedly deals with belief in God and the supernatural, most theologians place greater dependence upon the authority of revelation than upon human experience and reason. Some person who is believed to possess superhuman knowledge, some institution which is believed to be divinely sanctioned, some sacred literature which is regarded as superior to the writings of ordinary human beings —or a combination of these—is simply taken for granted. And though theologians may seek to reconcile the findings of science and philosophy with the content of revelation, the latter is regarded as normative.

Throughout the history of human thought there has been conflict between these two basic approaches—the scientific, with its appeal to human experience and reason, and the theological, with its confidence in the validity of divine revelation. Many times the conflict has been interpreted as a life and death struggle: reason *or* revelation, natural *or* supernatural, human *or* divine, sacred *or* secular, Christian *or* non-Christian, Catholic *or* Protestant. But the long course of Christian history should teach us this may not be the only way out. Perhaps we have reached a point in the progress of thought where we can recognize that there are at least "two roads to truth," [8] and that our problem now is to find ways of bringing these roads together into a better highway for the future.

Toward a More Adequate Conception of Human Nature

Part of our confusion and difficulty in formulating a satisfactory theory of personality for Christian education arises from the fact that we are confronted with a bewildering variety of views and theories, some of which are recognizably contradictory and exclusive, and from the further fact that there has been such limited communication between the specialized fields of study. Because of the complexity of the problem, most of us are disposed to look at it from too limited a perspective.

If we view a human being primarily from the standpoint of his body and note only the chemical elements of which it is composed, we find that he is made up of the same elements as the earth on which he lives. The various organs and the other component members of his body are quite similar to those of the lower animals. He shares with these similar instincts, impulses and appetites. Man is a part of the chemicophysical world. He is composed of hydrogen, carbon, nitrogen, phosphorus, calcium, and other chemical elements like the rest of nature. Some, noting these facts, have concluded that man is "merely" an animal, differing from the lower brutes only by having a more complicated organism and therefore more intelligence. He has an especially complicated structure and a more highly differentiated nervous system and is therefore biologically superior to other animals. He differs merely in degree, however, not in kind. At least, so say many scientists.

[8] Edmund W. Sinnott, *Two Roads to Truth.*

Others, taking into account man's direct dependence upon his fellows, have placed primary stress upon his social nature. No one can become a fully developed human being except in interrelationship with others. Anthropology and sociology have made it impossible for us ever to forget how much the individual owes to the groups with which he is associated.

It is unnecessary to deny the essential truth in either of these approaches in order to arrive at a Christian conception of man. In both cases, however, we may need a wider perspective if we are fully to understand his essential nature.

Man is an animal, a creature of earth, but he possesses qualities and powers which no other animal possesses. He can grasp ideas and communicate them, he can reason, he can direct his actions toward self-chosen goals, he can create and preserve culture, he can worship. Among all the animals, to man alone can be attributed such achievements as art, science, and religion. *Man is a social creature.* He is dependent upon his fellows but he can understand his relationships, criticize and evaluate them, and devise ways and means for their improvement. So that the animal and social views of man are true so far as they go. We are likely to gain knowledge and understanding of these sides of his nature more through the behavioral sciences than through theology.

These partial views, however, require supplement if human nature is to be understood in its entirety. Philosophers, poets, mystics, even men in the street have commonly felt that there is more to a man than a body and the capacity to deal with his neighbors. Not denying the physical and social aspects of his being, a comprehensive view must include also this other dimension. *Man is a spiritual being.* Physically he is joined to earth and to the other animals. Socially he is linked to his fellow man. But spiritually he belongs to God, and this relationship must be given legitimate recognition and cultivation if the fullest potentiality of human nature is to be realized. We are more likely to gain understanding of this dimension through the disciplines of religion, experience within the religious community, and theology.

It must be recognized, then, that the Christian doctrine of man is more than a "theory of personality," at least as this term is currently used in psychological literature. More than a theory, it is a statement of faith: faith in the existence and activity of God, faith that man is made "in the image of God," that he is a child of God. Whatever man may be in the physical and social aspects of his nature—and Christians have no reason to deny the findings of research in these fields—he can be fully understood only when his spiritual dimension is included in the total scheme of explanation.

Contemporary efforts to bring together the findings of experimental research into the nature of personality and the factors that influence its development seem to the present writer to offer exciting possibilities for a new statement of the Christian doctrine of man. Most of the contemporary personality theories tend increasingly to be organismic and attempt to deal with the individual as a whole rather than view him in terms of the separate component parts of his total being. Greater attention is being given to the striving, seeking, purposive aspects of human behavior. Hereditary factors and earlier conditioning are not overlooked, but increasing notice is given to the goals or "intentions" of the individual. The *self*, as a determinant of behavior, is a matter of growing concern. Even the terms religion and "spiritual" are not avoided as strenuously as they used to be, though as yet they are not central themes in most psychological literature.

We shall have an adequate conception of personality in philosophies of Christian education, not when we choose only some limited aspect of man's total being but when all aspects are included and seen in total perspective. We shall need all the insights that the behavioral sciences *and* theology can provide. Our problem is to find the dependable truth in both approaches and to combine them in proper proportion.

PART TWO

Psychological and Cultural Foundations

V. BACKGROUNDS OF
CONTEMPORARY
PSYCHOLOGICAL THEORIES

Scientists who have contributed most to knowledge and understanding of personality have worked within the fields of anthropology, biology, psychology, sociology, cultural anthropology, and social psychology. Of these fields, psychology has been most concerned with the formulation of systematized theories of personality.

Psychology as a field of study has had a long history, and this is not the place to attempt a full account of its development.[1] Some knowledge of historical origins is necessary, however, for a proper understanding of the difficulties that now confront those who seek to develop a satisfactory theory of human nature.

Speculative Psychology

Modern psychology had its roots in the thought of the ancient Greeks. For many centuries the views of Plato and Aristotle dominated the thinking of the Western world. These men had no tools except brilliant minds and keen powers of observation. They were philosophers, but they were also scientists in the only sense in which this term could be applied to the intellectual enterprise in ancient times. The wide range of data available to modern scientists and philosophers was simply nonexistent.

Plato's psychology drew a sharp line between psyche (soul, spirit) and soma (body, matter). The soul emanates from the eternal world

[1] For histories of psychology, see E. G. Boring, *A History of Experimental Psychology*; H. E. Garrett, *Great Experiments in Psychology*; Gardner Murphy, *Historical Introduction to Modern Psychology*; R. S. Peters (ed.), *Brett's History of Psychology*; Benjamin B. Wolman, *Contemporary Theories and Systems in Psychology*.

of spirit, while the body is part of the transient, shadowy world of change and instability. In the acquisition of knowledge, sensations come by way of the body, while the soul contributes ideas which are innate and reminiscent of the eternal world from which the soul has come. Sensations are only imperfect copies of reality and hence are the source of error.

Aristotle accepted dualism but went further than Plato in his analysis and description of the psychological nature of the individual. Central in man's makeup is the soul, the active life principle that gives shape and meaning to the body—just as the design of an architect gives form and meaning to the materials that make up a house. Men possess both soul (form) and body (matter). Human nature is a compound of vegetative, animal, and human characteristics. Man's highest faculty and the one that distinguishes him from other forms of life is reason, by means of which he can acquire universal knowledge. But the individual is endowed with other faculties by which he is able to function in various ways. This picture of human nature proved so attractive that it was accepted in philosophical and theological discussions for centuries. Thomas Aquinas was able to blend Aristotle's explanation of the soul in terms of its functions with the theology of the church, and this became the basis of the psychology of scholasticism.

As time went on, the word "soul" came to be regarded with increasing disfavor because of its vagueness; and "mind" became the term generally used in psychological discussion. But mind, too, eludes exact definition. Many attempts have been made to explain the relationship of mind, or consciousness, to the world of physical reality. Most modern thinkers have been influenced in one way or another by the views of three intellectual giants of the seventeenth century: Descartes (dualism), Spinoza (monism), and Leibnitz (pluralism). Other great thinkers have continued to wrestle with the problem of knowledge, one of the central themes of philosophy; and their perplexities have undoubtedly contributed to the rise of modern psychology.

British empiricism had its origins in the work of Locke, Berkeley, Reid and Hume. John Locke, who was suspicious of metaphysical speculation, sought to anchor his psychology directly in human experience. The mind at birth, he thought, is a blank slate (*tabula rasa*) on which personal experiences are inscribed; and it is only with these experiences that one can reason. He argued that objects in the material world have both primary qualities (such as weight and extension), which exist independently of mind, and secondary qualities (taste, color, and so forth), which are the sources of perception. This view was opposed by George Berkeley, who held that both primary and secondary qualities exist only in the mind and that therefore matter has no existence except in perception (*esse est percipi*). All reality exists in the observing mind of God, who arouses sensations in our minds and thus makes possible the apparent existence of material objects.

Thomas Reid contended for a "common sense" philosophy, holding that we have self-evident knowledge by means of which we know objects in the external world in the true sense and not just in copies or ideas. David Hume, however, pushed the logic of Locke and Berkeley to the extreme of skepticism with respect to the real existence of a substantive mind. When we examine experience, he argued, we do not find a mind but only a series of sensations. We simply infer causal relations from the combination of two or more sensations and must fall back on faith and common sense for ways out of the difficulty.

The problem of finding a way by which sensations and ideas may be related, so as to build up a body of knowledge, stimulated the interest of such men as Condillac, Hartley, James Mill, and Bain. Étienne de Condillac tried to simplify Locke's concept of knowledge and developed a theory of sensationalism. While retaining a Cartesian dualism of mind and body, he argued that all conscious experience is the result of passive sensations. David Hartley, a physician, held that the mind results from the association of sensations arising from vibrations in the brain and spinal cord. James Mill, who accepted Hume's skepticism regarding a substantial mind, held that when ideas appear frequently together, they form combinations by association which later leave no trace of the original elements from which they were derived. Alexander Bain applied mechanistic principles to the development of a neurological theory of association. The evolution of the mind comes about as a result of the development of nerve tissues and their connections. As the brain increases in size and complexity, there is a comparable advance in the functions of intelligence, emotion and will.

From these earlier beginnings, a psychology of learning known as *associationism* was formulated by John Stuart Mill and Johann F. Herbart, in which they sought to combine a realistic conception of the external world with an empirical conception of the nature of knowledge. They denied the validity of the faculty psychology and tried to reduce mental activities to a process of association.

Herbart was one of the last to develop a complete system of speculative psychology. He objected to current conceptions of change and maintained that the universe consists of "reals," each of which is simple and independent. Change is but alternations in the relationships among reals. The soul does not consist of faculties, as Aristotle thought, but of ideas which themselves are reals struggling for self-preservation. The mind is formed by the process in which simple perceptions of external objects become associated in the individual with other perceptions, thus resulting in more complex perceptions and ideas. The associated ideas become an "apperceptive mass" and it is the business of education to present ideas and perceptions in ways that will facilitate their association.

Immanuel Kant objected to the view that ideas must conform to an external reality independent of knowledge and he proposed instead that the world can be known only in so far as it conforms to the essential structure of the knowing mind. The things of experience (phenomena) may be known; but we can never know the thing-in-itself (*das Ding an sich*). We can have knowledge of natural events but only in terms of the categories of our understanding. Knowledge of the phenomenal world constitutes the subject matter of science. Although we cannot gain knowledge of the noumenal world through reason, we can know through our ideas that it exists; and its aspects can be revealed through ethical and aesthetic experience. Ethical judgments are based upon faith in the necessity of moral law, which is expressed in the forms of a categorical imperative; and beauty is disclosed in the immediate perceptions of noumenal value as we view nature from within. Only faith can justify belief in freedom of the will, immortality, and God. Science cannot invade the realm of ethics, aesthetics, and faith; and neither can these overthrow science. Thus, Kant set in motion an "anti-Copernican revolution" in regard to knowledge which has affected psychological thought down to our own day.

As contrasted with the halting progress in the development of psychology, growth in the physical sciences had gone on apace. Astronomy had surged forward after the publication by Nicholas Copernicus of his views on the universe and improvements of the instruments of observation by Tycho Brahe, Galileo, and Kepler. Newton had greatly advanced the study of physics by his experiments with light and formulation of the theory of gravitation and the laws of motion. Experimental studies of the nervous system by Charles Bell, Johannes

Müller, and Ernst Weber had put anatomy and physiology on a firm basis. And, although Francis Bacon made no outstanding discoveries himself, he gave added momentum to the advancement of science by his clear statement of the principles of the inductive method, as contrasted with the a priori methods then in vogue. It was inevitable that these attitudes and methods would permeate the field of psychology.

Psychology as an Empirical Science

After its beginnings in English empiricism, the modern science of psychology received its greatest impetus from two developments during the latter part of the nineteenth century. One was the theory of evolution, foreshadowed by Erasmus Darwin, an English physician, who published a book in the 1790's explaining organic life according to evolutionary principles. Charles Darwin formulated a theory of evolution on the basis of explorations, investigations and correlation of the facts observed during his five-year cruise on the "Beagle," which he published in the *Origin of Species* in 1859.

Another development was experimental work in the laboratories of Ernst Weber (physiologist), Gustav Fechner (psychophysicist), Hermann von Helmholtz (physicist and biologist), and Wilhelm Wundt (physiologist and psychologist), in Germany. Wundt established the first laboratory in experimental psychology at Leipzig in 1878. He defined psychology as *Erfahrungswissenschaft,* a "science based on experience."

G. Stanley Hall, who had studied in Germany, organized a psychological laboratory at Johns Hopkins University in 1882. He founded the *American Journal of Psychology* in 1887 and was one of the organizers of the American Psychological Association in 1891. Edward B. Titchener, who had studied under Wundt, became head of a new psychological laboratory at Cornell in 1892. William James, who had majored in medicine at Harvard, published his brilliant and epoch-making *Principles of Psychology* in 1890.

Thus the new science of psychology, which had been so tardy in getting started, was well established on an empirical foundation at the beginning of the twentieth century. That it had plenty of problems should be evident from this brief picture of the backgrounds out of which it developed.

Modern psychology has required a considerable period in which to define the limits of its field and to determine its methods of investigation. Although there is much better agreement over these than at the beginning, there is still wide disparity of viewpoint among those who make equal claim to the scientific validity of their work. The various schools are still influenced by basic philosophical presuppositions which are inherited from the past. Some of the problems proposed by Plato and Aristotle, and later elaborated by Descartes, Spinoza, Leibnitz, and Kant are not resolved by any means, though possibly most psychologists are sure that their particular system is superior to that of other systems.

Some present-day psychologists seem to be dualists but they are not satisfied with a sharp dichotomy between the mental and the material as was Descartes, nor can they be content with the vaguesness of Plato and Aristotle. Many are inclined to agree with Spinoza that reality is basically one, but there is no final agreement as between materialism and idealism. Pluralists all have something in common with Leibnitz, though none can accept his concept of monadism. Some would agree with Kant that a distinction must be made between phenomena and values, but they are not sure how the line can be drawn between them. About the only thing that all psychologists agree upon today is that a sound psychology must be based upon experience and the rigorous use of observation, research, experimentation, and reason.

Some Early Lines of Development

Some of the viewpoints adopted by leaders in psychology during its early development as an empirical science are no longer central emphases, though some have left their traces on subsequent thought. Only a brief résumé can be given of these beginnings.

STRUCTURALISM. The view held by Wundt, and elaborated by Titchener in his laboratory at Cornell, was that the problem of psychology is the analysis and description of the states of consciousness, the structure of personal experience. It was a protest against the faculty psychology which was declared to be a metaphysical rather than a scientific psychology. The method of study was that of introspection by trained observers, as the observer analyzed his own sensations, ideas, and feelings and the ways the elements and attributes of these are combined in experience. Titchener solved the problem of mind-body relationship by means of a psychophysical parallelism. Structuralism was soon challenged by child psychology—children and untrained observers were unable to report reliably their inner experiences—and by developments in animal psychology, mental testing, and psychiatry.

FUNCTIONALISM. Darwin's theory of evolution, Galton's studies of heredity and eugenics, and Spencer's philosophy of evolutionism were precursors of a new viewpoint that came to stand in opposition to both faculty psychology and structuralism. William James, a biologist and expert in anatomy and physiology, found it natural to base psychology upon the concept of adjustment to life. Mind, he thought, is not some primordial substance but a product of evolution. And mental processes should be thought of as functions or operations of an organism in its efforts to adapt to and modify its environment. James included a classified list of instincts in his explanation of human action. These instincts he regarded as inherited patterns of behavior which the individual has retained because he has found them useful.

According to Dewey's instrumentalism, the various forms of human behavior were regarded as instruments developed to help man solve his individual and social problems. Rather than a mind that acts upon the organism, or a system of instincts that impel action in predetermined ways, Dewey thought that the mechanisms that control interactions with environment are habits, which have been learned. Routine habits enable an individual to adjust satisfactorily to a more or less stable environment, but intelligence is required to transform a chaotic or disturbing situation into one that is coherent and harmonious. Hence the chief aim of education is to teach men "how to think."

Other proponents of functionalism were James R. Angell, Harvey A. Carr, and Edward R. Robinson.

CONNECTIONISM. Edward L. Thorndike combined the neurological theory of association proposed by Bain with a functional concept of behavior in his famous S-R bond, the stimulus-response theory of learning. Both animals and men act in accordance with their drives, seeking pleasure and avoiding pain. The reflex arc is the hereditary unit of behavior, and learning consists of forming specific connections between a situation S and a response R. When an individual faces a problem, he proceeds by trial-and-error until he succeeds in making a satisfying response. Connections tend to be stamped in when the response is satisfying and pleasant, and stamped out when it is otherwise. Connections may be strengthened by exercise or weakened by disuse. Intelligence depends upon the number of connections that have become stamped in the brain rather than upon any over-all mental capacity, though hereditary factors may affect the number of connections that may be made.

Robert S. Woodworth's "dynamic psychology" was in a sense a continuation of the functionalism of James and Dewey, though he placed greater emphasis upon motivation and the causative factors in behavior than they. It is important to discover the *what* of behavior but it may be even more important to learn the *why*. He expanded Thorndike's S-R bond into an S-O-R chain, the O representing the structures and functions of the organism.

BEHAVIORISM. The earlier tendencies toward a monistic theory of psychology, implicit in functionalism and connectionism, came to complete and explicit expression in behaviorism, exemplified best perhaps in the views of John B. Watson and Ivan P. Pavlov.

Watson described behavior strictly in terms of physiological responses to stimuli and rejected outright the method of introspection and all references to mind or consciousness. Personality in his view was simply the totality of behavior patterns conceived in terms of a rigid determinism and environmentalism. Psychology should restrict itself to overt and observable data and should exclude all subjective factors. Given a number of healthy babies, he wrote, he could take one of them at random and train him to become any type of specialist regardless of abilities, tendencies, or other inner dispositions. Purpose is a useless concept.

Pavlov, who became renowned for his experiments with animals to demonstrate the conditioned reflex, also adopted a completely materialistic and monistic concept of personality. Human beings are parts of nature, and nature is only the sum of matter and energy. All behavior is a flow of energy regulated by relatively simple laws. Hence psychology should be a study of reflexes, which are the basic elements of interaction between an organism and its environment.

Among the followers of Watson in America was Albert P. Weiss, who insisted that there is no world except the physical world and that consciousness, mentalism and introspection should be completely banned from psychology. Other behaviorists who in various ways modified Watsonianism were Holt, Hunter, and Lashley. Edward S. Holt held that not all human behavior is the result of conditioning— behavioral preferences established in childhood may persist into later life through the process of canalization. Walter S. Hunter suggested the combination of an environmental orientation and a naïve realism as the basis for psychological study (*anthroponomy*). Karl L. Lashley, through a study of brain mechanisms and injuries, postulated the laws of "mass action" (the brain functions as a whole rather than in terms of synaptic connections) and "equipotentiality" (when one part of the brain is injured, the remaining parts are able to carry on the action).

PURPOSIVISM. William McDougall shared with functionalism the view that psychological data have to do with the functions of living organisms, but he was a convinced opponent of behaviorism. All nature he believed to have purposive tendencies, and human behavior is goal-directed. Evolution is possible because of a basic *horme,* an urge to live, a desire to survive. The purposive tendencies in human behavior he called instincts or "propensities" and he gave considerable attention to the definition and classification of instincts, emotions, and sentiments. Like Lamarck, he believed in the inheritance of acquired characteristics and regarded learning as the modification of innate tendencies.

GESTALT. Some psychologists were dissatisfied with the analytical methods of structuralism and the mechanistic principles of behaviorism, which they regarded as too atomistic in their approaches to behavior. A new approach took shape in the studies of Wertheimer, Köhler, and Koffka. Max Wertheimer discovered the Phi phenomenon and demonstrated that a series of still pictures can be perceived as one continuous motion. Wolfgang Köhler, in experiments with chimpanzees, concluded that these animals learned not by trial and error as Thorndike thought nor as the result of conditioning as Pavlov believed but by *Einsicht* (insight) as they perceived a situation in relation to their own needs. Kurt Koffka attempted to reduce the results of such experiments to a theory of learning. According to this psychology, human behavior is organismic and is affected by goal-seeking tendencies. The individual responds as a whole organism to complex patterns of stimulation and tends to shape his experiences into a *Gestalt* (form, configuration). Two basic principles are included in this approach: one, the membership character of all behavior (each element in a situation, through dynamic participation, alters its individuality in becoming part of the whole); and the other, the law of *Pragnanz,* by which the dynamic attribute of self-fullment in structured wholes allows small gaps in a *Gestalt* to be disregarded (perception moves in one direction, toward a "good" *Gestalt*).

PSYCHOANALYSIS. Around the 1920's a new influence invaded American psychology, stemming from experimental studies by Charcot, Breuer, and Freud, which was to profoundly affect the future development of personality study in this country. Jean Charcot had established in Paris a noted clinic for diseases of the nervous system, in which he gained new insights into the nature of hysteria. Josef Breuer and Sigmund Freud, physicians in Vienna, collaborated in the use of hypnosis and the method of catharsis in the treatment of hysterical patients. Freud then began the formulation of the system of psychoanalysis, which is both a theory of personality and a method of treating neuroses. According to this theory, mental ailments are caused not by organic changes in the nervous system but by emotional disorders. The basic postulate in psychoanalysis is the concept of a dynamic unconscious which interacts with conscious processes in all human behavior. Personality, therefore, cannot be understood merely in terms of the environment and the conscious reactions of the individual; but its understanding must include consideration also of instinctive drives and emotional factors which exist far below the normal processes of consciousness. Because this system will be discussed at length in the following chapter, no further reference to it seems necessary here.

Other factors in the early development of American psychology as a scientific discipline doubtless could be listed than those mentioned here, and each of those mentioned might be analyzed further; but these would seem to be the most important for the purpose at hand. Attention will now be directed to some of the most important of the contemporary theories and systems.

VI. SOME CONTEMPORARY
THEORIES OF PERSONALITY

Since psychology has become established as a scientific discipline, many psychologists have recognized the need for a coherent theory which systematizes present knowledge about personality. Quite a number have developed theories that richly deserve the careful study of those who are engaged in Christian education. It would be impossible within the scope of this book to make a complete exposition of any one of the theories, much less of all, and the author certainly recognizes his lack of competence to undertake a complete analysis, appraisal and synthesis.

The purpose here is not to give a full account of any theory, nor to choose "the best," but merely to indicate that the findings of psychologists are important resources for building an adequate philosophy of Christian education. Brief references will be made to most of the current theories, but emphasis will be placed upon the distinctive characteristics of each theory rather than upon completeness. And the material as presented will support the thesis that, even in the variety of approaches to personality theory now being made, the tendency is away from narrow confinement within any one system and toward a more inclusive view that contains elements from several original sources. In such a presentation there is danger, of course, that the total viewpoint of any given theorist may be somewhat distorted, though not intentionally so. The interested reader should be on his guard against the possible bias of the present writer and is encouraged to make a comparative study of his own.[1]

[1] Excellent introductions to current theories of personality are to be found in Benjamin B. Wolman, *Contemporary Theories and Systems in Psychology;* Calvin S. Hall and Gardner Lindzey, *Theories of Personality;* and Sigmund Koch (ed.), *Psychology: a Study of a Science,* Study 1, Vol. 3, "Formulations of the Person and the Social Context."

Basis of the Present Grouping

One writer has recently grouped the leading contemporary theories and systems in three principal divisions, on the basis of their "common roots": (1) "theories that started with the orientation toward natural sciences," Pavlov and Watson being regarded as the leading exponents of this trend; (2) those that stem from psychoanalysis; and (3) "all the theories that have been influenced by Kant, Windelband, Husserl, Dilthey, and the cultural sciences." [2] But this scheme of classification seems a little too neat, since many of the theories seem to spill over the narrow boundaries thus set, and it was necessary for the author to point out many divergencies from the main streams.

The following sketches will follow the principal groupings outlined in the previous chapter, in so far as clear relationships can be discovered between the authorities cited and their precursors. But even with this broader basis of classification, there are instances in which divergence is as obvious as kinship.

Neo-Behaviorism

None of the behaviorists has worked out a full-fledged theory of personality. Such a theory is hardly possible if one confines his attention strictly to "overt and observable" data. But several neo-behaviorists have developed elaborate learning theories.[3] Among the more important of these have been Guthrie, Hull, Skinner, and Tolman. Thorndike's "connectionism" is primarily concerned with learning, but it has obvious implications for personality theory and it belongs clearly within the behaviorist family.

GUTHRIE. Edwin R. Guthrie has been one of the most consistent of the learning theorists in applying rigorously the concepts of behaviorism.[4] His "contiguous conditioning" is based upon the assumption that the fundamental principle of learning—the one from which all other principles are derived—is *association by contiguity* of the "cue" (stimulus) and the response. Capacities, drives, motivations, rewards, and punishment are of secondary importance and not mat-

---

[2] Benjamin B. Wolman, *op. cit.*, p. ix.

[3] For detailed outlines of many of the contemporary theories of learning, see Ernest R. Hilgard, *Theories of Learning;* W. K. Estes, *et al., Modern Learning Theory;* and Sigmund Koch (ed.), *Psychology: A Study of a Science,* Study 1, Vol. 2, "General Systematic Formulations, Learning and Special Processes."

[4] Because only a thumbnail sketch is offered of each theory, no attempt will be made at documentation. The principal works of each theorist included in this discussion are listed in the bibliography.

ters of primary concern. An individual learns what he does at the time, nothing more. A student does not learn from what is in a lecture or book, he learns only what the lecture or book causes him to do. Even Guthrie found it necessary to deal with the problem of purposefulness or intention and explained actions in terms of preparatory and consummatory responses. But intentions, he believed, always include action tendencies that have been affected by previous experiences. Hence, they can finally be reduced to some form of conditioning.

HULL. Clark L. Hull's "deductive behaviorism" is an attempt to formulate a theory of learning in terms of a set of formal postulates, expressed in mathematical equations, from which a series of theorems may be deduced for experimental verification. Within the behavioristic tradition, the theory is avowedly mechanistic and avoids all reference to consciousness. Behavior is related to muscles, nerve cells and brain; and, in the final analysis, it can be reduced to physico-chemical factors. Habits are but persisting patterns of behavior acquired by the organism through reinforcement.

Hull sought to measure environmental influences upon the organism (which he called "input variables") and the responses (output variables); to infer what goes on in the organism (intervening variables); and to express these relationships in quantitative terms. Since the "intervening variables" were always the product of inference, Hull was never able to perfect his total schema and he spent much of his life testing and recasting his propositions. As might be expected, the system is highly involved and complex, its final formulation including seventeen postulates, seventeen corollaries, and more than a hundred theorems.

SKINNER. B. F. Skinner's "operant conditioning" is an inductive system in contrast with the deductive method of Hull. It differs from other behavioristic systems in that its main emphasis is upon "operant" behavior rather than simple stimulus-response reflexes. Such activities as cooking a meal, playing a piano, or driving an automobile cannot be described as immediate responses to specific stimuli. These are instances of operant behavior. In cases where operations are obviously related to previous stimulation, Skinner regarded these as "discriminated" operants as distinguished from true reflexes. He was unwilling, however, to introduce "mentalistic terms," to posit an "inner self," or to use terms that implied supposedly "nonphysical" events such as emotions, drives or habits.

Although Skinner recognized the presence of operants in human behavior, he rejected a speculative approach to scientific inquiry. He argued that attempts to solve the problems of dualism by appealing to mind or consciousness stood in the way of a unified account of nature. Instead of drive, for example, he preferred the term "deprivation," which can be measured. Instead of emotions (fear, anger, and so forth) he chose to describe behavior in terms of strengths or weaknesses in the responses induced by operations. Thus, while he admitted the inadequacy of typical behavioristic explanations, he did not entirely overcome the difficulties these signified.

TOLMAN. Edward C. Tolman's "purposive behaviorism" is eclectic in its approach to human learning and attempts to combine essential elements of several contemporary theories, while rejecting elements that seemed objectionable. Tolman agreed with the behaviorists that observable behavior constitutes the legitimate subject matter of psychology and that introspection as a method must be discarded. He was in strong disagreement, therefore, with structuralism. As opposed to other behaviorists, he was determined to give his system a "psychological" rather than a "physiological" base. He held that an act of behavior is "molar" rather than "molecular"—that is, it must be interpreted in terms of the whole organism and has distinctive properties of its own, regardless of the muscular, neural and glandular processes it may involve. The learner is following "signs" toward a goal (or away from an undersirable outcome, as the case may be) and is learning *meanings* as well as movements. Even an animal seems to be following a kind of "map" toward a goal rather than blind habits. Like the Gestaltists, he placed greater emphasis upon perception than upon stimulus-response connections. He agreed with McDougall that behavior is goal-directed, but he found no place in his system for instincts. Contrary to the view of McDougall, purposive behavior does not imply a teleological metaphysics but is regulated by ends that can be objectively determined. Tolman's theory is inviting because of its friendliness to new ideas and its attempts to avoid a narrow partisanship, but it is often criticized because of its apparent ambiguity.

As has been stated, the neo-behaviorists have been concerned primarily with problems of learning and have not attempted to formulate complete theories of personality. But a learning theory has its *raison d'être* from the fact of its relationship to personality. Those who attempt to formulate personality theories are under inescapable debt to those who have stuck to their determination to understand the learning process, and they cannot ignore the results of these efforts; but they must go beyond this limited field if they are to understand the persons who are doing the learning. Even behaviorists have moved in the direction of admitting their inability to encompass all the facts within a tidy stimulus-response connotation.

Psychoanalysis and Its Derivatives

Psychoanalysis had its inception and original development in the medical practice and philosophical speculation of Sigmund Freud, though a number of his associates and students have built systems that have modified, and in some instances have sharply diverged from, some of his basic ideas.

FREUD. Sigmund Freud was an empiricist and moved from observable phenomena to generalization and interpretation. But, when there were gaps in the data, he did not hesitate to round out his system by speculation and the use of analogy. He accepted some postulates that he did not attempt to prove: causation, mental energy, the economy of energy, the constancy principle, the pleasure principle, and others. He seemed to vacillate between monism and dualism. He held, on the one hand, to the unity of man and nature and believed that mental processes somehow stem from the same physical sources as anything else. Psychic energy is but a transformation of somatic energy. But, on the other hand, he held that a human being may be transformed from an impulsive animal that mirrors the chaotic irrationality of the universe into a purposive agent exercising rational choice. He was a determinist and held that constitutional factors and experiences in childhood are the prime conditioners of personality, and that the individual is often unaware of the power of these forces. In order to understand human behavior, he insisted, it is necessary to understand the processes at work beneath observable phenomena. At this point, he seems to hold something in common with Kant.

One of Freud's basic concepts was that of a dynamic *unconscious*, an area of great psychic energy which influences all human behavior but operates upon materials not subject to recognition by the normal processes of thought. Many of life's experiences are forgotten, as a result of the operation of a mechanism known as *repression*, and these are prevented from recurring in consciousness by the process of *resistance*. These repressed memories are the occasion for many neurotic and pathological tendencies in behavior. On the basis of these convictions and concepts, Freud sought to build a systematic explanation of conduct.

Freud held that the cause of all behavior is *Trieb* (drive, instinct), which consists of the psychological concomitants of biological processes. He did not attempt to draw up a list of instincts but assumed that they all could be subsumed under two general headings: *eros,* the sexual instinct, the totality of the forces that serve pleasure and enhance the vital functions, and which moves toward affectionate, erotic, and constructive behavior; and *thanatos,* the death instinct, which impels toward aggressive, hostile, and destructive behavior. These two instincts are constantly at work operating in contrary directions. The aim of eros is to bind together, to preserve by fusion, to establish greater unity, while that of thanatos is to disperse, to disrupt connections, to destroy unity. The two forces may combine, but more frequently they fight each other. In properly adjusted individuals, the two opposing drives are made to interact so that each neutralizes the overt primitive expressions of the other.

The form of energy by which the instincts perform their work is called *libido.* The growing child goes through several developmental stages, during which his libido seeks outlets progressively through different body areas; and he receives pleasure in activities associated with the respective *erogenous zones* (the oral, anal, urethral, phallic, and genital stages). Following the genital period at the conclusion of early childhood, the latency period emerges when the sexual interests subside considerably. Then, at puberty, physiological changes lead to full-scale development and interest becomes centered in interpersonal relationships.

During the course of physical growth, libido development is successively directed toward different objects: first, toward the child's own body (narcissism); then, toward parents (Oedipus complex); and finally, toward persons and objects in the outer world. If development is arrested or thwarted, the individual will be retarded in emotional growth with inevitably harmful consequences in later life. If an adult is continually frustrated, and his libido must be diverted from its normal genital outlet, he may revert to objects and satisfactions associated with childhood (regression). A person thus frustrated may be unable to respond effectively to the complex demands of adulthood. In the emotionally mature person, most of the libidinal energy may be deflected from its unconscious aim toward socially useful goals (sublimation).

According to Freud, personality is divided into three functional parts. First, the *id,* the representative of instinct, the reservoir of instinctual drives, which contains the biological determinants of behavior. It is dominated by the *pleasure principle,* which aims at immediate gratification of instinctive impulses. It is an automatic aspect of mental activity and operates entirely within the unconscious. It knows no ethical values, no good nor evil.

Second, the *superego* is that part of the person which has been influenced away from the self-centered primitive impulses toward social ideals and motives as the result of experience. It manifests itself as conscience, as socially acquired inhibitions that limit the expressions of natural impulsiveness. The superego originates in the child's identification with parents and others and in response to social pressure. It acts as an effective *censor* of the instincts, often with accompanying mental distress. The unrestrained pleasure principle comes into inevitable conflict with the environment constituted by nature and society.

Third, the *ego* is that part of the id which has been modified by contact with the outer world and includes elements which are both conscious and unconscious, but is made up for the most part of what is usually referred to as consciousness. Its business is to reconcile instinctual human nature and society's coercive demands in conformity with the *reality principle,* the ability to modify or postpone the immediate discharge of energy. The ego is the mental agent that mediates between (1) the drive for immediate satisfactions that arises in the id; (2) the claims of the superego; and (3) the outside demands of social pressure and external reality.

Freud was essentially pessimistic about the outcome of the human struggle. An individual must always encounter frustrations exacted by reality. The resulting struggle will inevitably bring him anxieties and feelings of guilt. Men become neurotic because they cannot tolerate the privations that society imposes by means of its cultural ideals. So every individual becomes virtually an enemy of culture and maintains a deep resentment against a civilization built upon coercion and renunciation of natural instincts. He may seek various means of escape, but religion is one of the worst, being essentially an "illusion" and a regression to primitive forms of wishful thinking. Thus it may retard his progress toward mature adulthood. Psychoanalysis is one means by which he may be anabled to understand his problems, face them realistically, and live as effectively as he can.

The history of the psychoanalytic movement has been one of misunderstanding, heresies, schisms, and deviations in interpretations of the basic doctrines.[5] The limitations of space prohibit more than the most cursory review of some of the best-known modifications of the Freudian postulates.

ADLER. Alfred Adler, one of Freud's early associates, broke with Freud over the latter's insistence that sex is the universally predisposing factor in mental disorder. Adler's "individual psychology" placed the emphasis rather upon the *striving for superiority*, the will to power. All personality derangements, he maintained, have their roots in feelings of inadequacy from physical handicaps or from conflicts with those who restrict one's efforts toward power and self-assertion.

In contrast with Freud's rigid historical determinism, Adler held that man is motivated more by his expectations than by past experience. If hampered in the realization of his goals by real or imaginary handicaps, the individual may develop an *inferiority complex* and may seek to overcome his limitations by various forms of *compensation*. Demosthenes compensated for speech defects by becoming a great orator; Theodore Roosevelt, for physical weakness in his youth by systematic exercise. Compensation may take neurotic forms. It has been conjectured, for example, that Hitler tried to compensate for sexual impotence by a predaceous grasping after world domination.

According to Adler, every person has the goal of superiority but there are many different ways of striving for this goal. One may seek superiority by struggling for political power, another may pursue eminence in the intellectual world, another may devote his energies toward becoming a great athlete. But whatever his goal, he arranges the details of his life with reference to this goal. All behavior springs from one's *style of life*. The style of life is the expression of one's own individuality, for each individual sees the goal of life in a unique way. The important thing is not what one inherits, or what the environment may do to him, but what he does with what he has.

Man is influenced in his pursuit of superiority by his *self-ideal*, his vision of what he means to become, just as the character created by a good dramatist guides the performance of an actor in a play. This goal may even be unrealistic and fictional ("fictional finalism"), but it affects present behavior as truly as if the fiction were a reality. And,

[5] G. S. Blum, *Psychoanalytic Theories of Personality;* Ruth Munroe, *Schools of Psychoanalytic Thought.*

in Adler's view, a normal person can free himself from the influence of fictional goals and adjust his self-ideal to reality, something a neurotic person cannot do.

Adler placed great emphasis upon the social determinants of behavior. Whereas Freud had seen man's chief motivation in inborn sexual instincts, Adler found it in social urges. Man is inherently social. He seeks association with others. He co-operates with his fellows in community enterprises. He may place the public welfare above his own selfish interests. He tends to acquire a style of life that is basically social in orientation.

One of Adler's principal contributions as a personality theorist was his concept of the *creative self*. According to this doctrine, the individual creates his own personality. Heredity furnishes him with certain abilities, environment gives him certain impressions; but the manner in which he "experiences" these is his own creative way of building up his attitudes toward life. And it is attitudes toward life that determine one's relationships to the outside world. The basic principle of personal development in Adler's view, then, is not deterministic nor mechanistic as Freud believed, but teleological, idealistic.

JUNG. Carl Gustav Jung, like Adler, rejected Freud's pansexualism. His "analytic psychology" was based upon the concept of libido, but not in the sense of Freud's all-powerful sexual instinct nor of Adler's drive for mastery. Libido is psychic energy, a manifestation of the life energy of an organism as a biological system. Psychic energy is a continuation of physical energy, and each of the two types of energy can be transformed into the other. Life energy is generated by inner conflicts between the components of a given system.

According to Jung, the structure of human personality consists of three interacting parts. At the center is the *ego*, the conscious mind, which is made up of perceptions, memories, thoughts, and feelings. It is the means by which the person maintains his sense of identity and continuity. In a region adjoining the ego is the *personal unconscious*, which consists of subliminal perceptions and all experiences that have been suppressed, ignored, or forgotten. The *collective unconscious*, which has been the most controversial aspect of Jung's psychology, is the repository of acquired traits and cultural patterns inherited from the ancestral past.

A constellation of memories, thoughts, and feelings may form around some object as a nucleus and persist as a *complex* within the personal unconscious in ways that affect external behavior. For example, a "mother complex" may form from a combination of racial experiences with mothers and the child's experience with his own mother. Jung developed the free word association test as a method of identifying and studying the complexes. These exist as independent and autonomous, but partial, systems in the mind; and they vary according to the variety of experiences which different individuals may have.

Jung believed that racial memories exist as unconscious forces in the deeper layers of the individual mind. These "great primordial images" are transmitted by heredity from generation to generation. They take the form of *archetypes,* which are universal ideas that make up a part of the collective unconscious. They are the psychic remainder of human evolution and accumulate as a result of repeated experiences over many centuries. Mythology Jung regarded as the continuing influence of the early childhood of the race. Religion had its beginning in an autonomous system of archetypal nature. The principal archetype of religion is God.

Jung is well known for his distinction between two basic types of personality orientation. The *extrovert* is one whose libido moves toward the outer world. He thinks and lives so as to correspond with objective conditions and claims, whether good or bad. The *introvert* is self-centered and is deeply involved with his own inner life. For either type, life energy may perform four basic functions. It may take the form of rational processes (thinking and feeling), which are determined by what Jung calls "objective values." Or it may be spent in irrational processes (sensation and intuition), which are determined by "accidental perceptions," more or less illogical associations, and chance. Either extroversion or introversion may be organized mainly around one of the four functions, thinking, feeling, sensation, or intuition. The basic orientation and the function around which life energy is centered are important factors in determining the type of personality.

In his total view of personality, Jung combined the concepts of causality and teleology, and insisted that both principles are necessary if full understanding is to be achieved. The individual is conditioned by his own experience and by racial history (causality); but he lives by his own aims and aspirations (teleology). The self is not a "given" but develops gradually as the conflicting elements of the conscious and the unconscious come into harmony through the unifying function of the psyche. Self-achievement is the goal of life.

RANK. Otto Rank, rejecting the Freudian concept of the Oedipus complex, gave the *birth trauma* a central position in the causation of neuroses. He held that, prior to birth, the individual enjoyed a feeling of wholeness and security as he rested warmly and comfortably in the womb of his mother. At birth, he is thrust forth in separation from his mother's body into a cold and unfeeling world where he must learn to accept himself as a separate and independent entity. The separation is so traumatic that it becomes the source of an overpowering anxiety. Any subsequent experiences of separation may revive his feelings of anxiety. His development is an admixture of the struggle for independence and the fear of it. The process of education becomes primarily a matter of "will therapy."

An individual, according to Rank, goes through three developmental stages. First, he accepts blindly the social pressures that come from his parents and the sexual urges that come from within. Next, an inner conflict arises and he begins to form his own concepts and values. Lastly, he strikes out on his own way toward individuality. Similarly, there are three stages in the development of the will. The *counter will* is the first and is usually expressed in opposition to prohibitions imposed by his parents. The *competitive will* is an expression of the desire to do or possess things for himself. And the *positive will* is evidenced when he sets his own goals and standards.

Rank distinguished three personality types, depending on how the individual succeeded in mastering the three developmental stages. One is the *conforming* type who gives ready assent to the will of others. He may pretend to play a role of his own, but he really lives in a world of illusion and ignorance, in virtual abnegation of his own inner desires. A second is the *nonconforming* type who does not accept the collective will but cannot live independently. He cannot accept others nor can he tolerate separation from them. Remote from others he feels lonely, tense, and inadequate. The individual who successfully masters all three stages is the *creative* type, the whole person with an autonomous will, who neither has to compromise nor tamely accept the popular will. Such a person can develop his own ideals and standards beyond mere identification with the morality of the superego. He can evolve his ego ideal from within, not just in terms of ideals imposed upon him by others but from self-chosen goals for which he consciously strives.

SOCIO-CULTURAL PERSPECTIVES. As the psychoanalytic approach to personality gained wider acceptance, emphasis shifted from a focal interest in the instinctive drives of the individual to the larger social and cultural context in which behavior takes place. As we have seen, Adler gave attention to the importance of social urges in fashioning a person's style of life. Jung stressed the effect of inherited racial patterns, or archetypes, in determining the outlook of an individual.

New data bearing upon the motivation of behavior came from the advancing field of cultural anthropology. Bronislaw Malinowski's studies of the Trobriand Islanders showed that the stages in individual development are greatly dependent on cultural factors and he suggested at least the possibility that it may be mainly a product of these.[6] Ruth Benedict found that a particular culture tends to dictate the mores of the community and, in turn, dominates the lives of individual members and shapes their personalities.[7] Margaret Mead discovered that sex behavior in primitive societies, among both men and women, is primarily determined by their culture.[8] Abram Kardiner, in comparative studies of the institutions of several different cultures, concluded that child-rearing practices are culturally patterned and that personality structure depends upon environmental factors more than upon developmental stages.[9]

These and many other studies in cultural anthropology and sociology provided the basis for a new orientation for psychoanalytic theory. Neo-psychoanalysts, particularly in America, have tended to place much greater emphasis upon cultural determinants of personality than Freud had done. Notice can be given here to only a few of the innovators.

HORNEY. Karen Horney acknowledged her indebtedness to Freud and claimed that her theory fell within the framework of psychoanalysis, but she tried to eliminate certain concepts of Freud which she regarded as fallacious. She agreed that psychic processes are strictly determined, that unconscious factors affect motivation, that desires may be repressed and reappear in the form of dreams, and that sex is an important element in personality development.

But she denied that sex is the predominating factor. She rejected the concepts of eros and thanatos, and of libido, and was convinced

---

[6] Bronislaw Malinowski, *The Sexual Life of Savages in North-western Melanesia.*

[7] Ruth Benedict, *Patterns of Culture.*

[8] Margaret Mead, *Sex and Temperament in Three Primitive Societies* and *Male and Female.*

[9] Abram Kardiner, *The Individual and His Society.*

that psychoanalysis should outgrow its dependence upon an instinctive and genetic psychology. In fact, she was skeptical about the existence of instincts at all. Behavior is a product of cultural influences rather than of instinctive forces. She felt that neurotic behavior is evidence of social maladjustment rather than of conflicts between the ego and the id and superego.

Horney held that Freud overworked the pleasure principle (*Lustprinzip*, the principle of immediate, urgent discharge of energy) and based her own theory upon two guiding principles: "safety and satisfaction." The need for safety, to be secure and free from fear, she regarded as one of the basic human needs. People need to be accepted, to be loved. When children lack acceptance and love, they develop a basic anxiety which affects all their later development. They fear punishment or desertion and feel that the environment is menacing. In contrast with Freud's view that love and hate are the basic emotions, Horney regarded acceptance and anxiety (the result of a lack of it) as primary. People also have other fundamental needs, such as food, rest, and sex; and these needs must be satisfied if normal development is to ensue. These are all brought together under the heading of seeking satisfaction.

Horney agreed with Freud that character as well as neurosis develops in early childhood, but she denied the validity of Freud's concept of developmental stages which are biogenic and universal. There is no such thing as universal anal and phallic stages, no universal Oedipus complex. Development does not depend upon predetermined stages but upon how the child is treated. She listed ten "neurotic needs," which are acquired in the course of trying to find solutions to the problem of unhappy human relationships. Later she classified these under three headings: (1) the need for love, *moving toward people;* (2) the need for independence, *moving away from people;* and (3) the need for power, *moving against people.* The common denominator of all these trends is social maladjustment. They may be obviated or ameliorated in an atmosphere of acceptance and love where basic satisfactions are assured.

Horney was closer to Adler than to Freud in her confidence in the possibilities of social progress and of personality changes in adult life. She denied the strangle hold of instinctual forces and recognized a general human tendency toward constructiveness. She believed, therefore, that a human being has both the capacity and the desire to develop his potentialities and to go on changing throughout his life.

SULLIVAN. Of the American psychoanalysts who have developed theories of personality, perhaps Harry S. Sullivan has departed farthest from Freud. He constructed his own conceptual system, though at certain points he was strongly influenced by Freudian concepts.

Like Freud, Sullivan recognized certain *developmental stages* in personal growth, though he did not connect these directly with libido nor with specific erogenous zones. These stages were associated rather with stages of growth *in interpersonal relations*. These stages are six in number from birth to maturity: (1) *infancy,* from birth to the articulate use of language; (2) *childhood,* from the emergence of speech to the capacity to play with one's peers; (3) the *juvenile* period, from the first school attendance to (4) *preadolescence,* in which the child feels the need for intimate relationships with a person of his own sex; (5) *adolescence,* during which he moves from indeterminate patterns of heterosexual activity to the establishment of a fully mature repertory of interpersonal relationships in (6) *adulthood.*

During the entire course of this development, particularly in his early years, the individual is actuated by two basic purposes, satisfaction and security. *Satisfaction* is primarily a matter of relieving somatic tensions—the need for food, air, exercise, rest, sex, and the relaxation of tensions through the satisfaction of these needs. *Security* is related to cultural stresses. The feeling of "euphoria" results from being accepted and loved by one's parents and other "significant" persons; while its opposite, anxiety, comes from disapproval or rejection. Anxiety may prevent satisfaction in relieving somatic needs, interfere with normal mental functioning, retard the growth of proper self-esteem, and hinder the capacity to develop desirable relationships with other persons. On the other hand, avoidance or relief of socially engendered anxiety will bring satisfaction, security, and self-esteem.

Sullivan did not deny that biological factors are conditioners of personality, but he did not believe that instincts are important sources of motivation. He rejected Freud's libido theory and placed greater emphasis than Freud upon the influence of environmental forces. From the beginning, a child "feels" the attitudes of others toward him and these attitudes deeply affect his self-concept. In fact, the self develops through the approbation or disfavor of others. One develops self-identifications on the basis of the treatment he receives from the significant persons in his life. If he is accepted, approved, and loved, he tends to identify with the "good-me"; if not, with the "bad-me."

Similarly, he projects these personifications upon others, the "good-mother" or the "bad-mother," as the case may be. Hence the individual cannot be studied as an entity in isolation from his associates and his environment. Psychology is concerned with the "field" or "situation" in which two or more persons are involved. Not individuals but "dyadic" interactions constitute the subject matter of psychology.

Persons become persons in relation to others. The other persons may not be perceived as they really are. But the individual reacts to them as they appear to him. And, if the real persons do not maintain with him the types of relation that will provide satisfaction and security, he may establish relations with "eidetic" or imaginary persons. And his behavior is oriented toward the persons and the situations as he perceives them.

FROMM. Erich Fromm departs from the orthodox Freudian approach, which explains social phenomena as outcomes of libidinal trends, and holds that the behavior of the individual is shaped by society. Society, in turn, is molded by external conditions that are embodied in the culture. A given person is a composite of (1) his "individual character," which is the totality of innate factors as these are shaped by the specific influences of home environment; and (2) the "social character" of the majority of those who share the same culture. Since parents themselves bear the stamp of the social character, its influence is compelling. Thus, Fromm shifts the focus of interest from the child's libidinal experience to the environment and the impact of cultural forces. Individual differences stem from the total sum of social relationships.

In the course of evolution, man has developed certain characteristic attitudes which involve him in emotional difficulties. An animal is a part of nature and he lives in accordance with nature. But, though he is a part of nature, man cannot completely identify himself with it. Primitive man tried to escape this dilemma by developing myths and religion and by completely identifying himself with his group or clan. For modern man, this proves impossible. His "escape from freedom" has involved him in existential dichotomies which he has been unable to resolve. As his life becomes more atomistic and highly individualized, he feels less secure than did men in former times. If he seeks to regain security by relinquishing his freedom in some form of totalitarianism, this too is deceptive. The only way out is to further develop his own powers. He may find productive outlets for his energies in creating material things, works of art, systems of thought. But by far the most important object of his productiveness is man himself—"man for himself."

In the search for selfhood, people develop different forms of relatedness to the outside world, different "orientations." Fromm distinguishes at least four types of "nonproductive" orientation. The *receiving* type is expressed by a person who expects to receive and accept from others—but not to give—material things, love, loyalty. The *exploiting* person, like the receiving, expects to get from others but only by his own strength or cunning. The individual with a *hoarding* orientation perceives the world and other persons as threatening and he tends to be grasping and miserly. He withdraws as much as he can from social interaction. The *marketing* type of individual, so typical in our modern era, tries to "sell himself" and to "meet the right people." A person's success depends not so much on personal qualities as upon salesmanship.

In the long run, Fromm thinks, all of these attitudes are self-defeating and cannot lead to an abiding sense of security. There is, however, a *productive* orientation, in which one's energies are guided by creativity and by love for others. If a person is actuated by devotion to the welfare of his fellow men and if he uses his energies in productive activities leading toward this end, even the negative aspects of the other frames of reference may be overcome and they may be turned into positive traits.

Our present culture, however, is hardly the type to encourage the development of productive personalities. Modern society is "sick," a victim of the "pathology of normalcy." It constitutes only another dangerous "escape from freedom." It results in further alienation and but intensifies the human predicament. Modern man's best hope is to take more seriously what he believes and teaches about the dignity of man and the redeeming power of love. Our primary task is to use our human powers in building a "sane society," in which "man relates to man lovingly," in which there is "the possibility of transcending nature by creating rather than by destroying," and in which the higher potentialities inherent in human nature may be increasingly realized.

Stimulus-Response and Factor Theories

This chapter will be concluded with a brief reference to certain theories of learning which, while not personality theories as such, have some bearing on our present problem. Consideration should be given to these in a total assessment of personality.

STIMULUS-RESPONSE THEORIES. A number of psychologists have concentrated their efforts upon learning theory in the tradition of Thorndike, Tolman, Skinner, Guthrie, and Hull, but have taken a wider view of the learner than did the behaviorists.

John Dollard and Neal Miller, for example, have sought to combine S-R concepts with unconscious processes as stressed in psychoanalytic theory. In their view, learning theory is "the study of the circumstances under which a response and a cue stimulus become connected." The learning process consists of four elements: drive, cue, response, and reinforcement. It takes place within a social context and cannot be understood except in relation to cultural influences. Unconscious factors, occasioned by conflicts between inner forces and environmental pressures, are important. The theory of *reinforcement* (reward) proposed by Dollard and Miller, which modifies Hull's concept in the direction of psychoanalysis, seems to be their most important contribution to personality study.

Richard R. Sears holds a position which in general is consonant with the theory of Dollard and Miller. He places special emphasis upon the importance of *dyadic units* in the study of behavior. Psychologists who fix their attention exclusively upon "monadic units" (single individuals) fail to recognize the significance of the dynamic interpersonal aspects of experience. It is action, not perception, that is crucial. The behavior of one individual is functionally linked to the responses of one or more other persons. An adequate theory of behavior, then, must include both monadic and dyadic units and these must somehow be integrated.

O. Hobart Mowrer has developed a *two-factor theory* of learning in which he distinguishes between (1) "solution learning," which occurs when a drive is reduced or a problem is solved and which is mediated by the central nervous system, and (2) "sign learning," which occurs when a formerly neutral stimulus accompanies drive induction or onset and which is mediated by the autonomic nervous system. Solution learning involves the voluntary responses (behavior), while sign learning involves the involuntary processes (emotions). Most learning situations are complicated and include both of these forms of behavior, but they are different and can be distinguished.

FACTOR THEORIES. A number of psychologists have approached the problem of personality through analyses of the basic factors that motivate and constitute behavior. These work within the main stream of the psychometric tradition and make extensive use of objective tests and statistical techniques. These owe much to the pioneer work done on mental abilities by Spearman and on individual differences by J. McKeen Cattell. Among the factor theorists whose findings seem significant for a total understanding of personality are H. J. Eysenck, Raymond Cattell, and J. P. Guilford. The limitations of space will not permit a discussion of their contributions here.

VII. CONTEMPORARY PERSONALITY THEORIES, CONTINUED

The influence of early leaders has continued to be felt in the later development of psychology, though it is increasingly difficult to group individual psychologists together in "schools" or systems. Structuralism, functionalism, behaviorism, Gestalt, and psychoanalysis are terms which are more useful when designating major viewpoints in the early history of psychology in America than they are today. As we move closer to the contemporary scene, it seems necessary to find other modes of classification, while at the same time keeping in mind the relationship of the newer tendencies to earlier trends.

Morphological Theories

In the popular mind human behavior is related in important respects to certain characteristics of physical makeup. Stout people are supposed to be more indolent and jolly than others, lean people more nervous and shy, and people with red hair more susceptible to explosive outbursts of sudden anger. This view finds some support in the investigations of serious students of personality. Hippocrates suggested that human beings can be divided into four basic temperament types, depending upon the "humors" within the body. Lavater proposed the study of physiognomy as a basis for "the promotion of knowledge and the love of mankind." Rostan and Viola worked out typologies which classified human beings according to body build. But Kretschmer and Sheldon are most noted for their "constitutional" approaches to personality, and their views will be briefly outlined here.

KRETSCHMER. Ernst Kretschmer became interested in the problems of human morphology in connection with studies of mental disorder. He observed that schizophrenia and manic-depressive psychosis seem to be related to certain types of physique. He developed, from an elaborate system of measurements of the major parts of the body, check lists which could be filled in with patients standing before him. He noted that there are four fundamental body types: (1) *asthenic,* lean persons with narrow shoulders, thin stomach and flat chest; (2) *athletic,* well-proportioned, middle-sized, with wide, projecting shoulders, superb chest, and firm stomach; (3) *pyknic,* with pronounced peripheral development of body cavities, rounded figure, broad face, and a "magnificent fat paunch" protruding from a deeply vaulted chest that broadens out toward the lower parts of the body; and (4) *dysplastic,* a relatively small group with strikingly deviant builds such that they appear even to casual observers as "surprising and ugly."

After comparing his psychiatric patients by means of this physique classification, Kretschmer concluded that there is a "clear biological affinity" between manic-depressive psychosis and the pyknic physique and between schizophrenia and the asthenic, athletic, and dysplastic types. He theorized that there is likewise a relation between physique and various patterns of normal behavior but provided no direct evidence to support this postulate.

SHELDON. William H. Sheldon represents a fairly distinctive approach to personality in American psychological circles today in that he places primary emphasis upon the physical structure of the human body and its parallel and correlated temperament dimensions as the principal determinants of behavior. He insists that psychology should be "biologically oriented" and that it requires a "physical anthropology" for its foundation support.

In developing a procedure for analyzing variables in physique, Sheldon secured some four thousand photographs of male college students, which were inspected by several judges for the purpose of discriminating the factors that account for variations in body structure. Three dimensions were discovered which form the basis for Sheldon's "somatotyping." The first is *endomorphy,* represented in people who possess softness of body and present a rounded appearance, with relative under-development of bone and muscle. The second is *mesomorphy,* characterized by figures that are hard and rectangular with a predominance of bone and muscle. The third is *ectomorphy,* found in figures that are linear and fragile, with flat chests and delicacy of body texture.

The four thousand subjects were ranked and rated in terms of these components, a technique was developed for objective measurement (the *Somatotype Performance Test*), and a machine was constructed for computing the somatotypes represented by a preponderance of each of the dimensions indicated. The somatotype is regarded as a reliable means of estimating the basic biological determinants of behavior. While the initial work was based upon a study of male figures, Sheldon has carried out extensive investigation of female somatotypes, which he says confirms his belief in the validity of this technique.

Parallel with the study of somatotypes, Sheldon has also analyzed the chief components of temperament which is regarded as the other chief variable in determining behavior. These components are also three in number: *visceratonia,* characterized by general love of comfort, sociability and affection, and voracious appetite for food and drink; *somatotonia,* evidenced by love of physical adventure and the need for muscular and vigorous physical activity; and *cerebrotonia,* manifest in people who are secretive, self-conscious, afraid of social activity, and who have a preference for solitude. Sheldon's *Scale for Temperament* is a device for rating subjects according to the dominance of one or the other of these components together with the defining traits of each dimension.

Sheldon reports that there is a close correspondence between temperament as measured by observer ratings on the Scale for Temperament and physique as measured by the Somatotype Performance Test. And he regards the results of these studies as presenting strong confirmative support for his conviction that there is a marked continuity between the physical structure of the individual and his behavioral tendencies. Sheldon has applied his methods to studies of mental disorders and delinquency, and reports that there are positive correlations between somatotypes, temperament, and various types of psychological and social abnormalities. He is convinced that there are important constitutional and behavioral differences not only between delinquents and non-delinquents but also between the subvarieties of delinquents. His conclusions offer at least a challenge to those who see abnormalities of behavior as stemming entirely from environmental sources.

Organismic Theories

Several contemporary psychologists who have contributed to the development of personality theory are nearer to McDougall's hormic theory than they are to behaviorism, psychoanalysis, or constitutional psychology. These will be considered together here because of their emphasis upon the *holistic*, or organismic, character of human behavior.

These psychologists dissent strongly from the dichotomy of body and mind which constituted the basis of Descartes' philosophy and from the atomization of sensations, feelings, and ideas such as was held by the associationists and structuralists. They have endeavored to construct theories that combine body and mind, somewhat on the same basis as the early functionalists, and to deal with behavior as functioning of the organism as a whole. They differ from the early functionalists in their emphasis upon the goals or purposes of the individual. Though they have much in common with the Gestaltists, their theories have been more inclusive. Whereas Gestalt psychologists have been concerned primarily with problems of perception and "insight," the organismic theorists have viewed perception as only one aspect of the experience of the whole person. Gestaltists have centered attention upon learning theory rather than upon the total concept of personality.

GOLDSTEIN. Kurt Goldstein came to formulate his concept of personality after a study of medicine, several years of teaching neurology and psychiatry, and research on brain injuries of soldiers during World War I. He concluded that illness symptoms are not manifestations of changes in specific functions or structures of the organism but rather forms of adjustment to total internal needs and tensions caused by environmental pressures. Behavior patterns are not isolated events but expressions of the whole person.

Goldstein's personality theory can be outlined in terms of certain basic concepts. First, *self-actualization*. Human behavior has the goal of full self-realization. It consists of efforts in the direction of becoming a whole person. Each individual has many potentialities, which are indicated by his interests, aptitudes, and preferences. Ordinarily he acts in ways that will give opportunity for the development of these potentialities. If he is placed in situations with which he can successfully cope, he will develop normally through experience and maturation. As new situations arise, he will construct new behavior patterns to deal with these. But if the environment presents conditions beyond his capacities to manage, he may react in ways that are inconsistent with the principle of self-actualization, thus leading to pathological conditions.

Second, *equalization of energy.* Goldstein believed that an individual has a constant supply of available energy which is fairly evenly distributed throughout the organism. The normal person tends to discharge his energies in the reduction of tensions and in efforts to return to the "average" state of equalization. When he is hungry, he eats to relieve hunger. When he is disturbed by sudden noises or other external threats, he seeks to restore order by attending to the stimuli which led to the disturbance. When he is subjected to social pressures that make extraordinary demands upon him, he tries to behave in ways that will protect his own interests and at the same time restore equanimity.

Third, *coming to terms with environment.* Although Goldstein found the principal sources of motivation in the constitution of the individual and in the goal of self-actualization, he did not minimize the significance of interaction between individual and environment. The outside world is the main source of supply for accomplishing the purposes of the self, and it presents many possibly disturbing factors with which the self must deal. A person must "come to terms" with the environment, regardless of personal aims, both because it provides the means for self-actualization and because it poses the principal challenges and threats to the attainment of these aims. When the environment is rich in resources and relationships that encourage growth, energies may be utilized in behavior that leads toward self-actualization; but when it is barren or threatening, energies may be diverted into channels that retard progress in the desired direction.

Goldstein is optimistic regarding the potentialities of human nature. He believes that there is nothing inherently bad in the individual, who will develop into a healthy, integrated personality if supported by a friendly environment; but he may be handicapped and crippled if he must struggle against a hostile and malignant external situation.

MASLOW. Abraham Maslow has adopted a "holistic-dynamic" or organismic view of personality. He agrees with Goldstein that an essential characteristic of persons is their "self-actualizing" tendencies. Man is a "perpetually wanting animal." He is motivated by needs which operate on ascending levels. Maslow has classified the various levels of need in a "hierarchy of prepotency." Those at the lower levels appear earliest and are more potent. When these are met, needs at the next "higher" level emerge and press for satisfaction.

At the lowest level are *physiological needs,* food, drink, shelter, sex. When these are satisfied, *safety needs* appear; and the individual seeks security in some kind of haven in which he may carry on his activities. When physiological and safety needs are assured of gratification, *love needs* are manifested in the craving for companionship and affection, particularly of members of the opposite sex. At a still higher level are *esteem needs,* the longing for the respect of one's fellows and the search for prestige in occupational and social relationships. At the highest level are *self-actualization needs* which can only be satisfied by creative work of some kind, intellectual, artistic, or humanitarian.

Maslow believes that human nature is essentially good. He scolds psychology for its "pessimistic, negative, and limited conception" of man. A distorted image has resulted from too much preoccupation with cases in which the satisfaction of legitimate human needs has been frustrated or denied. The picture might be quite different if attention had been directed more toward instances in which the nobler qualities in human nature have been given fuller opportunity for expression. It might be different if as much consideration were given to the tenderness, sympathy, co-operation, and love of men as has been given to their conflicts, hostilities, and guilt.

The true quality of human nature, Maslow holds, is best illustrated by "self-actualizing" people rather than by those who operate on a level of mere adjustment or "coping with needs." He supports this contention with a study of a number of individuals, some of whom were figures of history, such as Abraham Lincoln, Thomas Jefferson, and Walt Whitman; and others who were living at the time of the study, like Albert Einstein and Eleanor Roosevelt. Maslow was concerned with the qualities that distinguish these from ordinary people. All of his subjects, he found, were marked by a degree of optimum psychological health and made full use of their talents, capacities, and potentialities. Their personal development involved growth motivation and a drive toward self-realization. They developed to the full stature of which they were capable.

Maslow concluded that all of these shared in common certain "whole characteristics" which reached beyond the simple reduction of needs. (1) They had a more efficient perception of reality, with consequent freedom from superstition and prejudice. (2) They accepted themselves, other people, and nature without becoming perfectionists or absolutists. (3) They had a spontaneity, simplicity and naturalness, without artificiality and straining after effect. (4) They were able to submerge their self-interests in helping to meet the problems of others. (5) They had a quality of detachment and a capacity for solitude. (6) They were autonomous and independent of cultural and environmental pressures. (7) They had a continued freshness of appreciation, without boredom and ennui. (8) They were capable of mystical experiences and had a deep sensitivity for the wonders of the universe. (9) They had pronounced feelings of loyalty and affection for the rest of mankind. (10) They developed intimate relationships with a few well-chosen friends with whom they shared profound personal experiences. (11) They seemed unaware of class differences and were friendly toward persons of every class, creed, or color. (12) They were fair and honest and did not confuse means and ends. (13) They were philosophical, with a nonhostile sense of humor. (14) They had a special kind of inventiveness, originality, and creativeness.[1]

ANGYAL. Andras Angyal has protested against "atomistic" approaches to personality and has pleaded for a science which studies "the human person in his totality." According to his view, previous theories have tended to deal with "artificially separated single aspects" of the human organism as if it were nothing more than "the mere aggregation of physiological, psychological, and social functions." Knowledge of the "total person," he feels, cannot emerge from these "segmental" studies. Moreover, personality theory has tended to borrow its concepts from physiology and psychology, with the result that there are sciences *related* to the person but none *of* the person. A holistic theory should develop its own set of concepts.

As a step in the direction of an acceptable theory, Angyal proposes the term *biosphere* to denote an entity that includes both individual and environment. He holds that an arbitrary distinction between an organism and its environment cannot be made legitimately. They cannot be separated except by abstraction, since they interact and interpenetrate in such complex ways that attempts to disentangle them can lead only to oversimplification and confusion. Life is an "autonomous event" which takes place between organism and environment.

The dynamics of biospheric behavior arises from tensions that pull in seemingly opposite directions between the two poles of organism and environment. The trend toward "autonomy," or *self-determination*, is manifested in efforts to expand the self through assimilation and mastery of environment. This is expressed in specific channels

[1] Abraham H. Maslow, *Self-Actualizing People: A Study of Psychological Health.*

such as the desire for superiority, for acquisition, and for achievement. The opposite trend toward "homonomy," or *self-surrender*, is manifested in efforts to fit the self to the environment and to participate in something that is larger than the self. This is expressed in adaptations to nature and to social groups and in adjustments of the individual to his conceptions of a supernatural being. These trends, although they may seem to be opposed, are really but two aspects of a more general and inclusive trend of the biosphere, that of *self-expansion*.

The integrity of the biosphere is maintained when the various organic processes, or "systems," work in harmonious relationship. It may be disturbed by the segregation of the systems one from another. As the various processes become conscious, a person develops various ideas about himself, and the totality of these constitutes his *symbolic self*. This may not always be a reliable representation of the true self. Distortions may result in behaviors that interfere with the goal of self-expansion. This goal is best achieved when all the dimensions of the personality are blended into one consistent and realistic whole.

Field Theory

Kurt Lewin, who began his work as a member of the Gestalt group, attempted to weave together into a systematic theory all the many properties of the individual and the varied environmental factors which impinge upon behavior. He maintained that an adequate psychology must be based upon open-minded observation of what people actually think, feel, and do as well as the situations and settings in which events occur; and that these must be combined by logical construction into a total system of concepts in which due consideration is given to all of the parts. His "field theory" was an attempt to deal with the full empirical reality of human experience and behavior without neglecting any of its components.

Lewin's field theory borrowed some of its concepts from mathematics and the physical sciences but gave these a specifically psychological connotation. Modern physics defines a "field" as a region or space traversed by lines of electro-magnetic force. The boundaries of a field are not sharply delimited because they change continually as a result of varying currents. So Lewin used the term *psychological field* to denote the totality of coexisting and interdependent psychological events.

By use of "topology" (a geometry of spaces) and "hodology" (a geometry of paths), Lewin was able to devise a system of logical constructs within which he could describe behavior in terms of changing relationships between the individual and his environment. Positive and negative forces, *vectors*, attract or repel the individual according to the attracting or repelling characteristics, *valence*, of the various stimuli to which he responds. The total psychological field consists of *regions* whose "boundaries" vary in their degrees of remoteness, rigidity, and permeability. The positive or negative valence of these regions at a particular time propels *locomotions* along paths leading to the different boundaries.

The *life space* of an individual is the total concrete manifold of interdependent facts that influence his behavior, including all his inner dispositions and the changing aspects of his environing situation. Both individual and environment constitute a dynamic whole which must be understood as an operational entity. Hence, behavior cannot be understood if attention is directed exclusively toward the past history and present constitution of the individual nor toward the several aspects of the environment without reference to his needs and values. The life space, then, is a totality of person, environment, and behavior. Each of these components must be defined in terms of the others. The environment refers to the world *as it exists for the individual,* as it is perceived by him; and behavior is the way he responds to the environment as thus perceived. Behavior is determined by the concrete total situation in which it occurs. It is a product of interrelationships and cannot be accounted for in terms of isolated and limited aspects of the whole.

An important element in Lewin's theory is the *principle of contemporaneity.* Neither the past nor the future can affect behavior except as they exist in the person's attitudes, feelings, and thoughts at the present time. Every individual, however, has some kind of *time perspective,* though it be long or short, clear or hazy. Practically every person of consequence in history has had a time perspective that included awareness of the past and reached out into the future. But the time dimension is not peculiar to great men, as the billions of dollars in life insurance now in force can attest. The way the individual views the past and the future *now,* however, is the determining element in his behavior. Of course some knowledge of the past history of a person and some understanding of his goals as he views them are helpful aids toward the interpretation of behavior, and an individual may act in neurotic ways because his picture is distorted or unrealistic; but it is important to recognize that it is the contemporary situation that conditions behavior, not the past nor the future.

Behavior is also conditioned by one's *level of aspiration*, which depends upon the evaluation one places upon his past experiences of success or failure, the degrees of reality of the goals he accepts for himself, and his own potentialities (as he sees them). These are all products of the interrelationships between the individual and his environing situation. Experiences of success or failure do not depend upon some objective standard but upon the aspirations a person sets for himself. Feelings of success or failure result from performances that fall above or below this level of aspiration. Experiences of success tend to raise the level of aspiration for future performances; failures tend to lower it.

Lewin assumed the principle of *homeostasis*, a tendency toward the maintenance of stability and equilibrium between the individual and his environment. A disturbance of equilibrium brings about a tension which leads to "locomotions" that seek relief and the restoration of equilibrium. Behavior, then, is a continuing process of tensions, locomotions, and reliefs within the several regions of the life space. Since this process is dependent upon so many variant combinations of factors, Lewin was dubious about the validity of distinguishing discrete stages of development. The use of an age scale for describing development was regarded as inadequate for understanding psychological growth. Nor did he consider it worth while to make a catalogue of needs as many psychologists do. A need is aroused by an increase of tensions or the release of energy among the inner regions of the personality. It may be occasioned by physiological conditions, by a desire for something, or by an intention to go somewhere or do something. Thus a need is a concept similar in meaning to a motive, urge or drive.

The importance of the concept "life space" as the total situation in which individuals exist has tended to extend the interests of field theorists beyond problems of motivation and learning to the broader area of social psychology. It has become increasingly apparent to them that social, economic, and political relationships play a more important part in human behavior than would be expected from reading much current psychological literature. Lewinian theory has stimulated a great deal of research in "group dynamics" and in the effects of group associations upon the outlook and conduct of individual members. Early in his work in America, Lewin pointed out some extreme differences in the values held by the people of Germany and the United States and suggested that these variations must have their roots in different patterns of social and political relationships. His followers have investigated the effects upon participants in varying kinds of group association. Some of these have reported dramatic improvements in the functioning of groups as a result of training in the skills of democratic leadership.

Personalistic Theories

Kant made a distinction between the phenomenal and the noumenal aspects of experience and claimed that perceptions of phenomena are conditioned by patterns of interpretation already existing in the mind.[2] Many thinkers since his time have endeavored to overcome the dualism between perceptions and knowledge which he proposed. Some of these have laid the foundations for the personalistic psychology which is now to be reviewed.

THE NEO-KANTIANS. Wilhelm Windelband agreed with Kant that experience is governed by a priori principles which he called "values." He tried to solve the Kantian dilemma by making a distinction between the natural sciences, which he called *nomothetic* (that is, they seek general laws rather than knowledge of individual cases), and the cultural or historical sciences, which he labelled *idiographic* (dealing with unique events and individuals). The latter, he held, are concerned with values more than with natural causes. Heinrich Rickert, a disciple of Windelband, stressed the selective nature of thought and declared that the values of an individual are his starting point in the search for knowledge and truth.

DILTHEY. Wilhelm Dilthey agreed with Kant that knowledge of the physical world is knowledge of phenomena only but, in contradistinction to Kant, he insisted that knowledge of one's own mind is true knowledge though of a different sort. The physical world exists independently of our cognitive processes, but the perceiving mind and the perceived mind are the same thing. He rejected Kant's set of a priori principles and denied that mind and body are but constructs of the perceiving subject. He criticized the psychology of his day as being inadequate for a true understanding of man because

_____

[2] *Supra*, p. 60.

it overlooked some of his essential properties. In concentrating upon sensations and their associations, it had failed to reckon with man as he sees and feels himself. In the experience of a living person, all the processes of the mind work together. In humanistic studies the distinction between nomothetic and idiographic science breaks down because in these both general laws and the unique features of individual personality are involved. The distinction between the natural sciences and the cultural sciences, in Dilthey's view, lies in the fact that the former seek to "explain," *erklären,* while the aim of the latter is to "understand," *verstehen.* The human being as a whole should be the subject matter of psychology, and he cannot be understood without reference to the totality of his inner experience. Human life is teleological and, in its study, purpose is a prime factor for consideration. Psychology which views human nature in this complete and unified sense should become the foundation of all the cultural sciences.

SPRANGER. Edward Spranger agreed with Dilthey that psychology should go beyond analysis and explanation of sensations and their physiological foundations and should seek understanding of the individual as a whole. He doubted whether an "objective" study of human nature is ever possible because cultural influences help to determine the outlook of the investigator and his interpretations are inevitably shaped by his convictions. While natural sciences may properly end in explanation, psychology and the other human sciences may not stop short of understanding. And adequate understanding of the individual must include a recognition of his goals and values in relationship to the norms and standards of the culture of which he is a part.

Spranger distinguished six *types of men,* basic value types whose goal-directed patterns are related to six areas of culture: science, economic life, aesthetics, social life, politics, and religion. The *theoretical* type seeks a rational and systematic interpretation of reality, the truth about things. The *economic* type is primarily concerned with the practical and material aspects of life. The *aesthetic* type values the objects in nature that give evidence of harmony and beauty and are immediately satisfying. The *social* type finds value in the persons around him. He is friendly, congenial, and considerate. The *political* type views other people not in terms of personal worth but primarily as pawns in the struggle for power. The *religious* type seeks inner harmony and unity between himself and cosmic reality. These are to be regarded as "ideal" types, since no human being is entirely devoted to the pursuit of a single goal. But an important consideration in the effort to understand man is to see the relation of the individual to the cultural area with which he is most concerned.

STERN. William Stern decried the tendency of his contemporaries to fragmentize personality study by making a sharp distinction between idiographic and nomothetic sciences and then choosing between them, as though explanation and understanding can be separated. Being both an experimentalist and a humanist, he sought to effect a reasonable compromise between the two approaches. Science rightly seeks laws, hence all sciences have their nomothetic aspects. It is proper to acquire empirical data and to classify these in general categories. But explanation of a particular individual is not complete if he is considered only in terms of general principles. He is not just a collection of things (*sache*) but a living whole, self-contained, striving toward goals, capable of having experience, a *person*.

Personal life, for Stern, is expressed in three modalities. The first level is *biological vitality*, in which the functions of growth, maturation, and reproduction are predominant. The second is *experience*, which is under constant "cleavage and tension," and consists of the co-ordination of inner dispositions and the establishment of relationships between the person and objects in the outside world. The third modality is *cultural introception*, in which the cultural norms and standards of the social environment are accepted and assimilated. The person therefore is a *unitas multiplex*, a unity composed of many elements, and can be understood only when all the aspects of his being are seen in total perspective. Personality is the continuum, the persisting and consistent whole.

ALLPORT. Gordon W. Allport has been one of the leading American representatives of the personalistic emphasis in psychology. He has dealt with the problem of nomothetic versus idiographic approaches to behavior and, although he admits that people within a given culture tend to develop "a limited number of *roughly comparable* modes of adjustment," he insists that no two ever behave in exactly the same way. Hence each individual is unique, he is an "epiphenomenon," though his behavior is "lawful."

Allport holds that psychology in its systematic attempt to establish general principles "through the discovery of regularities and uniformative characteristics of a whole class" has slighted the dimensions of personality that constitute the uniqueness of a given individual. Personality, he writes, "is the dynamic organization within the individual of those psychophysical systems that determine his unique adjustments to his environment." [3] Thus it may be seen that his view has much in common with the views of Stern and Lewin.

The essential features of Allport's theory may be indicated by presenting briefly five of his fundamental concepts: drive, traits, functional autonomy, intentions, and proprium. The *drive* (which he subdivides into various drives) is conceived as a need-reducing mechanism grounded in physiological processes, though it does not operate in response to specific stimuli. The concept of drive provides a logical explanation of infant behavior. Tensions are produced in the child by basic needs, and he responds in his own way to reduce them. These original movements are gross and undifferentiated; but, as the child matures, his drives become differentiated in such dimensions as interests, values, and traits, all of which are "distinctive motivational systems" capable in themselves of arousing new modes of behavior.

A *trait,* according to Allport, is a determining tendency or generalized predisposition, a "neuropsychic system" within the individual which is capable of initiating and guiding his behavior. Traits are "*bona fide* mental structures in each personality that account for the consistency of behavior." They are not categories dependent upon the observer but are "really there." They have taken form in the course of personal development and are expressions of the individual's customary modes of adjustment to environment. The totality of traits constitutes what Adler would call the "style of life." Thus a person who has acquired through the years the type of behavior subsumed under the term "neatness" will evidence this characteristic in practically all situations. An "exhibitionist" tends to seek situations in which to project himself. A soldier who has been subjected to strict military discipline for many years will be likely to behave in harmony with his disciplinary training even when he returns to civilian life.

The principle of *functional autonomy* asserts the lack of dependence of various motives of the individual upon so-called primitive drives. It is opposed to the theory that motives may be reduced to innate drives out of which presumably they were developed. Allport holds that evidence from a number of sources suggests tendencies on the part of an individual to persist in particular modes of behavior even when the original reason for the behavior has passed. For most

---

[3] Gordon W. Allport, *Personality: A Psychological Interpretation*, p. 48.

adults, there is no longer any functional relation between present motives and their historical origins. Motives are contemporary. Whatever drives must drive now. The character of motivation changes so rapidly that adult motives must be thought of as supplanting the motives of childhood. This view challenges the concept of historical determinism and permits a relative divorce from the conditions of the past.

The present *intentions* of an individual are more important for an understanding of his behavior than anything that has happened to him before. If we would discover a key to how he will behave in the present, we need not go searching into his early history. We need only to find out what he is striving for in the future. His hopes, ambitions, aspirations, and plans are determinative of the direction of his efforts today. This stress upon present intentions, as contrasted with the overpowering influence of previous conditioning, marks a distinctive difference between the viewpoint of Allport and that of many other present-day personality theorists.

The term *proprium* is used by Allport to designate the totality of the self- or ego-functions of personality. He recognizes the importance of the functions usually ascribed to self or ego in psychological writings, but seeks to avoid the ambiguity that surrounds such terms. In his view, the self is not a homunculus, an agent, a "man within the breast" that organizes and administers the personality system. It is not innate but develops in time. The proprium is the totality of all aspects of the personality that makes for unity and includes bodily sense, self-identity, self-enchancement, ego-extension, self-image, rational thinking, propriate striving, and the function of knowing. Its most important characteristic is *becoming*. It is a continuous process of growth.[4]

MURRAY. Henry A. Murray, who calls his theory "personology," has included in his perspective more than the other psychologists whose views are subsumed under "personalistic theories," but his system may be grouped with theirs without too much distortion because of his primary concern for a full understanding of the individual person. He seeks to give due consideration to the past history of the organism, to the physiological concomitants of psychological processes, to unconscious motivation, to the effects of varied and changing forces within the environment, and to the organizing func-

---

[4] For additional features of Allport's theory of personality see *infra*, pp. 109-10.

tions of the personality. While his attention has been focused upon constructing means of assessing the variables that operate in individual behavior, he has not been unmindful of its tremendous complexity. Attention can be given here to only a few concepts that seem to constitute the core of his theory.

In representing the mental structure of personality, Murray borrowed from Freud the terms *id, ego,* and *superego* but modified these somewhat in the development of his theory. He agreed that the id is the root of human energy, the source of innate motives, and the respository of primitive impulses. But he holds that the id cannot be limited to unacceptable dispositions. It consists of all the basic energies, emotions, and needs, some of which are wholly acceptable. The ego, as in psychoanalytic theory, is conceived as the principal force in the organization and integration of personality. Its strength and effectiveness are important determinants of individual adjustment. The superego remains an internalized subsystem which acts to regulate behavior in somewhat the same manner as parents and other surrogates of the culture have done in the past, and its nature is determined by the kinds of experience to which the individual has been exposed. Murray adds to these influences, however, the impact of peer groups and the contributions of literary and mythological personages.

To these concepts of Freud, Murray adds a fourth, the *ego ideal,* which is a self "at its future best," combining the ambitions and aspirations toward which the individual strives. It is an integrate of imaginative identifications, of heroes and their worship, and is intimately related to the superego. The collaboration of the superego and ego ideal allows for more latitude in the alteration and development of personality in later life than is possible in the typical psychoanalytic view.

To Murray, human behavior is caught in a time dimension, and basic data concerning it are to be found in what he calls *proceedings.* A proceeding is "a goal-directed and goal-attaining course of action," a series of reactions that takes place between the initiation and completion of a dynamically significant pattern of behavior. It may be *internal* (day-dreaming, planning, problem solving) or *external* (interacting with other persons or objects in the environment). A number of proceedings may occur simultaneously (watching television, drinking a cocktail, smiling at a child). When a proceeding continues over a long period of time, it constitutes a *serial* (building a home, going to Europe). In serials, the orderly arrangement of subgoals constitutes a *serial program*. Conflicts among competing goals may be reduced by arranging *schedules* for the expression of tendencies at different times. The orderly arrangement of serial programs and schedules is an important function of personality.

Murray has given much attention to *motivation* and the dynamics of personality. Perhaps more than any other psychologist he has attempted to specify and define the types of variables that enter into motivation so that their existence and operation can be tested experimentally. Only a limited number of these can be discussed in this brief review.

One of Murray's motivational concepts is that of *needs*, which he has subjected to the most rigorous analysis and specification. After an intensive study, he made a tentative list of twenty needs[5] which, although modified and elaborated in later tabulations, is still representative of his analysis. According to his view, a need is a construct standing for a force in the brain region which organizes psychological processes in such a way as to transform an existing, unsatisfying condition. He classified his list of needs into several types: (1) primary or *viscerogenic needs*, which are linked to organic processes and refer typically to physical satisfactions (needs for food, water, air, sex, urination, and defecation) and secondary or *psychogenic needs*, which are derived from primary needs and are not focalized in specific organic processes (such as needs for acquisition, achievement, recognition, dominance, and autonomy); (2) *overt needs* (those permitted direct and immediate expression) and *covert needs*, which are usually inhibited or suppressed; (3) *focal needs* (linked to specific environmental objects) and *diffuse needs* (so general as to be applicable to almost any environmental situation); (4) *proactive needs* ("spontaneously kinetic" and determined from within the organism) and *reactive needs* (activated by events in the environment); and (5) *effect needs* (leading to desired states or ends), *process activity* (vision, hearing, thought, speech), and *modal needs* (involving quality or excellence in performance).

Murray recognizes that needs do not function in isolation from one another and he provides in his theory for their interaction. When important needs are in conflict, certain ones may be *prepotent* and cannot be denied, in which case these must have at least minimal satisfaction before the others can operate. In certain circumstances,

[5] Henry A. Murray, *et al.*, *Explorations in Personality*, pp. 152-226.

multiple needs may be combined by *fusion*, the several needs being gratified by a single course of action. In some instances, the operation of one need may be instrumental to the gratification of another and their relation may be designated as one of *subsidiation*.

Murray does not locate all the motivational factors within the individual. A concept complementary to "needs" (which originate within the person) is that of *press*, the term Murray uses to represent the determinants of behavior that have their origin in the environment. His list of press is almost as impressive as the list of needs.[6] Press is divided into *alpha press* (the properties of objects as they exist in reality or as they are disclosed by objective inquiry) and *beta press* (as they are perceived by the subject). Murray uses the Freudian term *cathexis* (value) to denote the power of an environmental object to attract or repel desire on the part of an individual. *Sentiment* is the correlative tendency within the individual to be attracted or repelled by external objects.

A significant variation in Murray's theory from that of most other theorists in his concept of *tension reduction*. He agrees with the conventional view that needs arouse states of tension, that the satisfaction of a need involves a reduction of tension, and that an organism will repeat acts that in the past have been associated with tension reduction. But he holds that another consideration must be added. It is not a tensionless state, as Freudians suppose, that is most satisfying to a healthy organism. It is rather the *process* of reducing tensions. A normal person does not seek a state in which there is absence of positive need-tensions. To have no appetite, no curiosity, no need for companionship, no zest would be most distressing. An individual accordingly may develop tensions in order later to reduce them. The satisfaction he gets from tension reduction may be enhanced by increasing the amount of tension he will have to reduce.

Murray has taken great pains to explain the *directionality* of behavior. His analysis of proceedings, serials, schedules, press, and needs is illustrative of the conceptual richness of his analysis. But he goes further in his efforts to connect inner behavioral tendencies with the continuing effects of environmental events. When an instigating situation (press) is combined with an operating need, the result is called a *thema* and must now be dealt with as a "molar" and interactive element. Themas may vary from simple responses, as when

[6] *Op. cit.*, pp. 291-92.

a child goes to the cupboard for food when he is hungry, to the more elaborate behavior associated with preparation for a family picnic. When themas involve relations between two interacting persons, they constitute *dyadic units.* Sometimes an individual comes to connect particular responses to particular needs, in which case the integration of need with the image or thought of the environmental object is called a *need integrate.* When the pattern of related needs and press has its origins in childhood but continues to influence behavior in later years, particularly when it operates as an unconscious force, the resulting behavior is known as a *unity-thema.*

All these behavior tendencies operate with respect to ends or values. Consequently Murray believes it necessary to develop some scheme to include values in the total explanation of motivation. At this point he utilizes the concept of *vectors,* which is taken over from field theory. Value concepts such as physical well-being, property, authority, affiliation, knowledge, aesthetic form, and religious adjustment provide powerful incentives to action. Their operation may be represented by vectors such as rejection, acquisition, conservation, transmission, and destruction. The values and vectors may be arranged in a matrix of intersecting rows and columns so that each cell represents behavior that corresponds to a particular vector in the direction of a particular value.

In Murray's view, psychological processes have closely linked physiological concomitants. Thus he believes that constitutional factors play an important part in determining behavior. He believes that the brain is functionally related to all aspects of behavior and is the locus of personality. The dependent processes that constitute dominant configurations in the brain are called regnant processes, and the totality of such processes in a given instance is referred to as *regnancy.* All conscious processes are regnant, though not all regnant processes are conscious. Consciousness, therefore, is only one aspect of a dominant psychological process, since it may not be present at a given moment.

Self Theories

With the rise of psychology as a scientific discipline, such terms as soul and self came to be regarded with suspicion. There seemed to be no way of locating such an entity within the total complex of personality and no way of analyzing and measuring its activity as distinguished from physiological and psychological processes. All forms of behaviorism bluntly denied the validity of the concept. In recent years, however, there has been a resurgence of interest in the nature of the self and in its relation to the total personality.

MULTIPLE APPROACHES. Psychologists of a wide variety of orientation have been concerned with these problems. William James included a chapter on the self in his famous *Principles of Psychology* in 1890. As we have seen, Freud, Jung, Adler, McDougall, Sullivan, Goldstein, Angyal, Maslow, Stern and Allport have all posed questions concerning various manifestations of personality that seemed to imply an underlying substantial basis for human behavior. Other writers, including Percival M. Symonds, Arthur T. Jersild, Peter Bertocci, and Gardner Murphy, have added contributions to a growing literature on the subject. Attention will be directed here to only two theories in which the self-concept seems to have reached fairly clear formulation.

COMBS AND SNYGG. Arthur W. Combs and Donald Snygg have outlined what they call a "perceptual" approach to "individual behavior." This is an attempt to understand the behavior of the individual from "his own point of view." These writers hold that "People do not behave according to the facts as *others* see them. They behave according to the facts as *they* see them. What governs behavior from the point of view of the individual himself are his own unique perceptions of himself and the world in which he lives, the meanings things have for him." [7]

This point of view has much in common with the field theory of Lewin, but Combs and Snygg place a somewhat different interpretation upon the relation of the perceiving self to the remaining components of the perceptual field. According to them, the total perceptual field may be thought of as areas circumscribed by three concentric circles. At the center is the *self-concept*, that part of the total field which the individual refers to as "I" or "me." This area is confined to the self from one's own point of view, regardless of how he may be perceived by others. It is the central core of personality around which the other parts revolve. However, it is affected in development by its relation to the other fields, particularly by the attitudes of other persons toward himself. Surrounding this center is a second, broader area which includes the self-concept and all other aspects of the total field perceived as having directly to do with the

---

[7] Arthur W. Combs and Donald Snygg, *Individual Behavior: A Perceptual Approach to Behavior*, p. 17. Italics in the original.

individual's own interests and needs. This is the *phenomenal self*. And surrounding both of these is the still broader area which includes all additional elements of the individual's perception and experience, which is the *phenomenal environment*, the "not self."

The relationship of these several components is illustrated by an imaginary story of the behavior of a professor who is driving his car to work in the morning.[8] He is driving along at a leisurely pace and listening with varying interest to the contents of a news summary on the radio. He pays little attention to the livestock quotations from the local stockyards, since these have little or no relation to him. The stockyard is away out toward the perimeter of the "not me" in the perceptual field. The radio next announced a bad automobile accident involving a Mrs. Ethel Martin. This comes a little closer to the center of attention because he knows the hazards of driving in crowded traffic, and he may drive more carefully in light of the news item.

But suppose he knows Mrs. Martin whom he met at a tea a few days ago, and who happens to be the wife of a student in his department. Now the accident begins to set off a whole new chain of thoughts about the student, his family, his ambitions, and possibly many other details. He will remember the news report when he reaches the office and may talk about it with others. He may telephone the hospital and ask whether the student has been informed and what he may be able to do. The incident has moved away from the perimeter and toward the center of his perceptual field.

Now suppose that Mrs. Martin is his next-door neighbor with whom his whole family has been on especially good terms for years. In this case, he will telephone his wife, offer to lend Martin a car, and make plans to take care of the Martin children. When he returns home, he will take in the wash Mrs. Martin had left on the line, pick up the tools Martin had left in his driveway, and discuss with the neighbors what they severally may do to help out in the emergency.

Finally, suppose that Mrs. Ethel Martin is the name of his married daughter! The simple radio announcement now moves immediately directly into the center of the perceptual field and affects behavior with great intensity. Everything else is completely forgotten as he wheels around and heads straight for the hospital.

Combs and Snygg use this motif in considering the needs, goals, and values of the individual; the manner in which the phenomenal

[8] *Ibid*, pp. 147-49.

self takes form; the effect of the self on perceiving, learning, forgetting, and problem solving; the nature of capacities, emotions, and feeling; and the behavioral characteristics of adequate and inadequate persons. They regard the self-concept as only a convenient approximation and not as synonomous with the whole personality. The self does not exist as a discrete physical entity but must be inferred in order to understand the complexities of human behavior. Implications of the perceptual approach for human relations and for education are treated at some length.

ROGERS. Carl R. Rogers states that he began his professional work with the settled convictions that "self" was too vague and ambiguous a term to be scientifically meaningful and that it had gone out of the psychologist's vocabulary with the passing of introspectionism. He became aware, however, that clients always tended to talk in terms of the self when they were given the opportunity to express attitudes and problems in their own terms. His clinical experience has confirmed his feeling that the self-concept is necessary in effective therapy and this has spurred his interest in clarifying and defining the nature of the reality which the concept symbolizes.

Rogers postulates that the human infant is capable from birth of experience and that he tends to perceive his experience as "reality." He reacts to his reality as an organic whole, in terms of a basic and inherent *tendency toward self-actualization*. His behavior is a goal-directed effort to satisfy the needs for actualization as he perceives them. He behaves with "adience" toward those experiences perceived as maintaining and enhancing the organism and with avoidance toward those perceived as negating these values.

In the process of development, part of experience is differentiated and symbolized in the awareness of being and functioning, and this may be designated as "self-experience." This awareness becomes elaborated in the give and take of interaction with the environment and forms a *concept of self* as a perceptual object in the whole experiential field. The total concept includes a *self-ideal*, which denotes the self which the individual would like most to become. It is deeply affected by the experiences of approval or disapproval of others with whom the individual comes into contact.

With the emergence of self-awareness, there arises a *need for positive regard* (warmth, respect, sympathy, acceptance), which is universal in human beings and pervasive and persistent in the individual.

The satisfaction of this need is based upon inferences from interrelationships with others and is associated with a wide range of experiences. It is very potent, and the individual may become more "adient" to positive regard than toward other experiences of value in actualizing the organism.

A *need for self-regard* develops out of experiences associated with the satisfaction or frustration of the need for positive regard. The individual tends to introject within himself the attitudes which he perceives in the "significant others" of his acquaintanceship. These attitudes may then operate independently of transactions with others. If he experiences only positive regard, he will develop self-regard and will remain psychologically well adjusted. But if the regard of others becomes negative or conditional, his own self-regard also suffers. In such a case, *conditions of worth* develop which may deter wholesome growth. That is, if a child experiences love and acceptance from others regardless of his behavior, he tends to acquire feelings of self-respect and confidence. But if his relations with others are negative, this will be reflected in lack of self-regard.

Because of the need for self-regard, an individual tends to be aware of those experiences that are in accord with his conditions of worth, but experiences contrary to these conditions will be distorted or denied to awareness. In the latter case, there is *incongruence* between the self and experience, resulting in psychological maladjustment and *discrepancies* in behavior. Under such conditions, experiences incongruent with the self-structure are subceived as *threats* which the individual will attempt to meet by various *defenses,* such as inaccurate perceptions of reality or "intensionality" (rigidity of behavior).

Rogers has been especially interested in the *process of reintegration* in cases of discrepancies in behavior, neurotic behavior, and personality breakdown and disorganization. In therapy, the counselor seeks to communicate to the client an unconditional positive regard within a context of empathic understanding. When the individual perceives this unconditioned positive regard, he becomes able to reconstitute his self-structure and overcome the conditions which led to aberrant perceptions and discrepant behavior. With a decrease in the conditions of worth and an increase in unconditional self-regard, threats are reduced and the process of defense is reversed. Experiences ordinarily threatening are now accurately symbolized and integrated into the self-concept. The individual is then increasingly capable of behaving in ways that will actualize in self the valued aspects of the self-ideal.

VIII. WIDENING HORIZONS
IN PERSONALITY THEORY

In the two preceding chapters outlines were presented of some of the important contributions made by leading psychologists and psychiatrists to the development of personality theory. The attempt was made not to present the complete theory of any one of these but merely to specify some distinctive elements from the standpoint of their possible relevance to the task of developing a more adequate conception of personality. There was considerable overlapping, and it seemed necessary from time to time to point out common emphases and borrowings of various writers sometimes from those whose basic orientations were quite dissimilar. Some positions seemed contradictory to those held by others.

At this stage in the development of psychology, there is doubtless no such thing as a completely novel and original theory. It is perhaps inevitable, as indeed it seems fortunate, that anyone who fixes his gaze upon human nature with the intent to see it clearly will find many of the things his colleagues find, even though their respective vantage points may be different. Attention will now be directed toward efforts which have been frankly eclectic and which have achieved a degree of comprehensiveness not found in most of the theories previously considered.

Eclectic Approaches in Psychology

Some contemporary psychologists recognize the inadequacy of fragmented approaches to human nature and have deliberately included in their own theories important elements obtained from the formulations of others.

MURRAY. Some of the main emphases in the theory of Henry A.

Murray have already been considered.[1] Murray does not seek to minimize the extent of his indebtedness to other investigators in a wide variety of specialized fields. His own training cut across disciplinary lines, including an undergraduate major in history at Harvard; an M. D. degree, followed by an M. A. in biology, at Columbia; and a Ph.D. in biochemistry at Cambridge.

In a recent discussion of his preparations for the "scaffold of a comprehensive system," Murray acknowledges his debt to thinkers in widely separated fields, including a family physician; Henderson, Russell, and Ritter in biochemistry; Darwin, Bergson, and other evolutionists; McDougall and Lewin in psychology; Freud, Jung, Prince, Alexander, and Sachs in psychoanalysis; Whitehead in philosophy; social psychologists, cultural anthropologists, sociologists, and many others. He pays special tribute to colleagues in the Department of Social Relations at Harvard, particularly Clyde Kluckhohn and Talcott Parsons. And he specifies many elements in his own system that have their roots in the thinking of other men.[2]

ALLPORT. One of the pioneers in attempts to bring into a unified picture of personality the findings of other psychologists was Gordon W. Allport, whose general position has already been outlined.[3] Allport observed as early as 1937 that an account written exclusively in terms of a single psychological system is inadequate. "Better to expand and refashion one's theories until they do some measure of justice to the richness and dignity of human personality," he wrote, "than to clip and compress personality until its fits one closed system of thought." [4] He stated that in his book he had the two-fold purpose of (1) gathering the most important fruits of the psychological study of personality into one comprehensive survey and (2) supplying whatever new co-ordinating concepts might be needed to equip personality study to handle more effectively its "endlessly rich subject matter." [5]

The range of Allport's treatment may be suggested by the following brief outline of his book: a review of the various approaches to personality; a study of the many attempts at definition in general literature, theology, philosophy, jurisprudence, sociology, and psychology; the foundations and basic aspects of growth; various methods of

---

[1] *Supra*, pp. 99-103.
[2] Henry A. Murray, "Preparations for the Scaffold of a Comprehensive System," in Sigmund Koch (ed.), *op. cit.*, Study I, Vol. 3, pp. 7-54.
[3] *Supra*, pp. 97-99.
[4] Gordon W. Allport, *Personality: A Psychological Interpretation*, p. vii.
[5] *Ibid.*, p. ix.

analysis; and the many problems involved in attempts to gain a complete understanding of the many facets of personality.

He has continued to insist that one of the goals of psychology is "to reduce discord among our philosophies of man, and to establish a scale of probable truth, so that we may feel increasingly certain that one interpretation is truer than another," but feels that the goal is not yet attained.[6]

Our censure should be reserved for those who would close all doors but one. The surest way to lose truth is to pretend that one already wholly possesses it. For narrow systems, dogmatically held, tend to trivialize the mentality of the investigator and of his students. Sad to relate, we have examples of such trivialization in psychology today.[7]

Of particular interest to Christian educators is Allport's recognition of the place of religion in the growth of personality.[8] He followed up his early attempt to give a psychological interpretation of personality, in which he made an important place for religion, with a later study of the relations between psychology and religion.[9] In one of his most recent books, he observed:

While religion certainly fortifies the individual against the inroads of anxiety, doubt, and despair, it also provides the forward intention that enables him at each stage of his becoming to relate himself meaningfully to the totality of Being.[10]

And he has continued to chide those who neglect this important consideration.

We find many personalities who deal zealousy and effectively with all phases of becoming except the final task of relating themselves meaningfully to creation. For some reason their curiosity stops at this point.[11]

MURPHY. Gardner Murphy's theory is avowedly eclectic and he borrows unashamedly from a variety of sources. Because he is aware of the extreme complexity of personality and is willing to utilize relevant data from whatever source, his view is one of the most com-

[6] Gordon W. Allport, *Becoming: Basic Considerations for a Psychology of Personality* (New Haven: Yale University Press), p. 17.

[7] *Ibid.,* p. 17.

[8] *Personality: A Psychological Interpretation,* p. 226.

[9] *The Individual and His Religion.*

[10] *Becoming,* p. 96.

[11] *Ibid.,* p. 97.

plete and comprehensive available. He calls his theory "a biosocial approach to origins and structure" and emphasizes the necessity of combining biological and social factors in an effective synthesis. Though he examines the entire fabric of modern personality theory, selects strands of many textures and weaves these together into an attractive and consistent pattern, he stresses the inadequacy and tentativeness of the product. For, says he, "there is no danger that anyone will succeed in this century in getting the perspective completely right or, indeed, in defining clearly what personality is." [12]

Murphy uses the figure of the staircase to indicate the different levels that must be traversed in building an adequate theory. First, personality must be considered as a *biological organism*. Here he treats heredity-environment as a single developmental fact. The organism, with its hereditary dispositions, is the "nodal point," but it is not the complete functioning system. It is subject always to the influences of environmental pressures. In adjustment to environment, new tendencies, habits, and traits emerge but these are not simply "plastered on," for the organism *grows* into new phases of behavior as long as life continues. Murphy makes much of the incompleteness, the indeterminateness, the becomingness, the variable potentialities, and the uniqueness of the individual. Neither the genetic nor the environmental factors are as simple and homogeneous as they seem. A multiplicity of factors are at work in both the organic and the environmental components of behavior.

At a second level, which includes the organic system with its capacity to respond to stimuli, Murphy tackles the problems of *learning*, which he defines as "the process by which the organism becomes able to respond more adequately to a given situation in consequences of experience in responding to it." [13] He uses two principles to account for learning: conditioning and canalization. The process of *conditioning*, however, is much more complex in Murphy's view than in that of most behaviorists. Some conditioned responses become dominant in relation to competing response patterns, and the latter may disappear; there is a tendency to transfer or to generalize responses; conditioning may lead to differentiation as stimuli vary; the mechanisms of suggestibility, imitation, and sympathy play important roles in stylizing behavior around cultural norms; motives may be affected by conditioning; and conditionings are arranged in a hierarchical system as

[12] Gardner Murphy, *Personality: A Biosocial Approach to Origins and Structures*, p. 11.
[13] *Ibid.*, p. 990.

growth and experience lead into complex integrations or into conflict.

Murphy borrows the term *canalizations* from Janet and defines it as "progressive shifts in differential response to the various means of satisfying a drive." [14] This process is responsible for the acquired tastes of the individual and occurs in all major types of motivation. The distinction between conditioning and canalization is whether (1) the stimulus puts into action the consummatory response (conditioning) or (2) the preferences of the individual play a large part in determining the type of stimulus to which he will respond and the form the response will take. Personality traits are dependent upon the life history of the individual; and behavior is motivated both by outer and inner stimuli, the latter including the system of symbols which has been built up in the course of experience.

On the third level, beyond behavior modifications of the organic system which result from learning, is the *personal outlook* of the individual, his world of perception and thought. This more complex world includes the behavior system, which it presupposes, but goes beyond it to include also the cognitive-affective system, the structure of sense perceptions, imagery, feeling, imagination, and reflection. The fundamental principles which operate at the lower levels are essentially unchanged—one has *learned* to perceive and feel as he does —but a "private world" is now entered which is more difficult to explore. Murphy borrows from Bleuler the term *autism* to denote "movement of cognitive processes in the direction of need satisfactions.[15] Each individual tends to make autistic responses in terms of previous drive satisfactions. Imagination, fantasies, dreams, curiosity, creativeness are products of autisms. When competing systems of autism exist in the same individual, the result is "multiple personality." In so far as individuals share factors that make for uniformity of outlook with others, autisms are socially shared.

At a fourth level of complexity is *the self* with its capacity to perceive, think about, and respond to itself. A study of the self-functions involves all the previous levels but presents problems of its own. It is thus an extension of the organic-behavioral-cognitive system. With facing of the problems of self comes realization of struggles taking place among inherent tendencies, of differences between the self and nonself, and of the influence of *unconscious processes* which lie below the level of conscious awareness. Full understanding

[14] *Ibid.*, p. 981.
[15] *Ibid.*, p. 980.

of the self must include consideration of its origins; its evolution; its ways of enhancement and defense; unconscious mechanisms (such as identification, projection, rationalization, repression, regression, introjection, symbolization, transference, and compensation); tendencies toward introversion-extroversion; and how all these tendencies develop and are modified.

On a fifth level, beyond study of the dynamics of self, is the problem of unity or *wholeness*—or the lack of it in varying degrees of conflict and disunity. The various components or *traits* of the self are not unrelated and separate but are aspects of a totality. They have a "membership character" which places each in a contextual system. Traits are tools which are related to each other in functional modes of organization. Seen in a time perspective, they operate in ways that give evidence of continuity of both structure and function. Through damage or maltreatment, they may manifest discontinuity and disorganization. There is a sufficient degree of generality in the patterns of function and organization to make possible classification in terms of various typologies. But no individual ever quite fits into a given category. Every individual has unique qualities of his own.

The last level attempted by Murphy is study of the relations of *individual and group*. "Each individual is a member of a community; is guided, inhibited, molded, structured by the life of the community; each personality is a reflection of a developmental history in a specific cultural whole." [16] This is the view of the social sciences. Murphy gives attention to many phases of interpersonal relationships, including the outcomes of group membership, economic determinism, social roles, ethos, the effects of historical change, and the family as a mediator of culture. He then outlines two special views that have developed from the social science approach: *situationism* (personality at any given time both reflects and is an epitome of specific cultural requirements) and *field theory* (personality is a flowing continuum of organism-environment events). He concludes his study with consideration of the fitness of American culture for the development of adequate personalities.

Reference has already been made to Murphy's stress upon the need for a deeper exploration of personality than has yet been made by psychology.[17] He does not depreciate the significance of the advances

[16] *Ibid.*, pp. 20-21.
[17] *Supra*, pp. 47-48.

already made but considers them important only as they point toward more adequate understanding in the future.

The future course of personality research will plainly be governed not so much by the continuation of the methods borrowed from psychoanalysis, Gestalt psychology, physiology, and cultural anthropology, to which emphasis has been given in this book, as by altogether new modes of attack. . . . The present promising leads will guide us for a few more decades into better physical time-space definitions of man. But just as evolutionism and field theory make eighteenth-century rationalism seem rather childlike, so the systematizations achieved in a later century will show the puerile insufficiency of all that present day science can offer.[18]

In a later book,[19] Murphy discusses "three kinds of human nature." The *first human nature* was a product of the evolutionary process. At this level primitive man was an animal, retaining many of the traits of his simian kinsmen. But he was possessed of sensitivity, modifiability, and the capacity for learning and for adjustment to the world in which he found himself. His nature was not fixed but capable of alteration as new environmental conditions made their impact. He was "precariously balanced" and always ready for a new equilibrium. In the course of further evolution he developed "humanness" and individuality. Upon original nature ever-changing forces are at work and an evolving human nature has responded to cultural molding.

With the emergence of culture came the *second human nature* which "involves the development of new ways of feeling, or 'acquired tastes,' shared by men with their fellows and transmitted blockwise to the world of the young, who grow up knowing only the culture thus transmitted to them." It is human nature "molded, channeled, 'cabin'd, cribbed, confined,' made ready to move in one course rather than another." [20] Much of its potentiality is thwarted and finally snuffed out by the inertia, rigidity, and great resistance of the culture to change.

Murphy believes it is possible, by "breaking through the mold" and by the "creative thrust" of free intelligence and self-directed change, to realize a *third human nature* which would be

not simply the fulfillment of the known biological nature of man or the

---

[18] *Personality: A Biosocial Approach to Origins and Structures* (New York: Harper & Brothers, 1947), pp. 925-26.

[19] *Human Potentialities.*

[20] *Ibid.*, pp. 17, 18.

elaboration of the known potentialities of culture but a constant probing of new emergent qualities and realities given by a system of relationships that can today hardly be glimpsed; a leaping into existence of new realms of experience; *not an extrapolation of the present, but new in kind.*[21]

In presenting his conception of the types of effort required if the larger possibilities of the "third human nature" are to be realized, Murphy makes a strong plea for the freeing of intelligence, the nurture of individual creativeness, encouragement of the "yen to discovery," frank facing of the moral issues arising from the control of society by forces set free by science, and movement in the direction of extending the limits of freedom in choosing among the possible futures toward which posterity may move.

As in his earlier book, Murphy makes use of a wide variety of sources to support his thesis, citing evidence from anthropology, biology, genetics, psychology, psychiatry, social psychology, history, sociology, and philosophy.

Broad Surveys of Contemporary Psychologies

Several excellent surveys of current psychological systems are now available which enable the reader to identify major areas of agreement and disagreement, and in which the authors offer their own conclusions and raise crucial questions that require further investigation.

WOLMAN. Benjamin B. Wolman has published a survey of contemporary psychological theories and systems, with emphasis upon methodological problems such as concept formation, relationship to other sciences, methods of research, and interpretation of empirical data.[22] He warns against any easy assumption that knowledge of psychological theories will enable one to devise a completely satisfactory theory of personality as a whole. He concludes that most psychological theories can apply their principles toward understanding of the individual but, agreeing with Allport and Murphy, he holds that "When we deal with such complexity, a great many problems must be considered: heredity and environment, organic and psychogenic factors, motivation and perception, conditioning and canalization, and the organization of the individual and his interaction with the environment." [23] In a final summary he states, "Finally, several unsolved

[21] *Ibid.*, pp. 328-29. Italics in the original.
[22] Benjamin B. Wolman, *Contemporary Theories and Systems in Psychology.*
[23] *Ibid.*, p. 548.

problems and the lack of an all-encompassing psychological theory are presented as a scientific task for the future." [24]

HAIMOWITZ. In a book of selected readings, Morris and Natalie Haimowitz provide a wide range of viewpoints regarding the goals of education, the kind of children we want; what scientific knowledge tells us about children and about how they grow and develop into various kinds of personalities; and how this knowledge can be applied to help children grow.[25] Their book has the merit of including many kinds of scientific studies and also psychological insights contained in poetry, philosophy, and religious literature. They admit that many issues in the area of human development are highly controversial and that "Much of what we know to be true today may be found false tomorrow." [26] But their collection of readings will enable the uninitiated reader to establish connection with an important and growing body of literature which is exceedingly important for the philosophy of Christian education.

HALL AND LINDZEY. Calvin S. Hall and Gardner Lindzey have presented a review of some of the major personality theories that have been derived from psychological study and research. They helpfully discuss the nature of personality theory, some of the similarities as well as some striking divergencies and disagreements among the leading theories, and some difficulties confronting anyone who attempts to make a synthesis or integration at the present state of our knowledge.[27]

Psychological Symposiums

A number of attempts have been made to develop a greater degree of mutual understanding among psychologists by conducting symposiums and publishing compendiums contributed to by representatives of different viewpoints. Three of these can be mentioned here by way of illustration.

UNIVERSITY OF HOUSTON. In 1954 the University of Houston devoted its annual lecture series to a symposium on personality. Six psychologists, holding widely divergent positions, outlined their approaches to personality; and one attempted at least a measure of

---

[24] *Ibid.,* p. 553.

[25] Morris L. Haimowitz and Natalie Reader Haimowitz, *Human Development: Selected Readings.*

[26] *Ibid.,* p. viii.

[27] Calvin S. Hall and Gardner Lindzey, *Theories of Personality.*

integration by indicating similarities among the various viewpoints presented and suggesting possible ways of moving toward a more adequate and complete theory.[28]

INTERNATIONAL UNION. The International Union of Scientific Psychology devoted its 14th International Congress to the consideration of "perspectives in personality theory." [29] A total of twenty-three internationally known psychologists from America and several countries of Europe discussed their understandings of personality. In the introductory chapter of a book issued by the Congress, Gordon Allport outlined some basic differences in the philosophical assumptions of American and European contributors. He called attention to a prevalent smugness and provincialism in America and some dangers from the rationalization that often accompanies it: "We have nothing to learn from European psychology." [30]

AMERICAN PSYCHOLOGICAL ASSOCIATION. Over a period of several years the American Psychological Association has carried on a thoroughgoing study of the "science" of psychology, with aid of funds granted by the National Science Foundation. It is intended to cover both the status and current tendencies of psychological science at the present time. Some eighty distinguished authors have contributed essays dealing with: "(Study I) major theoretical formulations of recent importance; and (Study II) the structure, mutual interrelations, and associations with other sciences of the main empirical areas in which psychological research is pursued." [31]

Study I has been reported in three volumes already published. The third of these is entitled *Formulations of the Person and the Social Context*. It contains Murray's summary of the theoretical backgrounds of his own theory; David Rapaport's analysis of the structure of psychoanalytic theory; Carl Rogers' account of the theory underlying client-centered therapy; Ramond B. Cattell's report on theory based upon "multivariate quantitative research"; Solomon Asch's "perspective on social psychology"; Talcott Parson's "approach in terms of the theory of action"; and additional chapters by Franz J. Kallmann, Theodore M. Newcomb, Daniel Katz and Ezra Stotland, Paul F. Lazarsfeld, and Herbert A. Thelen.

[28] J. L. McCary (ed.), *Psychology of Personality.*
[29] Henry P. David and Helmut von Bracken (eds.), *Perspectives in Personality Theory.*
[30] *Ibid.,* p. 4.
[31] Sigmund Koch (ed.), *Psychology: A Study of a Science,* Study I, Vol. 3, p. 1.

Interdisciplinary Studies

As psychologists have worked together toward a more comprehensive view, there has come increasing realization on their part that a completely valid theory of personality cannot come from psychology alone, as Allport and Murphy had already pointed out. Hence there has been a noticeable trend toward interdisciplinary efforts. Only a few of these can be cited here.

ANGYAL. Twenty years ago Angyal argued that "A holistic theory of personality should not borrow its concepts from either physiology or psychology but *should develop its own set of concepts*." [32]

SLOTKIN. A decade later, J. S. Slotkin "tried to develop a systematic theory of personality development, out of the hypotheses and evidence from various relevant sciences." [33] Being a social anthropologist, he naturally placed chief emphasis upon the social and cultural factors in personal development.

THORPE AND SCHMULLER. Louis P. Thorpe and Allen M. Schmuller have adopted a "patterned electicism" as a rationale for the study of personality and have attempted to develop a rounded theory from a synthesis of the latest research drawn from cultural anthropology, psychology, sociology, social psychology, and education.[34] They conclude that "many gaps and obstacles to a 'closed' theory of personality still remain. It seems evident, however, that the scientific method is our most effective tool for filling in those gaps and sorting out the conflicting hypotheses submitted by scholars in the various areas of knowledge." "Personality," they say, "involves the interplay of many factors, all of which must be considered." [35]

Personality Research Centers

Several universities have developed centers in which problems of personality are approached from multiple points of view. In these specialists in various branches of behavioral science have worked together. Mention can be made only of some of the well-established centers in which studies have been under way for comparatively long periods of time.

[32] Andras Angyal, *Foundations for a Science of Personality*, p. 19. Italics in the original. Cf., *supra*, pp. 91-92.

[33] J. S. Slotkin, *Personality Development*, p. ix.

[34] Louis P. Thorpe and Allen M. Schmuller, *Personality: An Interdisciplinary Approach.*

[35] *Ibid.*, pp. 354-55.

YALE CLINIC OF CHILD DEVELOPMENT. For nearly a quarter of a century the Yale Clinic of Child Development has been making studies of the patterning of children's behavior and has reported its findings in a number of carefully written publications. In one of the earliest, detailed descriptions were offered of the behavior patterns of children from birth to five years under the headings: motor development, adaptive behavior, language development, and personal-social behavior.[36] The data were based upon extensive clinical studies and were presented in the form of age characteristics and developmental sequences. In a succeeding volume, more direct attention was given to the guidance of development in the home and nursery school.[37] In this, a more complete "Behavior Profile" and more elaborate descriptions of the "Behavior Day" at various stages were given of the growing child from birth to five.

The studies were continued for children from five to ten and were reported in a third volume in which the information was organized into a year-by-year series of "psychological portraits," with concrete guidance suggestions for the following areas of child life: motor characteristics, personal hygiene, emotional expression, fears and dreams, self and sex, interpersonal relations, play and pastimes, school life, ethical sense, and philosophical outlook.[38] Youth from ten to sixteen are subjected to similar analyses in the latest volume of this series. Typical youth of each of these ages are described in great detail with respect to (1) "maturity profiles and traits" and (2) "maturity trends and growth gradients." [39]

HORACE MANN-LINCOLN INSTITUTE. The Horace Mann-Lincoln Institute of School Experimentation, Columbia University, made an analysis of personality needs in terms of "persistent life situations" which are met by individuals and groups in everyday living. These recurrent situations arise in the family, in civic-social activities, in work and play, and in moral and spiritual life. As seen by this group the situations call for growth in three areas: individual capacities, social participation, and ability to deal with environmental factors and forces. Analyses of these areas were made and typical situations

[36]Arnold L. Gesell, *et al.*, *The First Five Years of Life.*
[37] Arnold L. Gesell and Frances L. Ilg, *Infant and Child in the Culture of Today.*
[38]Arnold L. Gesell and Frances L. Ilg, *The Child from Five to Ten.*
[39]Arnold L. Gesell, *et al.*, *Youth: The Years from Ten to Sixteen.*

119

faced by individuals were indicated at four age levels: early childhood, later childhood, youth, and adulthood.[40]

COMMITTEE ON HUMAN DEVELOPMENT. The Committee on Human Development of the University of Chicago has carried on many studies dealing with individual development and with the effects of various social forces upon the individual. Among the best known of these studies perhaps are the researches on "developmental tasks," under the direction of Robert J. Havighurst, and the studies of social class structure and function by W. Lloyd Warner and his associates.[41]

HARVARD LABORATORY OF SOCIAL RELATIONS. The Harvard center has included internationally known psychologists, anthropologists, sociologists, and leaders in other branches of the social sciences. Allport's and Murray's theories have been outlined in previous sections of this book and references have been made to the contributions of Kluckhohn and Parsons. Some indication of the extent of the investigations of this group may be seen in a symposium published several years ago[42] and in articles and books published by various members since that time.

These are only a few of the centers that have made significant contributions to our knowledge of personality. Others that should be mentioned are the Institute of Personality Assessment and Research of the University of California, the Laboratory of Personality Assessment and Group Behavior of the University of Illinois, the Research Center for Group Dynamics at Massachusetts Institute of Technology, the Institute for Human Adjustment and the Research Center for Group Dynamics of the University of Michigan, and the Center for Advanced Study in the Behavioral Sciences at Stanford, California.

Religious Dimensions of Personality

There still persists in American psychology a general reluctance to recognize religious values as factors in human behavior. This is due in part, doubtless, to the delimitations which many psychologists have set for their work. They propose to deal only with phenomena that can be subjected to measurement, prediction, and control. A rigid

[40] Florence B. Stratemeyer, et al., Developing a Curriculum for Modern Living.

[41] Robert J. Havighurst, Human Development and Education; Havighurst and Hilda Taba, Adolescent Character and Personality; A. B. Hollingshead, Elmtown's Youth; Robert F. Peck, et al., The Psychology of Character Development; W. Lloyd Warner, et al., Democracy in Jonesville and Social Class in America.

[42] Clyde Kluckhohn and Henry A. Murray (eds.), Personality: In Nature, Society and Culture.

behaviorism is still widely prevalent. And too many behaviorists forget the self-imposed limits they have themselves established in their attempts to be "scientific." When they assume a "nothing but" attitude toward personality, their dogmatism belies their claim to objectivity. Some avoid religion like the plague because they accept uncritically the dictum that all religion is illusion or superstition. Apparently many of them are unable to see the real thing!

One recently published textbook on personality, intended for upper-division college students, devoted just one-half page (of a total of 491 pages) to "religionism," of which, according to the author, "The three defining indicators are belief in God, low belief in evolution, and rejection of birth control." [43]

Such blindness is not true of all American psychologists. Reference has been made to Allport's recognition of religion as having an important integrative function in personality and as contributing to wholeness and mental health.[44] "A man's religion," he writes, "is the audacious bid he makes to bind himself to creation and to the Creator. It is his ultimate attempt to enlarge and to complete his own personality by finding the supreme context in which he rightly belongs." [45] Allport acknowledges the differing viewpoints from which psychology and religion approach human nature, but he insists that there is "inherent absurdity" in supposing that they must be permanently and hopelessly at odds. He asks, "Why should not science and religion, . . . differing in axioms and method, yet cooperate in the production of an improved human character without which all other human gains are tragic loss?" And he believes that "From many sides today comes the demand that religion and psychology busy themselves in finding a common ground for uniting their efforts for human welfare." [46]

Only a few additional examples can be given of psychologists who have found a place for religion in their understanding of the nature and growth of personality. A group of Catholic psychologists have recently attempted "to formulate an integrated theory of personality based on a Christian conception of human nature." [47] They

[43] J. P. Guilford, *Personality*, p. 465.
[44] *Supra*, p. 110.
[45] *The Individual and His Religion*, p. 142.
[46] *Ibid.*, p. vi.
[47] Magda B. Arnold and John A. Gasson, *The Human Person: An Approach to an Integral Theory of Personality*, p. iii.

examined the basic assumptions of scientific theories and of personality theories in particular, developed a theory of personality which they believe includes human values and yet rests on a valid scientific basis, and sought to show that this personalistic conception provides the theoretical foundation for a psychotherapy that respects Christian concepts and values.

Pressey and Kuhlen devote one of thirteen chapters on psychological development through the life span to a consideration of moral and religious values in human behavior.[48]

Ernest M. Ligon has devoted the major portion of his life to experimental testing of the effects of the use of religious concepts upon the development of character. He concludes:

> Psychologists are becoming increasingly agreed that value dimensions are indispensable to any complete study of personality. They are not agreed that some of these dimensions must involve religious faith. . . . Religion to many psychologists . . . seems not much more significant in personality than fashions or ethical mottoes hanging on the wall. In making such judgments they are violating the first rule of science, an unbiased sample. It is still inconceivable to me how psychologists have been able almost to ignore a force which has exerted such power in society as has religion.[49]

The Psychology of Religion

William James, one of the most eminent of American psychologists, gave impetus to the development of a new branch of psychology when he published his now famous *Varieties* at the turn of the twentieth century.[50] Since his day the psychology of religion has become a well-established field and it has enlisted a host of competent scholars, including Edward Scribner Ames, Walter Houston Clark, George Albert Coe, Paul E. Johnson, James H. Leuba, Wayne E. Oates, James B. Pratt, Edmund D. Starbuck, Henry Nelson Wieman, to mention only a few.

At least two of these have given special attention to modern studies of personality and have each contributed a theory of his own. Wayne Oates has been concerned with the continuities between the scientific and the Christian understandings of man and with the uniqueness

---

[48] Sidney L. Pressey and Raymond G. Kuhlen, *Psychological Development Through the Life Span*, Chapter 10.

[49] Ernest M. Ligon, *Dimensions of Character*, p. 209.

[50] William James, *The Varieties of Religious Experience*.

of the Christian view.[51] And Paul Johnson has proposed a theory of "dynamic interpersonalism," in which he explores what it means to be a person psychologically and religiously and how a person attains wholeness through the resources of "psychoreligious" growth.[52]

It would seem, then, that some beginnings have been made to bridge the "chasm" between psychology and theology, but the bridge is still shaky and insecure. Whether or not there is sufficient foundation to build a bridge that can carry all the traffic that may need to cross it remains to be seen. Our consideration of the theological approach must await treatment in a subsequent part of this book.

[51] Wayne E. Oates, *Religious Dimensions of Personality.*
[52] Paul E. Johnson, *Personality and Religion.*

IX. THE SCIENTIFIC IMAGE OF MAN

In the preceding chapters emphasis was placed upon the central place of psychology in the scientific approach to personality. But it became increasingly clear as the study proceeded that psychology is only one of the disciplines dealing with the complex problem of human nature. Additional contributions to a total understanding come from several other fields, notably biology, anthropology, and sociology. Findings from these several fields must be brought together and combined in a coherent synthesis before we can have a dependable view of man. This must include consideration of at least the hereditary and constitutional basis of "original" human nature; the physical, social, and cultural factors that condition its development; and the effects of experience and education upon the total outcome.

Is it possible to build a consistent theory of human nature in light of the many varying viewpoints held by competent observers in the several fields of study? The present writer believes that it is, though prominent features of some of the theories must be omitted and choice must sometimes be made between theories that seem contradictory. The following outline of the "scientific image of man" contains elements selected from conclusions of many responsible theorists and seems to have adequate foundations in research.

Original Human Nature

Human nature is a very complex and mysterious reality. The truth of this statement can be best understood perhaps by those who have tried to take into account the many factors that enter into its development.

BIOLOGICAL ORGANISM. The biological basis, first of all, is much more important than is commonly supposed. Studies in the fields of genetics and eugenics have revealed that physical characteristics are largely determined by genes and chromosomes, which are the bearers of heredity. Constitutional factors such as physique, the functioning of the glands and nervous system, and the differing degrees of metabolic activity, all play important roles in the formation of personality. During the prenatal period, such factors as malnutrition, endocrine disturbances and infections may retard the normal growth of the embryo. Birth injuries, physical deformities, and glandular deficiencies may have profound later effects.

In the process of physical growth, there are certain "natural" stages and principles of development that must be respected if "normal" growth is to be realized. Marked irregularities will result in varying types of abnormality, though the human organism has an amazing capacity to overcome difficulties if general provision is made for the satisfaction of basic needs. No theory of personality can be regarded as satisfactory that neglects the hereditary and constitutional ingredients of human nature.

ORGANISM-ENVIRONMENT. From the beginning of individual existence, however, there is no such thing as "pure" heredity. The process of development is jointly influenced by both heredity and environment. The health and well-being of the mother, for example, and her attitudes toward herself and her offspring will influence the development of the child, perhaps even before birth and certainly ever after. The emotions, once considered innate, are more likely to be learned responses acquired in dynamic interaction between the individual and the other persons who constitute his world. Most personal qualities are acquired as the result of learning. In fact, the individual and his environment are so closely interrelated that it is difficult to draw clear lines of demarcation.

MOTIVATION. The individual is endowed with certain energies which he expends largely in the search for satisfaction of basic needs, in maintaining a reasonable degree of equilibrium within the component parts of his organism, and in adjustment to environment. His basic needs may be roughly classified in four categories, though these overlap and interpenetrate so that exact differentiation becomes impossible. He has *physiological* needs which are associated with organic processes. Their satisfaction requires air, food, water, exercise, sleep, and excretion. He has *psychological* needs that are derived from an inherent drive for self-realization. His *social* needs are related to the other significant persons in his environment. And he has *spiritual* needs which grow out of efforts to relate meaningfully to the total reality of which he is a part. The degree and the manner in which these needs are met determine in large measure the direction of personality development. While certain needs may be predominant at a given moment, all demand satisfaction and none can be met ultimately until all are given their proper recognition. The response to any need is a response of the total organism.

Environmental Determinants

In spite of the constant interrelationship of organism and environment and the difficulties of demarcation, it is necessary to deal with factors external to the individual.

PHYSICAL ENVIRONMENT. The physical environment has obvious effects upon personality. Orientals and Occidentals are products of different natural settings, as are Bedouins and Eskimos. Their differing physical environments have conditioned the development of their bodies and also their ways of life. Climate affects body size, facial appearance, and color of skin. The presence or absence of available food supplies makes lonely nomads in some parts of the world, while densely populated cities grow up in regions where climate is more favorable and food resources more abundant. The effects of conditions imposed upon living by the physical environment are evident in every culture, and human behavior in considerable measure is a reflection of man's adaptation to the vicissitudes of nature.

SOCIAL ENVIRONMENT. The social environment is also a focal point in personal development. An individual's actions are not the sole products of biological heredity and reactions to natural surroundings; these are acquired from interractions with social groups. As a person, one cannot help reflecting at least in some measure his sociocultural universe. Persons are biosocial.

Evidence of the influence of group associations is extensive. Identical twins, though similar in temperament and emotional stability, have been found to vary considerably in educational and intellectual development when placed in differing cultural situations. Children from barren environments show the results of deprivation when their achievements are compared with the achievements of those who are reared under more favorable circumstances. Children of inferior stock often excel the intellectual and social development of their parents and siblings when adopted into socially adequate and superior foster homes.

There is a general tendency within given groups to develop common attitudes and prejudices. Such terms as Indian, Frenchman, and American suggest a tendency toward stereotypes at the national level. Unitarians, Presbyterians, and Catholics acquire characteristic beliefs and attitudes which are not the direct result of individual thought and critical judgment.

FAMILY. Of the social groups that influence the personal development of an individual, the family is undoubtedly the most powerful. The unique core of each personality arises out of the dynamic influences and experiences of childhood. The roots of emotional maturity, or of personal inadequacy, are laid in the home. Faulty parental behavior, the lack of love between parents, the rejection of a child by either parent, or a broken home, all leave tragic consequences in the future adjustments of the child.

Children who are deprived of love in their families find it difficult to love and trust others. Severe and unmerited punishment forms the basis for hostility and often delinquency in adolescence. There is a definite correlation between affection in family relationships and later personal and social adjustments. Unhappiness in childhood leads to later mismanagement of children, while happiness in childhood is an important ingredient in the making of a good parent. In homes where parents love each other and warmly accept their children, share enjoyable times together, participate in common recreational activities, respect children as persons and guide them in the growth of understanding and the acceptance of responsibility, foundations are laid which, properly built upon, will lead to the flowering of wholesome personality in later maturity.

GENERAL CULTURE. Culture is a coercive force that helps to shape the ideas, beliefs, and actions which influence the individual and mold his character. It is a dominant factor in establishing the basic personality patterns of various groups within a society as well as the personal characteristics of each individual. The typical forms of behavior of both children and adults are conditioned by family traditions and the community mores. Social stratification results in differing behavior patterns, moral standards, conceptions of self and of society among the several socio-economic classes in any community.

Thus an explanation of the personality of any individual must include an account of the social and cultural influences that have

127

impinged upon his life. To understand a person is to take into consideration the cultural atmosphere in which he spent his formative years. Personality tends to become structured in terms of the social practices of the groups with which the individual has been associated.

Knowledge of the total effect of the social and cultural environment upon individual development is sketchy and incomplete, but it has been enhanced in recent years by an increasing body of research literature in such fields as anthropology, social psychology, and sociology. As the results of these studies are better synthesized, understanding will be even more enriched. One who attempts to formulate a philosophy of Christian education can ill afford to neglect the insights that may come from the work of social scientists.

Education as a Conditioning Factor

Education is the organized effort of a society to enrich and control the experience of its younger members so that they may participate effectively in the ongoing life of the society. In making provision for education, society determines the structure and function of its formal educational agencies (schools); it chooses the leadership of these agencies (administrators and teachers); it selects from its total accumulated experiences and records the particular aspects it deems appropriate for emphasis (curriculum); it fixes limits to the initiative and freedom of those who take part in the processes of education (discipline); and it rewards or punishes those engaged in education in accordance with their accomplishment of the tasks imposed upon them (promotion, failure). Particularly in the strategic early years, the individual has little control over either the content or the method of instruction. Hence education exerts a powerful external influence upon the formation of personality.

Uniqueness of the Individual

It would be easy on the basis of the foregoing considerations to arrive at a thoroughly deterministic concept of personality. Thus far, there seems little possibility of freedom for the individual. Many cards are stacked against him: by original nature, over which he has obviously no control; by the social and cultural milieu that impinges upon him, regardless of his wishes, and circumscribes the arena of his action; and education, whose form and content are controlled largely by those who seek to fit him into already established patterns of thinking and living.

Education, however, is not merely a matter of writing upon a *tabula rasa,* of stamping in impressions from an external environment upon inert and wholly malleable material. There is something stubborn in human nature that refuses to be shaped completely by outside forces. Experience is always the result of interaction between two dynamic realities: the learner, who is seeking his own goals and therefore responds selectively to elements in the total situation; and the environment, which presents opportunities and incentives to action but cannot completely override the capacity of the individual to choose among the alternatives offered.

No two individuals are ever exactly alike, regardless of the seeming similarities in their respective environmental situations. Each person is the product of his own responses to the forces that have played upon him. He does not merely absorb his social and cultural environment but, at least in some measure, he creates his own by selective adaptation. The degree of freedom, of course, depends upon past experience and the relationships sustained with other people. In some situations, maximum self-development may have been retarded by deprivations in the physical environment, preventing the satisfactions of many of the normal human drives. In others, unfortunate interhuman relationships may have impeded wholesome growth. Parental discipline may have been too harsh and repressive. Powerful pressures toward conformity may have been exercised by groups with which he has been associated. A totalitarian state may have subjected him to regimentation, imposing extreme penalties for disobedience. In all such circumstances, the achievement of personal autonomy and responsible selfhood has been obstructed.

In the process of adjustment, the individual may have adopted patterns of behavior that stand in the way of his optimum self-realization. In more favorable circumstances, the growth of selfhood may have been encouraged and nurtured by adequate provision for basic needs, the security that comes from the love and companionship of understanding parents, mutuality in social relationships, and responsible citizenship in a democratic state. But, whatever the situation, the individual has played an important part in determining what he is now. And what he may become tomorrow is equally dependent upon the use he makes of the opportunities and resources that may open for him today. He is a *unique* personality and meets experience in his own way. Attempts to "handle" him without recognition of his own contribution to the total outcome may backfire. An adequate philosophy of education must take into account both the fact and the significance of individual differences.

Worth of the Individual

Two opposed positions may be taken with respect to the relative worth of the individual as contrasted with that of the total society of which he is a part. In some societies, the group is supreme; and efforts are put forth to make the individual conform to its standards of belief and action. Certain beliefs are "right," others wrong. The knowledge that may be needed is already in possession of the group and the individual is expected to acquire the elements selected for him by those who provide instruction. Behavior must be in accord with established norms. Nonconformity is frowned upon and an individual is "bad" to the degree of his nonconformity. Education is a means of transmitting the culture and of habituating individuals in the prevalent folkways. It is designed to condition individuals so that they will accept and appropriate values that have already been adopted. Freedom of the individual is restricted to limits that have already been set.

In other societies, the individual is supreme; and the group is judged on the basis of its possible contribution to the realization of the full potentialities of the individuals who compose it. The present accumulations of knowledge and the customary forms of behavior are regarded as but steppingstones toward broader knowledge and richer life for the individual and, through individual enhancement, for the group as a whole. A premium is placed upon initiative and freedom. Individual freedom is restricted only when it is apparent that the common good is endangered. Education is designed to enable individuals to make whatever use of present knowledge and customary behavior patterns as will lead to self-realization and individual growth. Education will provide opportunities for criticism and evaluation of present standards and attainments and will encourage change in the direction of ever more desirable goals and values.

Neither of these extreme positions with respect to the relative worth of the individual and his group is justified. In view of the integral relation of individual and group, the values of one cannot be fully realized without the fullest development of the other. A group is made up of individuals, and the totality of its values is inclusive of the values of every individual within it. When the values of particular individuals seem to clash, or when the goals of an individual seem to contravene the values of society, the tensions should be resolved in a spirit of compromise so that the fullest possible good for the whole may be realized. If a society operates consistently on this principle, the degree of individual intransigence will be progressively overcome. One does not continue to fight those who persistently seek his good. Social groups, then, should struggle against those forces in nature and in themselves that impede the development of the full potentialities of all their members. A particular society is limited only by its capacity to envision the whole of humanity, in which the good of one society finally involves the good of every other.

Toward a Coherent Theory of Personality

This discussion has attempted to identify some of the components that enter into the making of personality. These have included the original biological and constitutional basis of human nature, the social and cultural factors that have helped to shape the course of later development, the role of education as a determinant of personality growth, the effect of unique patterns of response to environmental stimuli that characterize the reactions of a particular individual, and the significance of differing value orientations with respect to the relative worth of the individual in influencing the form and content of instruction.

This should suggest the extreme difficulty of formulating a theory of personality that combines all these considerations into a coherent whole. Contributions of great potential value toward an understanding of human personality have been made in recent years by specialists in many fields of research. The accumulation of data from their many investigations has been so rapid and so vast that no complete synthesis is now possible. As a consequence, there is a variety of theories of personality, exhibiting certain trends but also manifesting tremendous complexity and diversity. All of these theories should be subjected to continuing study and experimental testing. But some results seem dependable, and these should be carefully taken into account by those who are concerned about gaining deeper insights into human nature as a basis for a philosophy of Christian education.

It seems clear, for example, that the human organism is a striving, dynamic, purposive entity that seeks to maintain selfhood in the midst of many conflicting and opposing influences. Present behavior is deeply affected by previous experience. Hereditary factors may be partly determinative, but personality is largely *acquired* through learning—through interaction with other people.

Especially significant for an understanding of behavior are events in early childhood, membership in social groups, the roles one is expected to play, and the degree of freedom allowed for individual expression and initiative. Standards of conduct are influenced much more by the behavior of associates than by the formal teaching of precepts.

The elements of behavior cannot be fully understood in isolation from one another. They must be considered as parts of the functioning of the "whole" individual, vis-à-vis the various groups with which he is associated. Behavior must always be judged in terms of its sociocultural context.

The subjective frame of reference (the situation as perceived by the individual) is much more important than objective reality as noted by an observer. Many forms of behavior that may be regarded as aberrant by an outsider may be merely the best way an individual has found to achieve his own goals in the midst of a hostile environment. Integrity of character is best maintained when the individual, within a supporting environment, has accepted a supreme goal to which all lesser loyalties may be subordinated and toward which all his energies may be directed. All of these findings have implications of the greatest consequence for the philosophy of Christian education.

PART THREE

Religious and Theological Foundations

X. PERSONALITY IN
CHRISTIAN PERSPECTIVE

The behavioral sciences have provided invaluable data on human personality in its physical and social settings. It would be very foolish to attempt the formulation of a philosophy of education without taking these data into account. But scientists usually recognize that rather strict limitations are imposed upon their several fields of investigation, and they do not pretend to deal with the whole of reality.

It seems proper to raise the question whether any theory of personality can be regarded as complete and satisfactory that neglects the religious dimension, that fails to see man in cosmic perspective. The Christian faith is not unmindful of biological and social needs, but it recognizes spiritual needs as well. Man does not live by bread alone, nor is he limited in his relationships to his fellow human beings. His wholeness depends upon proper relationships with God, the creator and sustainer of his being.

Jesus' Estimate of Human Nature

A valid starting point for a Christian view of personality would seem to be the estimate of human nature held by Jesus. The findings of the behavioral sciences must be taken seriously as far as they go, but they may need to be supplemented at important points by Jesus' intuitive understandings arising out of intimate day-by-day associations with real human beings in his own day.

TRADITION AND CREATIVITY. Jesus' outlook on life and his concept of human nature were the result of a skillful blending of tradition and creativity. He was well acquainted with the Jewish scriptures and selected from them elements which constituted the

135

core of his faith. Some elements he rejected, others he expanded until they seemed entirely new. But always his views of life and of reality squared with his own rich experiences, and he was able to express these views in a language that made an immediate impact upon the mind of his hearers. They understood him because he spoke to their condition.

Jesus' theology was quite simple. For the most part he accepted the concept of God embodied in the writings of the great Jewish prophets. God is an active spiritual presence who is working out his purposes in human history, and with whom man can establish and maintain personal relations through faith and prayer. But Jesus added to this conception the idea of God as a loving Father, which is only implied in the Jewish scriptures.

GOD'S LOVE. Jesus used many striking parables and figures of speech to illustrate the nature of God's love. No sparrow ever falls to the ground without his notice, and each human being is worth much more than many sparrows. Even the hairs of our heads are all numbered. Just as God clothes the grass of the field, so will he take care of all who trust him. God is like the father of a prodigal son who, when his son turns his back upon his family and squanders his property in dissolute living, watches yearningly for his wayward son's return. He is like a shepherd who, when one sheep is lost, leaves all the others to search for the lost sheep until he finds it. "There will be more joy in heaven over one sinner who repents than over ninety-nine righteous persons who need no repentance." (Luke 15:7.)

Jesus based his concept of human nature upon his understanding of God. He therefore regarded human personality as of infinite value because it is precious in the sight of God. God's relation to man is animated by love (agape), which is boundless and extends to all people. God's love is unrestricted; he makes the sun to shine on the evil as well as the good. Children are never to be despised, for it is not the Father's will that any of them should ever perish. No man can profit if he lose his soul, not even if he gain the whole world.

THE BASIS OF VALUE. All institutions are to be judged on the basis of their contributions to the rich and full life which God intends for all his children. The Sabbath was made for man and not man for the Sabbath. The rulers of the temple are to be opposed when they prostitute their sacred office for human gain. It would be better for a man if a millstone were hung around his neck and he were cast into the sea than that he should cause a child to stumble.

THE GROUND FOR SELF-ACCEPTANCE. God's love for human beings provides the ground for self-acceptance and makes it possible for them to love one another. Man's health and wholeness depend upon his maintaining love in all his relationships: with God, whom he must love completely, and with his fellow men, whom he must love as he loves himself. Though Jesus used the phrase, "kingdom of God," his concept of relationships can best be expressed in terms of the family. God is to be thought of as Father and human beings as his children. Therefore all men are to regard each other as brothers.

Men often reject God's love, disobey the principle of love, disregard the obligation to love others, and thus prevent the good that God wills. But when they repent, God is ever eager and waiting to forgive and to restore the broken relationship. The kingdom of God is a community in which its members are more concerned about the well being of others than about their own.

THE GOSPEL. Jesus thought of his mission as that of announcing the "good news" that God is engaged in saving action *now*, that his kingdom is "at hand," and that man's part is to offer a willing response to God. He ordered his disciples to go into all the world and preach this good news to everyone. The kingdom, he said, is like a tiny mustard seed that grows to be the biggest of all plants; it is like leaven that permeates the entire meal. And those who accept it are the salt of the earth and the light of the world.

The theory of human nature embodied in a philosophy of Christian education should combine Jesus' estimate of man with the best knowledge and understanding available from other sources. But the theory that underlies much of the recent literature in Christian education is in serious need of reformulation because it does not meet this test. It is based upon selected passages of scripture, to the neglect of other equally relevant passages, and it fails to take into account information and insights gained from investigation and research in other fields.

MISTAKEN CONCEPTS OF HUMAN NATURE. Not all Christian theology has been based upon Jesus' sane and wholesome view of human nature. Certain passages in Paul's writings and some of the works of Augustine reflect another view. In attempts to outline the "biblical view of man" and to recover a "Christian anthropology," some Christian theologians have magnified these writings to the almost complete neglect of the teachings of Jesus and the record of his dealings with the men and women of his day. Jesus, who "knew what was in man," never once referred to the "fall of man"; only three times in the Synoptic Gospels is he reported to have used the noun "sin" in its singular form; he made no utterance that can be made to support a doctrine of total depravity.

JESUS' REALISTIC VIEW. This may not be taken to mean that he was unaware of sin nor that he was casual in his attitude toward it. But it does mean that he placed his stress always upon human potential, upon the saving qualities that people have in themselves, particularly their love and their faith. His recognition of human failure and sin was counteracted by his sense of infinite human redeemability. He thought of persons primarily in terms of what they might become, rather than what they had been. And he loved them for what they were. The only people he ever condemned were those who put their doctrines and institutions above the value they placed on the individual. There seems little warrant in Jesus' attitudes and teachings for taking a jaundiced view of human nature. Surely a Christian theory of personality should take into account Jesus' belief in man.

It is understandable that the theology of the recent past should react to an overly optimistic view of man which pervaded much of the thinking of the early part of the twentieth century. *Man is not a paragon of virtue* whose progress toward perfection can be guaranteed by the improvement of material conditions and the extension of educational opportunity. An accurate reading of history and a recognition of the devious ways in which human beings have been led astray should have taught us that. But if we are to be "realistic," the picture must not be distorted from the other side. *Man is not by nature a diabolical creature* who must be damned unless God chooses to extend an arbitrary proffer of redemption. An obsession with the fact of sin may be quite as damaging as belief in the inevitability of progress. *The possibilities of both sin and righteousness*, we may believe, are woven deep into the very fabric of human nature. And a proper understanding of man must await deeper insights into the forces and conditions that lead to the ascendancy of one over the other.

The Conditions of Christian Growth

The Christian way of life is *learned*—it is not automatic nor is it achieved without effort. If Christian education is to succeed in its attempts to enable persons to become faithful members of the family of God, some understanding of the conditions which stimulate Christian growth is required. It should be recognized that all persons are created as children of God and members of his family, but not all are *faithful* members. Each individual must be dealt with in terms of his own relationships and needs. A vast number have never come to confess membership nor to recognize its obligations. A great many have broken the relations which constitute true membership. Others who acknowledge membership have only the slightest notion of what this involves. And all are under the requirement of continuing growth.

Faithful members of God's family will perceive that everyone is to be accepted in respect and love because each is a subject of the infinite love of God. In a climate of understanding and accepting love, self-acceptance becomes a possibility. Acceptance of self and of others, rooted in the experience of being accepted by God and by others, is a prime condition of Christian growth. This is why the Christian church is so important, since it is a forgiving and sustaining fellowship when it measures up to its high responsibilities as an agency of Christian education. As such, it is a channel through which the individual may be brought into redeeming fellowship with God.

Self-acceptance is never to be identified with complacency and self-righteousness. Acceptance of the *actual* self must always be associated with the desire and effort to realize all the possibilities of the *potential* self. The Christian must "press on toward the goal for the prize of the upward call of God in Christ Jesus" (Phil. 3:14). He must never be satisfied with anything short of the *ideal* self, the self which God would make of each individual if he fully had his way. And the Christian accepts others in terms of what they may become.

Faithful members of the family of God are ever seeking to assist all members to realize their highest potentialities, since that is what God intends for all. They seek to overcome the influences that hinder and degrade personality and to sustain and augment those that build it up. "For we are fellow workmen for God." (I Cor. 3:9.) This involves self-denial and cross bearing, but these are accepted willingly for the sake of the larger good. Jesus' teachings are quite clear at these points: "I came that they may have life, and have it abundantly" (John 10:10); and "If any man would come after me, let him deny himself and take up his cross and follow me" (Matt 16:24).

There is an inseparable relation, then, between Christian faith and the major social problems in the world today. Taking a responsible part, according to ability and opportunity, in efforts toward improvement in such areas as economic life, race relations, health and public welfare, housing and slum clearance, human rights, intergroup education, interchurch co-operation and world peace is another necessary condition of Christian growth.

Christian Maturity

One of the pressing needs in the philosophy of Christian education today is a clearer concept of what constitutes Christian maturity. In the light of the central emphasis upon the concept of maturity in current educational and psychological literature, it seems strange that so little attention has been given to it in Christian education. It sometimes would seem that teachers think maturity is automatically achieved when one is able to repeat a set of verbal formulas, recite selected passages from Scripture, and follow stated rituals with exactness.

MENTAL HEALTH. Helpful insights into the nature of maturity may be gained from familiarity with the literature in the field of mental hygiene. Practitioners in this field have given a great deal of attention to the problem of maturity. They usually approach the matter of definition by suggesting some characteristics of a mentally healthy person. Some of these suggestions follow:

1. *A mentally healthy person is at home with himself.* He feels comfortable about himself and is not defeated by his own emotions, such as fear, anger, jealousy, guilt, and worry. He accepts his own shortcomings, neither underestimating nor overestimating his own abilities. He recognizes that he often makes mistakes and he can laugh at himself. He is able to pull his own weight and to take life's disappointments in stride. He has self-respect, accepts and esteems himself for what he is. He is an "integrated" personality.

2. *A mentally healthy person feels right about other people.* Having accepted himself, he is able to take a tolerant, easy-going attitude toward others. He expects to like and trust others and assumes that others will like and trust him. He can feel that he is part of a group and does not need to fight against it. He is able to give love as he expects to be loved. He feels a responsibility to his neighbors and to all his fellow men. The religious way of putting it is this: "Thou shalt love thy neighbor as thyself."

It may be noted that this commandment is bipolar. One must love himself. This of course can be an unhealthy attitude if self-regard is exaggerated, disproportionate and perverted, the connotation usually given to the term "selfishness." But to love one's self in the sense of mental health means to understand one's self, to accept one's self, to respect and esteem one's self. Only a person who thus loves himself is in a position to love his neighbor. So the requirement is bilateral: love your neighbor as you love yourself, but first your self-regard must be worthy.

3. *A mentally healthy person takes a positive, confident attitude toward life and toward external reality.* He is able to meet the demands in his situation without evasion and without shifting responsibility to others. He is able to think for himself and to make his own decisions. He welcomes new experiences and new ideas. He seeks to do something constructive about his own problems, as he is willing to assist others in meeting theirs. He reshapes his environment whenever possible and adjusts to it when necessary. He puts his best efforts into whatever he does and gets satisfaction and happiness out of it.

In summary, then, a mentally healthy person is at peace with himself; he is able to take a friendly, co-operative attitude toward other people; he feels at home with the world of nature and reality; and he meets the demands of life with creative effort and with a sense of joy and achievement.

A careful reading of the writings of competent psychologists by thoughtful Christians will reveal that there is much in common between the approaches to personality of psychology and of the Christian faith. Among the findings of modern psychology which seem likely to be regarded as secure are these: an individual remains mentally healthy if he is treated with respect and dignity and is allowed increasingly with growing experience to regulate his life in the direction of his own chosen purposes; he is handicapped if he is dominated by superiors who try to substitute their values for those which seem desirable to him; he is assisted in regaining his health, in the event of its impairment, only as he is able to understand his condition and is allowed to follow a course of action which he regards as consistent with his fundamental drives and wishes; the resources which lead to health are inherent in the very nature of things—man does not make them, he can only understand and utilize them; and health is enhanced as he removes the conditions that breed disease and allows the health-giving streams of the universe to flow freely through his total organism.

SPIRITUAL WHOLENESS. These generalizations are not out of accord with certain conceptions of religion which across the centuries have challenged and inspired men to reach up toward wholeness, godlikeness. Among these are the dignity and worth of personality; the love of God for all his children, rich and poor, healthy and unhealthy, good and bad; the necessity of humility and repentance for recognized infringements of the moral law; the validity of faith in redemption when man seeks restoration of right relationships with his fellow men and with God. Thus, mental health and true religion are not two opposed approaches to human nature. They are differing ways of stating one interpretation, couched on the one hand in the language of modern science, and on the other hand in the phraseology of religion. So far as the interpretation is true, one need not be concerned about its sources.

JESUS' ILLUSTRATION. As an aside, and for purposes of illustration, it may not be out of place to call attention to one of the most profound symbolic accounts of good religion and of sound mental hygiene to be found in the world's literature, the story of the prodigal son, told by a master student of human nature and the world's best exemplar of high religion.

According to Jesus' story of the prodigal son, there was a wealthy man who had two sons for whom he provided a home in which respect for personality was a dominant feature. In the process of maturing, one of the boys asserted his independence and requested his share of the inheritance. This was immediately granted by the father who understood the requirements of true maturation. Unfortunately, however, the great love of the father had not been coupled with an understanding of the process by which one arrives at autonomy and the capacity to make mature judgments. The boy had been shielded too much from the world of reality. As he went out into a world of his own, he was unfortunate in his choice of companions.

In the course of time, he wasted his entire substance and found himself destitute. His only means of livelihood was a task regarded as completely despicable by his father and by those who were his kinsmen. But along the way, the boy had learned at least to critically evaluate his outward circumstances as well as his inner desires. His experiences in his father's home had created for him a standard of values which he understood and accepted. Through his own willful choice he had brought himself into a condition where he could no longer regard himself as worthy of the love of his father and of an honored place in his father's household. Nevertheless, he arose and turned homeward, satisfied to ask for only a place of humble service. All he wanted was to be restored to health, to be reconciled to his father, and to have a chance to stay at home again. A humble position seemed to him consistent with the abuse he had given his privileges and former position.

But, to his complete surprise, his father was not angry; he did not condemn him as a sinner; he required no expiating sacrifice. All along the father's heart had yearned for his son's redemption and this redemption began at the moment the lad accepted himself for what he was and started back on his way to what he might become. We may be sure that the lad's growth toward maturity had been advanced even in his unfortunate experience.

THE MOTIF OF CHRISTIAN EDUCATION. Jesus meant this to be a parable of the proper relation of a father to his children. It surely suggests the proper attitude on the part of all more mature Christians toward those who are less mature. It suggests the proper atmosphere for effective Christian education. God's love is about us all the time. We may rebel against it if we choose, but we will suffer the consequences if we do. Sometimes temporary rebellion is a prerequisite to growing up, but health is restored as we recognize our condition and need and take advantage of the processes which are intended to promote health all the time and for all human beings whom God has created. If we have strayed away, we, too, may arise and go to our Father who has already taken the initiative in bringing about our reconciliation.

XI. THEOLOGICAL
FOUNDATIONS OF
CHRISTIAN EDUCATION

The term Christian education implies a theology. There are certain convictions at the heart of the Christian faith which must be taken into account in any valid attempt to state a philosophy of Christian education.

Theology is the discipline by which man seeks to organize his religious beliefs into coherent and ordered form. It is concerned with God and with his relation to the world and to man. It is one of the most important, and at the same time one of the most difficult, of the intellectual disciplines. It is of vital importance to religion because cult practices may degenerate into sentimentality and moralism unless they are brought before the bar of reason. Since religion is a way of responding to ultimate reality, one may be led astray unless the response is a total response, including the rigorous use of the mind. Of course theology is only one aspect of religion, not the whole. Theology without worship is not religion at all. Worship without theology can become little more than emotionalism and hence a poor substitute for religion.

Theology is more difficult than most of the disciplines because of the nature of its subject matter. Theology deals with the infinite, and man's knowledge must ever be limited. He sees through this glass darkly, and he must make most of his judgments on the basis of inference. He is forced to express his ideas of God in symbols and analogies which are never identical with the Reality which he seeks to describe. Moreover, all of man's ideas are culturally conditioned. An individual is inevitably influenced by what others think, by the books he reads, by the content of his individual experience, and by categories of explanation which he borrows from the culture. This is true in all areas, of course, but it makes for special difficulties in theology because of the complexity of the subject and the limited equipment of any one individual to deal with it.

A theologian usually takes his stance within some already existing theological tradition. If he is a Christian, he is also a Methodist, or a Presbyterian, or a Roman Catholic, as the case may be. And he is likely to be influenced more than he realizes by the established currents of thought within his group. It is easy to assume a finality for these which is hardly justified in the very nature of the human situation. If God is God, then human beings can never fully understand him. To assume finality for any system of theology therefore is to make theology god. This is idolatry.

In spite of these difficulties, theology is necessary in any adequate statement of the philosophy of Christian education. I am by profession an educator, not a theologian, and recognize my inability to deal adequately with the technical problems of theology. Nevertheless, I feel that a necessary preliminary to any statement of the philosophy of Christian education is some outline of the basic presuppositions upon which Christian education rests. I attempt this outline with considerable diffidence, knowing full well that my particular formulation may not prove acceptable to many other equally devoted Christians. The outline is not regarded as necessarily normative. It is made in the hope that it may be intelligible and that it may be found consistent with other aspects of the philosophy presented in this book.

God

Basic, perhaps, to all other considerations is the Christian belief in the existence of God. Conceptions of the nature of God have varied across the centuries. They vary today from individual to individual and from group to group, for the reasons already suggested: the limitations of man's knowledge and understanding, the difficulty of finding adequate media of expression, and the influence of cultural traditions. But variations in Christian beliefs about God usually have to do with his nature and his relation to the world and to man. The *existence* of God (however conceived) is taken for granted. Atheism and Christianity are incompatible. Christian education is based upon a theistic faith.

One of the terms commonly used to indicate the Christian conception of God is that of Creator, "the maker of heaven and earth." God is believed to be self-sufficient and eternal, the sole source of all existence: the physical universe, life, and man. Conceptions of the process of creation have varied, but about the fact that it was God who created there has been general agreement. As distinguished from their Creator, all creatures, including man, are finite, mortal, contingent, and dependent upon the sustaining power of God. And in the universe which he has created, God is sovereign. Upon him ultimately depends the history, the hope, and the destiny of all his creatures.

Another element in the Christian concept of God is his providence. God, as the author of the world, is active within it and has the power to direct and control its events. He exercises his power, not arbitrarily nor capriciously, but in an orderly and intelligible fashion. His creative activities are purposeful, they lead to ends which God foresees and wills. He makes himself known to his creatures in many ways, particularly through the orderliness, dependability, and intelligibility of nature; through the experiences of people who earnestly seek him; through the minds and spirits of great religious seers; and especially through unique events in human history which point to his presence and power.

Man

God created human beings "in his own image and likeness," in order that he might have the fellowship of creatures who are capable of understanding his purposes and of sharing with him in their realization. He offers to them the relationship of a loving Father "whose will is ever directed to his children's good." He places upon this fellowship only two conditions: complete obedience to his will as one may understand it and love for other human beings without restriction. He has provided for the habitation of man a world full of the richest resources to be subdued and used for the common good. He surrounds his children with influences which, if responded to with gratitude and faithfulness, can lead to development and well-being beyond possible calculation.

Their capacities for understanding, of course, are limited; but they are endowed with great potential for growth and with the freedom that makes growth possible. Whenever they have developed and used their capacities, with rightful recognition of creaturehood and with sensitivity to the direction of divine providence, they have increased their knowledge and understanding, deepened their fellowship with God and with one another, extended their mastery over nature, and thus have achieved a fuller measure of their stature as human beings. Thus the purposes of God in some measure have been fulfilled.

But men have not often realized their full potentialities. They have forgotten their creaturehood. They have refused divine guidance even when they recognized its proffer. They have substituted their own designs and goals for the known purposes of God. They have sometimes worshiped the false gods of class, race, or nation. They have set up arbitrary boundaries to human fellowship and thus have failed in their fellowship with God. Children of a loving Father, they have been disobedient and rebellious children. Separating themselves from the love of God, they have failed to achieve their highest possibilities and have created problems for themselves which they cannot solve, all as consequences of their alienation. And so in large measure the purposes of God have been thwarted.

The Bible

God has not left himself without witness. Throughout history and among peoples everywhere there are evidences of continuing response to what was believed to be the presence and power of God. Not all individuals have been sensitive to the claims of the divine, but in every generation there have been some who have acknowledged these claims. The universality of the religious response is significant, though not all forms of the response are of equal worth.

Christians believe that the Bible, consisting of the sacred scriptures of the Jewish and Christian peoples, contains the clearest revelation of God's will for mankind and the most dependable record of his initiative in seeking man's reconciliation and redemption. Hence a study of the Bible is basic in Christian education.

Not all parts of the Bible are of equal value. It is based upon a pre-scientific view of nature. It contains only fragments of history, and these are presented from a religious point of view. Its religious ideas reflect varying degrees of progress and retrogression. But throughout its pages are the clear indication of an enduring sense of the presence of God in human history and a record of attempts to specify what this means for the life of man.

Proper use of the Bible, therefore, requires more than a knowledge of its present text and immediate application of its contents to the practical problems of everyday living. Biblical conceptions of the natural order must be revised in the light of modern science. Secular history provides needed supplements to the historical records contained in the Bible. Many of the perplexing problems of our modern day were not even anticipated in biblical times. The Bible provides no consistent theory of human nature and no complete philosophy of education. But the view that God is the author of the universe and that man's dependence places him under special obligation is pervasive and this is not affected by modern science and history. It should be taken into account in any effort to see human experience in complete perspective.

The Old Testament deals with the experience of the people of Israel in the light of their recognition of the special claims of God upon them. They thought of their relationship with God in terms of a covenant: Israel undertakes obedience to God's commands in return for which God pledges his forgiveness and blessing, but always with the threat of punishment in the event of disobedience. In passage after passage, Israel's good fortunes are attributed to the goodness and mercy of God. Their hardships and misfortunes are regarded as a direct result of disobedience. Their concepts of God changed, particularly as a result of the contributions of the greater prophets, Amos, Hosea, Isaiah, Micah, and Jeremiah. And their ideas varied regarding the central requirements of the covenant, but their sense of direct obligation to God never wavered. It recurs like a symphonic theme throughout the Jewish scriptures.

The New Testament resulted from the conviction that in the life, teachings, and ministry of Jesus of Nazareth, God had appeared in a special manner to point the way to man's redemption and to establish a new covenant with his people. "At the beginning God expressed himself. That personal expression . . . was with God and was God, and he existed with God from the beginning. . . . So the word of God became a human being and lived among us." (John 1:1-14 Phillips.) "All this is God's doing, for he has reconciled us to himself through Jesus Christ; and he has made us agents of the reconciliation." (II Cor. 5:19 Phillips.) Out of this conviction arose the Christian church. It is the central motif of Christian education.

Jesus Christ

One must face the task of trying to determine what is basic in the gospel for a philosophy of Christian education only with great hesitation. Attempts to summarize the teachings of Jesus are myriad.

Statements of Christology are almost as numerous. But if Christian education is essentially the effort to enable persons to become faithful members of the family of God, expressing in all their relationships the attitudes and way of life exemplified by Jesus—and the present writer believes that it is—an attempt must be made to discover what this means. In the light of the great variety of interpretations, it is too much to expect that all Christians will agree with this one.

It must be recognized at the outset that any effort to completely recover the "historical" Jesus is bound to fail. The "Jesus of history" is forever obscured behind the "Christ of faith." Records of how he lived and what he taught have come down from those who were a generation removed from the actual events and who wrote for the purpose of witnessing to what he had meant to them and to other members of the early Christian community. It was history "molded by theological beliefs." Modern historical and critical studies of the New Testament, however, have provided a fairly clear picture of the times and the main currents of thought and make possible some distinction between fact and interpretation. But whatever is held to be true regarding his actual life and teachings can only be inferred from records which reflect the theology of the early church.

Jesus was born into a Jewish family whose members were evidently very pious and deeply devoted to their religion. He must have received the best religious training possible for a boy in his circumstances. Unfortunately, practically nothing is known about his "hidden years." But in the one brief glimpse provided of him at twelve, he is already pursuing a zealous search for the deeper meanings of his faith and acknowledging a special responsibility for fulfilling its requirements. (Luke 2:41-52.) He undoubtedly spent much time in a study of the Scriptures and in prayer. One can be confident that throughout his early life he completely accepted the terms of the Jewish covenant: perfect obedience to the will of God and absolute trust in his loving favor. By the time he reached manhood he must have had some very deep convictions regarding what God willed for his people and what he must do about it.

In contrast with his own experience and commitment, however, he found all around him evidences that his people had forsaken God. And their external circumstances seemed to indicate that the ancient faith of Israel was true: their troubles were due to their failure to keep the covenant. The nation had lost its independence and was under the ruthless heel of a foreign power which scorned the God of

Israel. Exorbitant taxes were wrung from an already poverty-stricken people to support a lavish and extravagant military dictatorship. Rebellion against the government was punished by crucifixion. Thousands of Jesus' contemporaries had been crucified and some of the towns he had visited as a boy had been destroyed. One can hardly imagine a more anomalous economic and political situation for a proud nation, the "chosen people" of Almighty God.

Religious conditions were no better. Some of the more pious of the Jews had concluded that nothing could be done to improve conditions and they were quietly waiting for the "day of the Lord." One group of super-patriots was actively fomenting a violent revolt against the forces of Rome. One influential party had compromised, and the high priests were openly conniving with the hated conquerors. They had made the sacred Temple a "den of thieves." Another group was advocating the strict observance of outward ceremonies, with apparently little concern for their deeper inner significance. And, worst of all, the groups were all fighting among themselves. The sense of fellowship which was to characterize the children of the covenant had been lost.

At the time of his baptism, by a wandering evangelist whose message was strangely reminiscent of the great Jewish prophets, Jesus was assured of God's approval and felt the call to a special mission. He then went aside to ponder what this involved. After a period of retirement, "Jesus came into Galilee, proclaiming the Gospel of God, saying, 'The time has come at last—the kingdom of God has arrived. You must change your hearts and minds and believe the good news' " (Mark 1:14-15 Phillips).

A primary concept in Jesus' teaching was that of the kingdom of God. By this he meant the rule or sovereignty of God in the hearts and lives of men. The establishment of the kingdom is not some far-off event but "the time is at hand." The kingdom is not to be ushered in by some striking manifestation of supernatural power. It is a gift, offered freely by a loving God and man may enter by a simple acceptance of the will of God.

The heart of Jesus' teachings has come down to us in a kind of manifesto, the Sermon on the Mount, in which he described the mind and spirit of those who submit to the rule of God and outlined the principles that should guide in their mutual relationships. These principles are too well known to require much comment. They include humility, meekness, righteousness, mercy, purity of heart, the pursuit of peace, forgiveness, patient endurance of persecution, love of enemies, complete trust in God, and active pursuit of the will of God.

These cut so clearly across the ordinary standards both of his own day and of ours that too few have taken them seriously. When their full implications were understood by Jesus' contemporaries, they were rejected and he was put to death. Modern Christians have excused themselves from giving them rigorous testing in practical experience by the device of labelling them "an interim ethic," "an impossible possibility," or some other defensive appellation. But Jesus apparently believed that he could persuade men to accept them and that thus the kingdom of God would come in power and the problems of the people could be solved. He himself accepted them without reservation and followed them with complete devotion throughout all of his life.

One of the clear implications of Jesus' way of life is the requirement that one minister to human need, even at the cost of self-sacrifice. Jesus saw this clearly and, with his natural love and compassion for others, he often stepped aside from the task of teaching to heal the sick, cure the mentally deranged, feed the hungry, comfort the bereaved, and counsel those who were in trouble. His reputation spread swiftly throughout the country, and he gained wide popularity among the people. Sometimes they crowded around him so eagerly he found that his ministry of healing was interfering with the more compelling task of helping others to see what is required of them if God's kingdom is to come. This realization deepened as opposition of the religious leaders became more intense. Somehow he was not succeeding in leading the people to repentance. So, late in his ministry Jesus retired for a period to rethink his calling.

A new understanding of the true relationship of his work to that of his Father came—possibly as he considered the nature and work of the Messiah for whom the Jews for so long had looked forward. There were two prevalent concepts of the Messiah who, the Jews believed, would come and solve all their problems: one, an apocalyptic being who would usher in the kingdom by the spectacular use of supernatural power; the other, a descendant of the royal line who would restore the political independence of the nation and re-establish the kingdom of Israel by military power. Jesus had rejected both of these concepts of Messiah early in his career.

But it had become increasingly clear that the multitudes were coming to regard him as Messiah. They were constantly causing trouble by ascribing to him this title and thus interfering with his real work. It was evident also that a commingling of elements in both of the current conceptions of Messiah was influencing their expectations. His healing had led many to attribute to him supernatural powers. Many of his followers, on the other hand, expected him to lead a revolt against Rome. It became necessary for him to consider whether he really was Messiah and, if so, in what sense.

He found his answer, apparently, in the concept of the Suffering Servant in the second Isaiah. He had pondered these passages many times before and had used them in his teaching. But Isaiah's description of "him who brings good tidings of good, who publishes salvation" (Isa. 52:7) took on a deeper poignancy now as he thought back over his work.

> He was despised and rejected by men;
> a man of sorrows, and acquainted with grief
> and as one from whom men hide their faces
> he was despised, and we esteemed him not.
>
> Surely he has borne our griefs
> and carried our sorrows;
> yet we esteemed him stricken,
> smitten by God, and afflicted.
> But he was wounded for our transgressions,
> he was bruised for our iniquities;
> upon him was the chastisement
> that made us whole,
> and with his stripes we are healed.
>
> . . . .
>
> Yet it was the will of the Lord to bruise him;
> he has put him to grief;
>
> . . . .
>
> he shall see the fruit of the travail of his soul
> and be satisfied.
>
> Isa. 53:3-11

He saw now that the way of God was not only the way of love but also of suffering, that Messiah was to be a Suffering Servant, and that God was calling him to that work. He was the Messiah! So he returned to his disciples, now with a sense of utter urgency. He inquired of them what the people thought of him. "John the Baptist," they said, or "Elijah," or "one of the prophets." But it was necessary to press for their own answer. Finally Peter blurted out, "You are the Christ." He then charged them not to tell others—the popular conceptions of Messiah were too blurred to serve his purpose. "And he began to teach them that the Son of man must suffer many things, and be rejected by the elders and the chief priests and the scribes, and be killed, and after three days rise again." Peter stubbornly refused to believe it—that was certainly not his concept of Christ! But Jesus rebuked him, "Get behind me, Satan! For you are not on the side of God, but of men." (Mark 8:27-33.)

The new concept was so startling that Jesus was quite unable to bring his disciples to understand and accept it. Soon he found them haggling over the chief places in the new kingdom he was expected to establish. As Jesus moved into Jerusalem for the closing days of his ministry, doubtless still with the hope that he could bring the religious leaders to repentance, events moved swiftly to their climax. His enemies cleverly plotted his downfall. One of his disciples betrayed him into their hands. With a curse, his staunchest follower disavowed any association with him. The rest of his disciples deserted. And soon he was nailed to a cross. His final understanding of the nature of his mission sustained him in his darkest hour. Once he had seen it clearly, he moved unflinchingly to the end. In the turmoil and confusion of the closing scenes, his was the only calm and unruffled spirit in all the mob.

There is a mystery about all this which still eludes the full understanding of his most perceptive followers. But Christians all agree, however they may differ in their ways of explaining it, that "God was in Christ personally reconciling the world to himself" (II Cor. 5:19 Phillips). That "strange man on a cross" still marches down across the ages, and he has done more to make men aware of God than any other figure in history.

The Church

Immediately after the crucifixion of Jesus, his disciples were scattered in confusion and despair. His promise of the kingdom now seemed without foundation. The fellowship which had been built up around him was dissolved. But soon thereafter it was reconstituted, never again to be completely dissevered. Those who had been associated with Jesus came together under a compelling conviction that their Master who had been crucified was alive again and that he was present among them. Some testified that they had seen him. Their stories were incorporated in the later written records, but they are difficult to piece together into one consistent account. Christians are faced, therefore, with one of the most baffling historical problems, a mystery to which perhaps no final solution can be given. But it is clear that, in a manner which the followers of Jesus themselves could not explain, they came to believe that he was still with them as a living presence; and on this certainty they built their faith. This faith became the dynamic of a new movement, the Christian church.

As the church began its efforts to fulfill its mission of reconciliation, it became necessary for its leaders to formulate Christian doctrine, to think through the new understandings of God and of his requirements which Jesus had taught and exemplified in his life. And they saw that the new theology must include their understanding of Jesus and his relation to God. The process went on for many centuries —as it must continue today. From the beginning, new problems were faced as the Christian message was shared with each new group. And always the Christian evangelists sought to adapt their message to the experiences and thought patterns of those to whom they went.

Two of the doctrines which have come down to us from that ancient time, couched in terms that are difficult for us to understand, are the doctrine of the Incarnation (the union of divinity with humanity in Christ) and that of the Trinity (the union of three "persons" in one God). Across the centuries, Christians have differed in their interpretations of these doctrines, as many still differ today. But the doctrines were attempts to combine in intellectual formulae three aspects of the nature of God: the eternal, the historical and the contemporary. From the beginning, God (the Father) is the Creator and continues to carry on his work of creation. Once in history, he was uniquely revealed in human personality (the Son). And he is present now and always (the Holy Spirit), whenever men recognize his presence and are responsive to his will. Though Christians may continue to differ in their understandings, the essential truths which these doctrines were meant to express will doubtless continue to challenge those who accept their places within the fellowship of the church. One of the tasks of theology is to assist the church to understand the doctrines in terms of the concepts which people hold today. Insistence upon the precise language in which they were stated at an earlier period may hinder rather than aid understanding.

This is not the place to trace the history of the church. But it may be noted that from its beginning as a small sect within Judaism, which soon distinguished itself by its open avowal of the Lordship of Jesus, it became separated from the parent body and began a growth that has continued until today it is the largest religious movement in the world. It contains within itself the most bewildering variety of forms of organization, statements of beliefs, methods of work; but Christians of all varieties are bound together by allegiance to the same Lord.

One of the tasks of Christian theology is to define the nature of the church so that it may be understood in all its manifold expressions of life and thought and that these may be seen in their proper relation to God as revealed in Christ. This is obviously not easy, for Christians differ in their interpretations of the church. As theologians have wrestled with these differences in recent years, they have seen more clearly the effects which historical and cultural factors have played in determining particular expressions of faith and practice. They seem to be determined to discover the "given unity" that underlies and transcends the differences and holds Christians together in spite of diversity. This may suggest a new approach to an understanding of the proper relation of theology to Christian education.

As was stated at the beginning of this chapter, Christian education implies theology. Some of the problems of obtaining a theology that can provide an adequate basis for Christian education have been indicated. One of these is the fact that it can hardly be said that there is *a* Christian theology. There are many Christian theologies. All of these, it may be hoped, contain some facets of the truth about God, about man, and about man's relation to God. The great variety of theologies should dispel an easy presumption that any one system contains the whole truth. Thus, while Christian education must have a theology, it must ever keep open to the possibilities of a better one.

XII. TOWARD A
NEW PERSPECTIVE IN
CHRISTIAN THEOLOGY

It may seem presumptuous for one who is not a professional theologian to attempt to deal with current tendencies in American theological thought and to suggest possible new directions for the future. But the effort to do so is necessitated by the nature of the work of a Christian educator. No one who works actively within the Christian movement can escape theology, whether he be pastor, evangelist, church-school worker, or college teacher of religion, though most of these are not professional theologians. Christian education necessarily involves the outcomes of theological effort and should be concerned about the quality and utility of the product. It is hardly a question of whether or not one has a theology, but whether the theology is good or bad.

Theology is the study of the intellectual aspects of religion. It is the disciplined effort to develop knowledge and understanding of God and his relation to the world and to man. Christian theology is the attempt of Christians to make clear and explicit what they think they know about God as revealed in Christ so that this knowledge may be communicated to others. Professional theologians are needed so that this special knowledge may be organized, systematized, and reduced to a form that makes it communicable. But the outcomes of their work may be of little value unless Christians who are not specialists in theology are able to make effective use of it. As a Christian educator the writer has discovered that too often there is a chasm between the thought worlds of theologians and educators which affects adversely the effectiveness of the ministry of both groups. He suspects that the "vocabulary of faith" has less meaning to the man in the pew than many preachers realize.

Essential Elements in a Valid Theology

A valid theology must be based upon an experienced relation with God, an understanding of the nature of this relationship, and an interpretation in terms that are intelligible to the contemporary mind. Christian theology today must be concerned with each of these elements.

To see the task in proper perspective, it may be instructive to note the chronological sequence which actuated the origin and development of Christian theology in the first place. (1) Christianity had its beginnings in the vital experience of a group of people who took seriously their relation to God. (2) They attempted to clarify their understanding of this experience by discussions among themselves and by testimony and witness to others outside their group. (3) They naturally couched their interpretations and explanations in the language and thought patterns that were prevalent at the time. (4) The verbal content of their testimony varied as it was presented by different individuals and to different groups.

Always their theology was an outcome of efforts to interpret experience in terms that made sense both to the interpreters and to those who heard the interpretation. The *experience* was primary. *Explanation* was related as realistically as possible to the experience. The *form* of the explanation was conditioned by the knowledge and mental outlook of the times.

Christian theology in every age, as in the early church, faces the same problems. The experience of relationship to God must be vital and real. Discussion must be based upon actual experience. The discourse must be relevant and intelligible. The content of Christian theology therefore must allow for flexibility and adaptation. Christian experience in its particulars may vary from individual to individual and the patterns of interpretation and explanation may change from group to group and from age to age. Hence richness and variety rather than fixity and rigidity are essentials of the Christian faith.

Creativity in Theological Expression

The problem of continuing theological reconstruction has faced Christianity from the beginning. Though his mind was steeped in the religious traditions of his people, it was because he was keenly sensitive to the requirements of a vital and continuing experience of God in the midst of changing times that Jesus was compelled to restate the elements of his faith: *"You have heard that it was said"* what the current theologians were saying, *"but I say to you"* something that seemed truer in the light of his richer experience (Matt. 5:21, 22).

Abundant evidence is presented in the four Gospels of the lack of complete unanimity in the understanding of their experience on the part of the companions of Jesus. Paul's understanding of his own faith was deepened and expanded as he sought to share it with groups of differing backgrounds. And a long procession of Christian witnesses have left a priceless legacy in their varying interpretations: Origen, Augustine, Aquinas, Calvin, Luther, Wesley, Temple, Niebuhr—and countless others. To take the testimony of any one of these and try to make it definitive and final would tragically impoverish the Christian witness for today.

It is true that some individuals and groups of our time have insisted upon the "unity" of Christian testimony to the neglect of its variety and diversity. But to choose only elements which support one's own presuppositions to the neglect of other elements is but to splinter the Christian faith, which transcends the capacity of any one individual to restrict its complete expression to his particular set of categories. Since God is infinite, as we must believe, and since man is finite, it must follow that man's knowledge of God must necessarily be limited. And hence there can never be a final and complete statement of theology.

This is not to minimize, but rather to dramatize, the importance of Christian theology for us today. In our attitude toward it, we may well take our cue from the writer of Hebrews: "Remember your leaders," he wrote, "those who spoke to you the word of God; *consider the outcome of their life, and imitate their faith.*" Note that he did not say to slavishly repeat their words; though, like him, we may well believe that "Jesus Christ is the same yesterday and today and for ever" (Heb. 13:7-8).

The Theological Revival

No one who is acquainted with the current religious situation in America can doubt that we are in the midst of a theological revolution. The study and discussion of theological problems have been more intense and widespread during the last quarter of a century than in any period since the Protestant Reformation. Ecumenical gatherings, national and regional conferences, local ministerial associations, individual clergymen and laymen in local churches have all been affected by this ferment. This is evidence of a wholesome desire to find a more adequate intellectual framework within which to express the Christian faith.

Interest in religion is not confined to the churches but spills over into the academic world and into general life. Perhaps it is incorrect to say that there is a general religious "revival," but surely there is a resurgence of interest in religion. The wistfulness of the common man for satisfying answers to the ultimate problems of his existence can hardly be denied. The world is sorely in need of a more adequate theology, a better understanding of God and man's relation to him. If Christian theology can meet this need, its ministry to contemporary civilization will be of incalculable value and significance. Its ability to meet the need will depend, as has already been suggested, upon the vitality of our experience of God, the adequacy of our understanding of this experience, and our ability to provide explanations that are intelligible.

Historic Development of Christian Theology

It may be helpful to review briefly certain theological trends during the last few decades and to make some assessment of these as resources for a restatement of Christian theology in terms of our present needs. A number of excellent popular treatments of theological tendencies have appeared in recent years, and each discusses these trends in greater detail than will be possible here.[1] For the present purpose, it seems necessary to call attention only to some of the main developments and alternatives. The discussion will be limited largely to trends within Protestantism.

PROTESTANT ORTHODOXY. For nearly four centuries, Protestant thought in America followed the main outlines set forth by the Reformers of the sixteenth century, though with many minor variations. These were based upon the commonly accepted interpretations of the Bible as these had been embodied in the historic creeds.

Distinctive emphases which were characteristic of all Protestant theologies were (1) a denial of the claim of Roman Catholicism to be

[1] *Infra,* pp. 184-87.

the exclusive expression of genuine Christianity; (2) substitution of the Bible for the church as the source of final authority; (3) the right of the individual to private judgment in matters of religion; and (4) the consequent priesthood of all believers. Each of these at least in some measure was contributory to the present unsettled state of Protestant theology and, unless all are seen within a larger context, may continue to retard the development of a theology which can meet the requirements of the Christian faith of tomorrow.

SECULAR HUMANISM. Paralleling the development of Western religion was secular humanism, a trend of thought that stemmed from the Renaissance. Protestantism and secularism throughout the modern period have had much in common, though at significant points they may be clearly distinguished. Secularism was accentuated by the development of science, particularly since the middle of the nineteenth century. For most of the last hundred years there has been what Andrew White called a "warfare of science with theology." Though they were mutually interactive and in countless ways influenced each other, Protestantism and secular science tended to draw apart and go their separate ways.

The medieval picture of the universe, with the earth as the center and man as a unique form of creation, was placed increasingly on the defensive by the impact of theories propounded by Copernicus and Darwin. The orthodox doctrine of the fall of man was opposed by optimistic hopes of man's continuing progress toward a more decent world order. Marx viewed religion as the chief enemy of man's hope for a better world. Freud claimed that religion was outmoded, being essentially wish fulfillment and a childish refusal to face the facts of life realistically. Belief in revelation as essentially an instrument in the hands of ecclesiastical authorities was placed in increasing jeopardy by insistent claims for the adequacy of human reason.

PROTESTANT SECTARIANISM. New problems arose within organized religion itself. Protestantism broke into innumerable sects, each insisting upon the finality of its interpretations of the Bible and of the church. Biblical criticism made it increasingly difficult to regard the Bible as an infallible guide in many fields in which it had been regarded previously as authoritative. The study of comparative religions brought a serious challenge to the claims of Christianity to final supremacy over the non-Christian religions.

Some of the time-honored doctrines of the church were seriously questioned by leaders within the church itself. These and many other influences seemed to present a serious threat to orthodox Christianity as it had been commonly accepted. The violent fundamentalist-modernist controversies, rising to their heights in the 1920's, resulted in an almost irreparable schism within American Protestantism.

ROMAN CATHOLICISM. The Roman Catholic Church has an effective way of meeting the tensions which arise between its forms of theological expression and the impact of secular culture. Salvation is made dependent upon the sacraments and ministry of the Church. Standards of morality and the main outlines of theology are determined by papal edict. "Modernism" is officially condemned. The findings of scholars and scientists are examined and censored so as to minimize the likelihood that the doctrines of the church may be undermined. Publications intended for the eyes of the faithful must bear the *imprimatur* of someone who knows what it is permissible to believe.

If civilization were monolithic, if cultural interchange could be curtailed, if education could be controlled by the Church—and Catholicism works energetically and ceaselessly to attain these ends—theology would not be under the continuing necessity of reconstruction. How well even the Catholic Church can succeed in maintaining uniformity and standardization in the changing world of tomorrow remains to be seen. But for Protestantism, its ways of standardizing doctrine are denied. The very nature of Protestantism precludes regimentation. Concensus with respect to the content of theology must come by persuasion and consent. It cannot be imposed by ecclesiastical authority.

Recent Trends in Protestant Theology

FUNDAMENTALISM. It was inevitable that Protestantism should seek some means of establishing stability in its ideological framework. And so fundamentalism arose in the early decades of the twentieth century as a movement intended to preserve orthodox Christianity. It substituted the Bible for the church as the source of authority and insisted upon acceptance of the Bible as the infallible Word of God. It published an outline of "The Fundamentals" of the Christian faith, doctrines deduced from the historic Christian creeds which it was claimed had been accepted by Christians in all generations.

The validity of any claim of science was judged in terms of its consistency with the contents of the Bible. Evolution was therefore condemned as being incompatible with the story of creation as contained in Genesis. The dignity of man was considered as hopelessly impugned if it were admitted that he is directly connected with other forms of animal life.

The miracles of the Bible, in spite of any seeming implausibility, were defended on the basis of a supposed sharp dichotomy between the worlds of nature and the supernatural. While the immanence of God was never denied, it was almost completely overlooked in a primary stress upon his transcendence. The significance of Jesus was believed to rest upon his deity and this was made to depend upon the literal historicity of his virgin birth and physical resurrection. His imminent "second coming" was a constant expectation of most, though not all, of the fundamentalists.

Revelation, as contained in the words of the Bible, was appealed to as the final arbiter of religious truth. Secularism in all its forms was excoriated. Thus, the warfare of science with theology could be finally consummated only by the complete surrender of one or the other. To the fundamentalist there could be no doubt of the final outcome. Truth, as contained in the Bible, would conquer all its foes.

MODERNISM. In protest against a rigorous biblicism arose a rather loosely organized movement known as modernism. Its proponents were convinced that fundamentalists were destroying Christianity by forcing it into the intellectual molds of the past and thus making it impossible for intelligent people to hold it today. They insisted that it is not only possible but necessary to "modernize" Christian theology, that the "abiding experiences" of Christianity are not necessarily to be identified with the "changing categories" in which at any given time they may be expressed, and that the essence of Christian faith may be retained even if the thought patterns in which it has previously been clothed were abandoned.

Views of the nature of the universe and of man were revised as the findings of science seemed to require. Scientific knowledge came to be regarded as revelation just as truly as the Bible or any of the ancient doctrines of Christianity. "Some call it evolution and others call it God." The results of biblical criticism were thought to make a literal interpretation of the Bible untenable. The miracles of the Bible were subjected to critical study and were explained as natural events interpreted in the thought patterns of a prescientific era. Stress upon the divine immanence overshadowed the concept of the transcendence of God.

162

The virgin birth, physical resurrection, and second coming of Christ were no longer considered the sole bases for belief in the divinity of Jesus. His authority was thought to rest, not solely upon supernatural sanctions, but upon his pre-eminence as an exemplar of the divine nature which is implicit in every human being. Jesus provided the clearest example of the life that every man ought to live; he exemplified the kind of spirit that must prevail if the potentialities of human nature are to be fully utilized in overcoming the evils of this present life. Opponents of modernism charged that in the acceptance of such views the warfare of science with theology had been resolved by the surrender of a definitive theology.

TOWARD RAPPROCHEMENT. From our ˌvantage point a quarter of a century after the battle between fundamentalism and modernism has subsided, we are able to see that Christian theology could hardly rest its case by accepting either of the extreme positions that have been sketched here. Indeed, in the effort to clearly delineate the nature of the struggle between them, the writer may have been guilty of exaggeration and possible distortion by over-simplification. The positions as outlined are extremes at the two ends of a continuum.

We need to be reminded that both fundamentalists and modernists were Christians, leaders of both groups seeking to express their convictions in terms which they thought consonant with the faith which stems from Jesus. Fundamentalists were seeking to *defend* Christianity, thinking that they could do this only by reiteration of its ancient formularies and time-honored creeds. Modernists were seeking to *remake* it by restating its affirmations in the current vernacular.

Seers in both movements soon began to realize that there were weaknesses in both positions that needed correction in the light of a truer perspective. It is difficult to find a simon-pure fundamentalist today. Most erstwhile fundamentalists now call themselves "conservatives" or "evangelicals." It is just as difficult to find a died-in-the-wool modernist—all modernists now call themselves "liberals."

In the midst of the controversy between fundamentalism and modernism, a leading liberal, Harry Emerson Fosdick, preached a sermon in which he pointed out some of the chief weaknesses of the movement which he had done so much to initiate.[2] A conservative, George W. Richards, wrote a book in which he sounded much the

---

[2] "The Church Must Go Beyond Modernism," a sermon preached in Riverside Church, New York, in 1935. William Hordern, *A Layman's Guide to Protestant Theology,* pp. 107-11.

same note.[3] These were forerunners of a vast literature which holds that Christian theology must somehow catch up the essential values in both positions and go beyond them toward a more adequate expression of Christian doctrine.

NEO-ORTHODOXY. The theological movement that has attracted the greatest attention in American Protestantism during the last twenty years is variously known as "Neo-orthodoxy," "Theology of Crisis," "Dialectical Theology," and "Reformation Theology." It cannot be identified with either fundamentalism or modernism, though it holds certain features in common with both. Like fundamentalism, it insists upon the validity of the biblical revelation; but, like modernism, it accepts the results of biblical criticism and agrees that the Bible cannot always be interpreted literally.

Many of the truths of the Bible are regarded as "myths" that are to be understood as symbols of truth which cannot be fully expressed in ordinary language. Though the Bible contains revelation, the Word of God must be sharply distinguished from the words of Scripture. Revelation is not knowledge about God; it is God giving himself. Man can only accept the revelation in an "I-Thou" relationship in which he gives himself to God in simple love and trust.

In neo-orthodoxy the transcendence of God is stressed sometimes to the point of a complete denial of his immanence. God cannot be found in nature nor in history; he can be known only through a mediator, Jesus Christ, who comes from God with the revelation which man could never find by himself. Man is entirely separated from God by his sin and guilt and hence is incapable of arriving at saving truth by his own efforts—he is completely dependent upon the initiative of God through divine revelation. Hence, there can be no such thing as "natural theology." Both fundamentalists and modernists are criticized for their preoccupation with doctrines, the intellectual propositions which have previously been regarded as the content of the Christian faith.

Faith, to neo-orthodoxy, is not acceptance of any body of doctrine but a radical commitment of life in the existential situation. Life comes full of paradoxes and contradictions and hence it is fallacious to suppose that truth about it can be reduced to a neat little set of rational principles. God is completely free, and his revelation cannot be confined to creeds, to the church, not even to the words of the

[3] George W. Richards, *Beyond Fundamentalism and Modernism.*

Bible. Science, being the product of man's experience and reason, is impotent in the search for divine truth. Christianity faces a crisis today because it has become embroiled in contemporary human culture. It can be saved only by disassociation from this culture. Thus, the reality of any supposed warfare of science with theology is disallowed. Science may be an appropriate discipline for those who seek an understanding of the physical universe, but in the quest for truth about God and his relationship to man it is wholly irrelevant.

A New Perspective in Christian Theology

The present writer would like to propose an attitude and approach to Christian theology which he believes is an advance beyond all three of the positions outlined in the foregoing, that of a *reconstruction* of Christian doctrine through an intensification of Christian experience and a more realistic interpretation of this experience in terms of contemporary thought through the pooled insights of thinkers who are specialists in a variety of disciplines. Through collaboration and communication we can develop a new "vocabulary of faith" that will better serve our needs in the present age. There are tendencies within American Protestantism which indicate that such an advance is not only possible but necessary.

Christian thought of tomorrow cannot go back to fundamentalism. Modern scholarship has made untenable a return to a literal biblicism. Conservative theologians themselves have retreated from this position and are seeking to bring their teachings more into accord with science and human reason. One leading conservative, who makes a "case for orthodox theology," admits that there can never be a perfect harmony between science and Scripture; but he believes that their spheres can be differentiated. "Scripture speaks of *ultimate* causes, while science speaks of *proximate* causes." [4] By making this distinction, he believes it possible to relax the rigorous denial of the claims of science, for example in the former controversy over the literal account of creation versus evolutionism, by making concessions to paleontology.[5]

Orthodoxy remains certain that God created man, but it does not know *how* he formed him from the dust of the ground.[6] It no longer

---

[4] Edward J. Carnell, *The Case for Orthodox Theology*, pp. 92-93. Italics in the original.
[5] *Ibid.*, p. 95.
[6] *Ibid.*

insists that God made the world in six literal days, since the evidence of geology seems to refute this view.[7] It no longer resists the light that higher criticism can throw on the literary and historical background of the Bible. Conservatives believe that they can make such concessions to science and still hold to the plenary inspiration of the Bible and to the plan of salvation it contains.[8]

We cannot return to modernism which lacked a sufficient recognition of the limits of human knowledge. Most liberals who are open-minded about the values of the historic faith now admit that there is something unique and permanently significant in Christianity which should be understood and appropriated.

A leading liberal theologian finds no inconsistency in exercising freedom of the mind while retaining the historic doctrines of the Incarnation and the Trinity.[9] He restates these doctrines in terms more nearly identifiable with the categories of modernism than with fundamentalism, but nevertheless he accepts them as essential elements in Christian theology. "The legitimate task of the Christian thinker is clearly to enter into genuine communication with the culture of his day," he writes, but it is equally important to "keep himself steeped in the historic teaching of the Bible and the church." [10]

Neo-orthodoxy would seem to be a passing mood which made valuable contributions but can hardly maintain its insistence upon a sharp breach between revelation and reason. Many contemporary leaders who had espoused neo-orthodoxy have parted company with Kierkegaard and Barth and are seeking ways of establishing more effective communication with religious leaders of other orientations. Some have gone so far as to insist that the Christian theologian is under inescapable obligation to relate the message of the Bible to the contemporary situation.

One theologian whose basic viewpoint might be considered within the main stream of neo-orthodoxy pleads for a "new Reformation theology" that avoids the danger of both "an archaic world view and an emotional tinge to modernity." [11] Such a theology will recognize the

[7] Ibid.
[8] Ibid., pp. 97-111.
[9] L. Harold DeWolf, The Case for Theology in Liberal Perspective, Chaps. III, V.
[10] Ibid., p. 59.
[11] William Hordern, The Case for a New Reformation Theology, p. 162.

need to speak to the age in which it finds itself. No matter how much it learns from Calvin, Luther, or Wesley, it cannot speak their truth in their words to this century. But the fact that it is a new *reformation* theology means that it is looking with the Reformers to the Word that God has spoken to all times.[12]

Is it not time to raise the question whether the seeming conflict between science and theology is really a legitimate struggle? Is it not rather a result of limited knowledge and understanding on the part of people who have specialized in certain restricted fields and who try to superimpose their judgments upon reality as a whole? Have we not been guilty of trying to confine religion to the cloister and of condemning as "secularism" the outcome of the legitimate efforts of scholars and scientists who do not use theological terminology? Do not religious leaders tend too much to keep to themselves and thus miss the growth of knowledge and insight that might come through interchange of experience and ideas with those outside their respective traditions?

We live in an age of specialization. Knowledge has increased so rapidly in recent years that no one individual can possibly know all that is to be known even in the limited field of his own specialization. Scientists and scholars in every field are daily discovering new data which bear upon their own areas and all are discovering how every field overlaps all the others. There is simply no hope that we can ever again have an Aristotle who can synthesize all existing bodies of knowledge. There is less hope that any modern Thomas Aquinas can write a *Summa* which integrates this knowledge in a new Christian synthesis. Certainly no theologian today, working alone, can draw up a complete system of doctrine which will serve the needs of all Christians for any considerable time.

Recent experience in the ecumenical movement should be instructive. Churchmen of a variety of theological orientations came together, each with the preliminary expectation that his system of doctrine was the true one and that others could be made to understand and accept it. But as they worked together, there came an increasing awareness of the limitations of all specialized points of view. In worship and fellowship, they all have been confronted by the living God who is greater than any system of doctrine. Those who have been so confronted are no longer seeking to convert the others,

[12] *Ibid*. Italics in the original.

but all are humbly seeking to learn more about God whom each knows only in part.

This ecumenical experience is good as far as it goes. But theologians in time may come to see that God has other paths than theology through which he may reveal his truth. If theologians could sit down together with men who have gained their knowledge through other disciplines, could share their knowledge and insights together in an atmosphere of mutual respect and trust, and could stay together until real communication is effected, the Holy Spirit might teach them all more than any one could ever learn working alone and independently.

As individuals, we need of course to know what the theologians can tell us. But we need also to learn from anthropologists, psychologists, and sociologists. Christian theology in the future must be centered around two foci. Our Christian faith had its beginnings in events centering around Jesus of Nazareth. There would be no Christianity without these beginnings. But our records of these events are embodied in documents conditioned by the thought patterns of a people who lived long ago and in a world quite different from our own. We shall be misled if we take these documents literally and attempt to explain the events in terms of ancient concepts. But we need to understand what these events were and how they affected the early Christians. We can be assisted in gaining this understanding by better use of the techniques of modern scholarship, many of which have been developed outside the technical discipline of theology.

Another focus of Christian theology must be our experience as Christians today. This experience must be vital and real just as that of the early Christians was dynamic and compulsive. We cannot fulfill our mission as Christians now merely by casting admiring tributes to our forebears nor by trying to repeat verbatim their explanations. We can believe that the God who worked through Jesus and his contemporaries is alive and working powerfully among us today. We need to see and recognize his activity wherever it may be found. We can be helped toward this larger vision through effective communication with many of his servants who now work outside our limited precincts.

The physical sciences have revolutionized our conceptions of the universe, and some of the biblical concepts of earth and heaven now seem obsolete. In a world of automation and space travel, we can hardly think of God in exactly the terms which seemed to serve the purposes of the ancients. The modern psychological and social sciences are giving us new insights into human nature and the effects of our social relationships. Shall we depreciate these insights because they come to us from sources outside the Bible and our ecclesiastical traditions?

No Christian theology adequate for today and tomorrow can neglect either the experience of Christians as recorded in the Bible nor that of Christians who live in the world of today. Somehow we must combine these two foci in a total perspective. We can gain this new perspective only if our experience of Christ is real and vital, only as our explanations are based upon experience itself, and only if our medium of discourse is understandable to ourselves and communicable to others. No present system of theology meets these tests adequately. But we can build one out of resources already available if we all work humbly and sincerely together.

PART FOUR

How Firm a Foundation?

XIII. EVIDENCES OF PROGRESS
TOWARD A MORE
ADEQUATE PHILOSOPHY

The thesis of this book has been that the "foundations" for a philosophy of Christian education are derived from two principal sources: (1) the behavioral sciences, which are concerned with the nature of personality, the ways of human growth and learning, and the effects of culture and education upon personality development; and (2) Christian experience and theology, which are concerned with man in his cosmic relationships.

The argument was advanced that in the past these two approaches have too often been divergent but that this need no longer be so; that communication between scientists and Christian leaders, and co-operative search involving both groups, might lead to enriched understanding and increased effectiveness on the part of all who are engaged in the total task of education. Whatever may be the attitude of others toward this problem, for *Christian* educators there is no legitimate alternative to continued effort to build bridges across the chasm that has existed between the behavioral sciences and Christian theology.

This, of course, is not a new view. Several instances have been cited of personality theorists who have insisted that the religious dimension must be included in a total view of man. Many examples could be given of attempts on the part of religious leaders to avail themselves of knowledge and insights that come from scientific investigation. The question perhaps should be pursued further. How firm are the foundations for a philosophy of Christian education which have been laid up to the present time by co-operative efforts between science and theology?

Many events in the past decade or so seem to portend greater possible progress in the direction of a more adequate philosophy of Christian education. Space will permit consideration of only a few illustrations. Doubtless the reader could cite many others which are equally pertinent.

Clearer Vision of the Relation of Religion to Culture

There are many evidences that religion may become increasingly a matter for the consideration of social scientists. Understanding of religion has been greatly advanced through research in anthropology, psychology, psychoanalysis, and sociology. Many specialists in these fields have encountered the force and reality of religious ideas and motives in their studies of the individual and society and have reported their findings in publications easily available to the interested reader. Although a comprehensive survey is impossible within the limits of this book, perhaps a few references to helpful sources may not be out of order.

Among the psychologists, Allport has already been noted as one who includes religion among the principal factors in personality development.[1] The effects of culture upon the stability of individual life has been a matter of deep concern to a number of psychoanalysts, notably Adler, Fromm, and Jung, who have interested themselves in the constructive role of religion and altruistic motives in personal growth.[2] Case studies of the value of religious therapy in overcoming emotional difficulties that have their roots in childhood have been reported by Johnson and Weatherhead.[3]

Among the anthropologists and sociologists, Yinger has dealt with the functions of religion in the life of the individual and society and has pointed out how religious activities may be distinguished from nonreligious activities which serve the same functions.[4] He has collaborated with Simpson in a study of the problems of minority groups and the extent and causation of racial and religious prejudice.[5]

[1] *Supra*, pp. 110, 121.

[2] Alfred Adler, *What Life Should Mean to you*; Erich Fromm, *Man for Himself*, *Psychoanalysis and Religion*, *The Sane Society*, and *The Art of Loving*; Carl G. Jung, *Modern Man in Search of a Soul*, *Psychology and Religion*, and *Psychology and Religion: West and East*.

[3] Paul E. Johnson, *Personality and Religion*; Leslie D. Weatherhead, *Psychology, Religion and Healing*.

[4] J. Milton Yinger, *Religion, Society and the Individual*.

[5] G. E. Simpson and J. M. Yinger, *Racial and Cultural Minorities*.

Studies of the serious effects of social class cleavages have been made by Gordon, Hollingshead, Hunter, and Mills.[6]

Parsons, Shils, Naegele and Pitts have made available an extensive and valuable collection of writings from a wide variety of sources which constitutes what they call "foundations of modern sociological theory." [7] The first volume contains a section on "Religion and Social Structure." [8] And the second is divided into three parts, each of which is relevant to our purposes here: "Personality and the Social System," "Culture and the Social System," and "Social Change."

The great variety of faith and practice in American religion has been reviewed and analyzed by Williams.[9] The effects of our changing culture upon the dynamics of religious groups and resulting patterns of church organization and activity have been studied by leaders of a wide variety of orientation, including Fichter, Hoult, Marty, and Shippey.[10] Benson has recently published a comprehensive survey and digest of the findings of social scientists regarding the scientific approach to religious phenomena and the nature and functions of religion in personal and social behavior.[11]

Students of history and philosophy have added their contributions. Of these, Toynbee has insisted that religious motivation has been a prime mover of human history, though he is pessimistic about the outlook for civilization unless mankind can face its challenges with greater courage than it now seems to be doing.[12] Trueblood makes a strong plea for empirical methods in studying religion, criticizes modern thinkers who disregard the power of religion in human life, considers the principal challenges to religious faith, and outlines a philosophy of religion which he believes in accord with scientific knowledge and religious experience.[13]

[6] Milton M. Gordon, *Social Class in American Sociology*; A. B. Hollingshead, *Elmtown's Youth*; Floyd Hunter, *Community Power Structure* and *Top Leadership, U.S.A.*; C. Wright Mills, *White Collar*, *The Power Elite*, and *The Sociological Imagination*.

[7] Talcott Parsons, Edward Shils, Kaspar D. Naegele, and Jesse R. Pitts (eds.), *Theories of Society: Foundations of Modern Sociological Theory*. 2 Vols.

[8] *Ibid.*, Vol. I, pp. 643-82.

[9] J. Paul Williams, *What Americans Believe and How They Worship*.

[10] J. H. Fichter, *Dynamics of a City Church*, and *Social Relations in the Urban Parish*; T. F. Hoult, *The Sociology of Religion*; Martin E. Marty, *The New Shape of American Religion*; Frederick A. Shippey, *Church Work in the City*.

[11] Purnell H. Benson, *Religion in Contemporary Culture*.

[12] Arnold J. Toynbee, *An Historian's Approach to Religion*.

[13] D. Elton Trueblood, *Philosophy of Religion*.

The series on "Religion in American Life" in the Princeton University's Special Program in American Civilization [14] provides perhaps the best single collection of essays on the relation of religion to American culture and should be studied carefully by anyone who seeks a better understanding of this complex problem. The bibliography contains an excellent guide to general surveys and histories; the evolution of American religion; religion and society; religion in the arts and literature; and intellectual history with special reference to the relations of theology, philosophy, and science.

All of these, together with a much greater volume of equally pertinent materials, seem to the present writer to make possible a much clearer vision of the relations of religion to culture than has ever been possible before.

Theologians have not been unmindful of the relation between religion and culture. Among those who have been most concerned about this problem are Richard Niebuhr and Paul Tillich. In an early book, Niebuhr discussed the concept of "kingdom of God" in relation to American culture.[15] Later he made a typological study of the social outlook in various theological positions.[16] In a recent volume he considers how "radical monotheism," supreme loyalty to "God beyond the gods," may transform the life of men in the fields of religion, politics, and science.[17]

The American theologian who perhaps is most at home in all phases of modern culture is Tillich. He regards the central task of theology as that of mediating between faith and culture and feels that theology can actualize itself only as theologians engage in encounter and continuous dialogue with others outside the field of theology—artists, natural scientists, economists, sociologists, depth psychologists, and philosophers. His many writings give evidence of encyclopedic knowledge and of sympathetic understanding of the problems of those who seek to find meaning in the several areas of their thought and action.

Tillich's famous principle of "correlation" provides a guide for theology as it seeks to relate to philosophy, science, and the experience of ordinary men in their "existential" situation. The wide range of

[14] James Ward Smith and A. Leland Jamison (eds.), Vol. I, *The Shaping of American Religion;* Vol. II, *Religious Perspectives in American Culture;* Vol. III, *Religious Thought and Economic Society: The European Background,* by Jacob Viner; and Vol. IV, *A Critical Bibliography of Religion in America,* by Nelson R. Burr.

[15] H. Richard Niebuhr, *The Kingdom of God in America.*

[16] *Christ and Culture.*

[17] *Radical Monotheism and Western Culture.*

his interests is well illustrated in a recent volume of essays prepared by friends and former students who from their several vantage points have "unearthed particular treasure in a field explored by one of the great minds of our day." [18] The essays cover such diverse areas of culture as psychiatry, language, music, science, philosophy, politics, church vocations, missions, and world order. An appended bibliography of Tillich's publications contains thirty pages of closely packed materials printed in small type.

Better Understanding of the Problems of Communication

Another area in which there has been notable advance is a converging interest in several fields of study and research in the problems of communication. Linguists have turned their attention increasingly from the formal structure of language to consideration of the relation of language to culture, the function of language in communicating meanings, and the effect of language upon the manner in which experiences are perceived, classified, and manipulated.

As was noted earlier, psychologists are becoming more and more interested in problems of perception; and field theorists have insisted upon the fact that people select, organize, and interpret their experiences in terms of their own perceptions. This emphasis has led naturally to a new interest in communication.

Anthropologists have become increasingly absorbed in problems connected with the relation of symbols to human behavior. Their recognition that ways of communicating have dynamic effects upon behavior and cultural change has provided new insights into the problems of intercultural communication. Mathematicians have been engaged in the construction of symbol systems which have only internal significance and are not related to objects outside the system, but the results have been of great value to scientists in unlocking many secrets of the universe. Philosophers accordingly have become occupied with the functioning of symbols as media of communication.

The science of cybernetics (information theory) has contributed greatly to an understanding of communication. Such terms as encoding, decoding, and feedback have become commonplace jargon in popular discussions of education. The development of "teaching machines" is forcing a new consideration of what is involved in learning. It is obvious that if factual knowledge is the aim of education,

[18] Walter Leibrecht (ed.), *Religion and Culture: Essays in Honor of Paul Tillich.* Quotation from dust jacket.

machines may conceivably be produced which will do the job better than mediocre teachers!

Certain theologians have given the problem of communication their attention increasingly during the last few years. Bultmann, by insisting upon the necessity of "demythologizing" the Bible, has forced churchmen to face the need of reinterpreting the Christian message in terms that can be understood by the modern mind and he has thereby stimulated thinking about the method of communicating religious meanings. His viewpoint, of course, is a matter of controversy among theologians at present, but in any case he has made it clear that the Christian preacher must speak *to* his hearers rather than *at* them if he is to communicate the gospel.

Tillich also has been concerned with the use of traditional symbols in translating the Christian message into the language of today. He contends that men are not now asking the really fundamental questions of human existence which must be raised if their deepest problems are to be solved, and that these questions cannot be settled by giving only superficial answers gleaned from the Bible and from the historic creeds. We must somehow discover what the real problems are and must find answers addressed to these problems. This is obviously the very essence of the problem of communication.

Nels Ferré has given considered attention to problems of communication between theologians and other thinkers. He writes that his latest book represents his "most recent thinking on many subjects, with a strong common core of the bearing of this thinking on contemporary theology, philosophy, social theory, biblical interpretation, and education." [19] Among other problems, he discusses the barriers to dialogue, the authority of the Bible, whether the theologians are undermining the Christian faith, and the kinds of revision that are needed in American education.

Buber's insistence upon the necessity of "dialogue" between persons in the comprehension and the communication of truth is but another illustration of the significance of this area for theologians.

Christian educators have not paid as much attention to these developments as they should. Fortunately, however, they are beginning to take an interest in this field. Eugene Nida has made the communication of the Christian faith one of his central interests over a period of years. His books provide an excellent introduction to this im-

---

[19] Nels F. S. Ferré, *Searchlights on Contemporary Theology*, p. ix.

portant problem. He discusses most helpfully the influence of the social context upon communication; the structure of communication; symbols and their meaning; and the dynamics, psychological relationships, and the theological basis of communication. Though he is concerned primarily with the translation and use of the Scriptures, his insights are applicable to many other areas of concern to Christian education.[20]

The recently projected Westminster Studies in Christian Communication should prove of great value in this connection. Two volumes have appeared at the present writing, and both should be studied carefully by all who are engaged in the work of Christian education. Moreau has made a penetrating analysis of the difficulties involved in the fact that words become so heavily laden with traditional associations of a particular culture their equivalents simply do not exist beyond the limits of that culture. And he shows clearly that it is not necessarily *words* that are important but the meanings that the words convey.[21] DeWire points out that real communication involves a *reciprocal encounter* between persons in which the deeper levels of experience must be brought to light and shared. The Christian therefore must not seek to impose his own beliefs upon another person, but must make friends with him, be ready to receive as well as give, and listen as well as speak.[22]

A Changing Climate in Psychology and Psychiatry

Attention has already been called to the willingness of certain psychologists to consider the religious dimensions of personality and to recognize the place of religious factors in its development.[23] There is considerable evidence that the "climate" of psychology is changing in the direction of a more favorable attitude toward religion than has obtained at any time since the rise of psychology as a scientific discipline. For example, the American Psychological Association in its 1957 convention—for the first time in its history—sponsored a symposium on "Religion and Mental Health." And in September, 1959, the same organization held another on "The Place of the Con-

---

[20] Eugene A. Nida, *Message and Mission: The Communication of the Christian Faith.* See also his *God's Word in Man's Language* and *Customs and Cultures.*
[21] Jules Laurence Moreau, *Language and Religious Language.*
[22] Harry A. DeWire, *The Christian as Communicator.*
[23] *Supra,* pp. 120-23.

cept of Sin in Psychotherapy," which gained nationwide attention and was reported in a number of the popular news journals.[24]

There has been a notable increase in the number of consultations between psychiatrists and clergymen in recent years, so that the insights of psychotherapy are increasingly used in pastoral counseling. This has resulted in the development of departments of psychiatry and religion in a number of theological seminaries. And, possibly as a result of the collaboration of specialists in these formerly separated fields, some psychiatrists are coming to question the adequacy of the earlier materialistic concepts in psychoanalysis.[25] Of course these facts do not point to a widespread conversion of psychologists and psychiatrists to evangelical Christianity. But at least doors are being opened for an exploration of the value of religion in the restoration of mental and spiritual health. Who knows what may happen if theologians can learn to speak a language that can be more generally understood by laymen? If scientifically minded students of personality can find between Christians and non-Christians more clearly defined qualitative distinctions?

One of the men who participated in the 1959 APA symposium was O. Hobart Mowrer, a research psychologist at the University of Illinois, who has worked for a number of years at the task of establishing *rapprochement* between psychology and theology. His paper was entitled "Some Constructive Features of the Concept of Sin." [26] In a recently published volume, Mowrer dramatizes *The Crisis in Psychiatry and Religion* and suggests tentatively some steps toward meeting that crisis. He claims that the "biologizing" of American psychology and the ready and uncritical acceptance in pastoral counseling of Freud's explanation of the origins of neurotic disorder have brought about a crisis from which we can escape only by a basic reconsideration of man's unique psychological needs and the possible contributions religion can make to their satisfaction. He insists that the crisis "has been occasioned by the pervasive acceptance of Freudian psychoanalysis, with its basically biological orientation and emphasis." [27] But this, he feels, has been misleading and pernicious in its total effects. "Long ago," he writes, "we were reminded that man

[24] *America*, September 12, 1959, pp. 686-87; *Newsweek*, September 14, 1959, p. 108; *Time*, September 14, 1959, p. 69.

[25] O. Hobart Mowrer, *The Crisis in Psychiatry and Religion*.

[26] *American Psychologist*, 14:356, 1959.

[27] O. Hobart Mowrer, *The Crisis in Psychiatry and Religion*, p. 60.

does not live by bread alone and it is none too early for us to turn our attention to the identification and better understanding of this 'something more.' " [28]

As a research psychologist and a practicing churchman, Mowrer has become convinced of the basic unsoundness of some of the major premises in modern psychology and psychiatry and has come to accept a "position which can be at least loosely identified as Judeo-Christian." [29] "Man's salvation must surely come, not from his looking and moving *downward,* but from an *upward* reach, toward reconciliation and community, made by means of confession and manifest restitution." [30]

But he does not believe that we can depend upon traditional Protestant theology for an adequate explanation of human nature. He regards the doctrine of original sin, for example, as "nonsense." [31] At the same time, he feels that to regard actual sin as simply "sickness" is to belie its real nature and to fail to cope with it realistically and effectively. Hence, he insists that the unconscious must be re-examined within a religious context. Most of our efforts to deal with the psychoneuroses are aimed at symptoms and are ineffective because they do not reach the roots of the difficulty. "Note how often we speak of *restoring* the individual to his *former* self, when not restoration but *reformation* is needed." [32]

Mowrer feels that a new look must be taken at the view of man contained in the biblical tradition, though due consideration should be given to possible misunderstandings of this view embodied in certain systems of Christian theology. "Although I hold no brief for the metaphysical baggage which the Judeo-Christian Ethic has accumulated in the course of 2,000 years, I do maintain that this Ethic embodies some perduring verities which we can today ignore only at our deadly peril." [33]

He points out that certain types of Protestant theology, along with secular psychotherapy, have stressed the *helplessness of man* and thus have minimized the responsibility of the individual for taking the necessary steps toward his own salvation. The doctrine of justification

[28] *Ibid.,* p. 16.
[29] *Ibid.,* p. 123.
[30] *Ibid.,* p. 122. Italics in the original.
[31] *Ibid.,* p. 147.
[32] *Ibid.,* p. 153. Italics in original.
[33] *Ibid.,* p. 154.

by faith, he feels, has often been interpreted as "cheap grace," relieving man of any responsibility for his own choices and actions.

Mowrer disclaims a thorough knowledge of contemporary trends in theology but states that his "casual impression here is a land of shifting sands." He fails to see "anything that looks much like the bedrock of perduring human realities." [34] The confusion, he believes, is "because theology, by becoming bookish and unredemptive, has lost its true center of gravity, its contact with basic human realities, and its leaders bob about like loose corks in a choppy sea." [35] To illustrate, he reports attending a three-day conference of seminary professors, parish ministers, psychologists, and psychiatrists called for the purpose of finding areas of agreement and developing new insights regarding human nature and its needs and potentialities. At the end of the first day, he says, he was "thoroughly mystified by what was being said and done, especially by the theologians." [36]

Those who may be concerned about the formulation of a more adequate philosophy of Christian education may well take seriously what psychologists like Mowrer are saying. Though they may not agree with all he says, they surely must accept his conclusion that the way out of our present difficulties lies not in uncritical acceptance of the current explanations of man brought forth by psychologists and psychiatrists nor in simple reaffirmation of traditional theological formulae. For, as Mowrer says, "there is urgent necessity for continued exploration, new insights, and social inventiveness." And they will surely agree with what he calls a truism: *"a sound psychology and a sound theology will show congruence, not conflict, and should generate personal practices and institutional forms decidedly superior to those we currently follow."* [37]

The Search for a "Living Theology"

Spurred by the deep probing of the Faith and Order Commission of the World Council of Churches, several denominations have conducted series of theological conferences in which the "central themes" of theology have been considered in the light of modern scholarship and cultural trends. As one example, the American Baptist Convention held its first national theological conference on the Assembly

[34] *Ibid.,* p. 169.
[35] *Ibid.,* p. 170.
[36] *Ibid.,* p. 177.
[37] *Ibid.,* p. 176. Italics in the original.

grounds at Green Lake in 1954. Papers were presented on a wide variety of topics; and a published volume contains discussions of problems of central concern to Christian education, including the biblical basis of the gospel, God and the natural order, the Christian doctrine of man, and a theology of church order.[38]

This example of the effort of a denominational group to restate its theology in terms of contemporary thought is a movement in the right direction. In this way theology may be brought closer to life as it is being lived today. But it falls short at the point of our present concern—enriching theology through "dialogue" with specialists in other fields. The writers whose articles are included in the symposium were all theologians or pastors. All the members of the study and discussion groups listed as contributors were likewise professionals in religion. The chapter on "A Christian Doctrine of Man: Man's Essential Nature" contains several footnotes referring to the works of theologians: Cairns, Thomas Aquinas, Luther, Tillich, and Barth. Only one reference is made to the contributions of a nontheologian (Carl Rogers).

Another example of denominational efforts was the work of a group of representatives of Lutheran colleges and theological seminaries which carried on for several years a study of the theological issues involved in Lutheran higher education. The published report deals with (1) *Presuppositions*—the role of the liberal arts in Christian higher education, the theological basis of Christian higher education, and "what man thinks of man"; (2) *Structures*—Objectivity in teaching, administration, and curriculum; and (3) *Implementation* in the various fields of study.[39]

The professional positions of the contributors to the Lutheran symposium are not indicated, but presumably they represent the various subject matter fields in higher education. The contributor of the article on "What Man Thinks of Man" gives a review of theories of human nature going back to the ancient Greeks. He regards as the three principal current options: "(1) classical cosmocentric rationalistic humanism, (2) neo-Epicurean-Democritean materialism of modern scientific naturalism, Marxism, and Nazism, and (3) polar theanthropocentrism of Christianity." He believes that "The Christian

---

[38] Lynn Leavenworth (ed.), *Great Themes in Theology.*
[39] Harold H. Ditmanson, Howard V. Hong, and Warren A. Quanbeck (eds.), *Christian Faith and the Liberal Arts.*

view of man is at home with both views [humanism and naturalism] and in conflict with both." [40] The summary of his "Christian view of man" contains eleven points, at each of which he indicates points of agreement and/or disagreement with the alternative views.[41]

Theology for the Layman

If theology is to make the kind of contribution it can and should make to the advancement of Christian education, theologians must find ways of communicating their understandings to laymen who carry most of the responsibility for leadership in the educational work of the churches. Most of these laymen are not conversant with the technical language of theology and hence are unable to grapple with the fine points of distinction between the viewpoints of individual theologians. The writings of men like Barth, Brunner, Bultmann, Kierkegaard, Niebuhr, and Tillich are so far above their heads as to leave them cold.

Preachers fresh from theological seminaries who build their sermons upon notes from theological study cannot help them much, for these sermons sometimes seem remote from the interests and thoughts of the laymen who people the pews. At the same time many of these are manifesting increasing hunger for theological insight. Fortunately some theologians are coming to recognize this problem and are taking steps to remedy the situation. Several have addressed themselves to the task of defining theological issues and surveying current systems of theological thought in terms that can be understood by laymen. Only a few examples can be given by way of illustration.

William Hordern has published a "Layman's Guide," in which he traces the growth of orthodox forms of Protestant thought since the sixteenth century as a background against which modern schools can be seen in perspective; explains the main currents in contemporary American theology under the following rubrics: (1) *fundamentalism*, or conservatism ("the defense of orthodoxy"); (2) *liberalism* ("the remaking of orthodoxy"); (3) *neo-liberalism* ("the remaking of liberalism"), (4) *neo-orthodoxy* ("the rediscovery of orthodoxy"), —special consideration being given in this connection to the systems of Reinhold Niebuhr and Tillich; and then sets forth his own attempt

[40] Howard V. Hong, *op. cit.*, p. 61.
[41] *Ibid.*, p. 60.

at a mediating position which he calls "orthodoxy as a growing tradition." [42]

W. Norman Pittenger for a number of years has been concerned with restating the Christian faith in terms that are understandable to the modern mind. Over a decade ago he surveyed the American scene from a cultural and political point of view and considered the relevance of the "historic faith" to the changing world of that period.[43] Five years later he sought "to present a point of view towards the Christian theological tradition . . . which can deliver us from the banality of much of our traditional language and yet give the essential Christian gospel an historically sound statement." [44] In a later book he registers his acceptance of "the essential affirmations of historical Christianity" but states his conviction that "one of our necessary contemporary tasks is the rethinking, reinterpreting, restating of these essentials in the light of the best knowledge of the times." [45] His presentation of theological thought should provide for laymen the kind of foundation they need for an understanding of the Christian faith.

Daniel Day Williams believes that specialists in theology "ought to say not only to one another but to laymen what theology is about, and what we think is being accomplished." And he recognizes that "This is a different task from technical scholarship; but a necessary one if the Christian message is to be interpreted at a critical level for all who would understand it." [46] In a revised edition of an earlier book he restated what he regards as the basic issues in current theological thought and illustrates these by references to some of the outstanding works.

He sees "three developments [which] may well dominate much of theological thought as we move into the second half of the twentieth century." These are (1) "an ever-deepening search for the meaning of authority in the Christian faith," (2) the relations of Christianity to other religions and to culture, and (3) "the relation of religious faith to the technological transformation of the face of nature and our power over the conditions of life." [47]

[42] William Hordern, *A Layman's Guide to Protestant Theology.*
[43] W. Norman Pittenger, *The Historic Faith and a Changing World.*
[44] *Theology and Reality,* p. viii.
[45] *Rethinking the Christian Message,* p. viii.
[46] Daniel Day Williams, *What Present-Day Theologians Are Thinking,* p. 7.
[47] *Ibid.,* pp. 10-12.

After describing at some length "the theological renaissance," Williams discusses the authority of the Bible, the relation of Christian ethics to modern life, the present status of Christological doctrine, and the nature of the church. He concludes that "theologians are an embattled company," but finds a basis for hope in the central emphasis in contemporary Christian theology upon "its own proper source, the reality we call Jesus Christ." [48]

Roger Hazelton has presented some of the "new accents" in contemporary theology in terms that laymen can understand. He defines the task of theologians as "that of understanding and making understandable the truth of the Christian faith." This task as he conceives it, however, is not exclusively confined to theologians but "must be shared by many disciplined workers who bring differing, yet finally complementary, perspectives to their common concern." [49] He admits that such movements as neo-orthodoxy have their place in theology when Christian faith turns "inward upon itself, asking what is authentically and ultimately its own kind of truth." [50] But he feels that self-discovery and self-definition should be balanced by rhythmic movements outward, as attempts are made to get back into touch with the world. "Theology today and tomorrow has for one of its major purposes the rediscovery and repossession, in Christ's name, of vast territories of human culture which have long been lost to the Christian intelligence." [51]

Contemporary theology in Hazelton's view involves four principal "accents": (1) *conversation* with the arts, the sciences, and philosophy; (2) *interpretation,* as Bible study is approached from a theological perspective and at the same time is set free from a world-view that is untrue for us because it is unscientific; (3) *consensus,* as theologians search for a greater degree of mutuality and common understanding in the ecumenical movement; and (4) *invitation* to deeper understandings and appropriation of Christian truth as it is shared with others outside the church and theological circles. Theology, so conceived, could become for laymen an exciting and challenging adventure.

Several of the denominational publishing houses have undertaken the publication of series of popular theological books for laymen.

---

[48] *Ibid.,* pp. 174-75.
[49] Roger Hazelton, *New Accents in Contemporary Theology,* p. 11.
[50] *Ibid.*
[51] *Ibid.,* p. 12.

Among the better known of these are the *Layman's Theological Library* by the Presbyterians and *Basic Christian Books* by the Methodists.

Victor Murray, in considering the relation of Christian theology to "natural religion," calls attention to the necessary dependence of theology upon its cultural associations. St. Paul's writings, for example, were directed to the problems his readers were facing and might have been different if they had been addressed to other groups who were facing different problems.

It is an interesting subject of speculation to ask what St. Paul's reaction would have been had he had to preach the Gospel to the Hindus or the Chinese instead of to the inhabitants of the Graeco-Roman world. How far was his theology dated by its times and specific as to its place? All the Pauline epistles except one are *ad hoc* and other questions than those which arose among Corinthian Christians might have brought other answers.[52]

From the standpoint of the need for "dialogue" between scientists and theologians, Canon Smethurst makes a case for the complementary nature of the two approaches. The statement of his purpose in a recent book must conclude our comments regarding the importance of developing a theology for laymen, and one that combines the valid findings of both science and theology. He stated that his purpose was twofold:

First, to attempt to show that, so far from there being ground for any distrust or hostility on the part of Christianity towards science, there is so close a connection between them that there ought to be mutual trust, understanding and co-operation between scientists and Christian theologians; and secondly, to face and discuss frankly the very real problems and difficulties which arise, for Christian faith, in various fields of science, biological as well as physical or astronomical, and for scientists, in some aspects of Christian teaching.[53]

A Methodology for Formulating a Philosophy of Christian Education

If the viewpoint developed in the present book is sound, it seems unlikely that any individual is capable by himself of formulating an adequate statement of the philosophy of Christian education. Such a statement must be the product of group thinking and must pool the

---

[52] A. Victor Murray, *Natural Religion and Christian Theology*, p. 102.
[53] Arthur F. Smethurst, *Modern Science and Christian Beliefs*, p. xix.

knowledge and insights of competent persons representing a wide variety of specialized disciplines. And the statement must be regarded as tentative and subject to improvement and revision as additional knowledge in relevant areas of experience becomes available.

The possible outcome of such co-operative effort may be indicated by a statement prepared by a group working in the university with which the present writer is connected. It is reported here by way of illustrating a methodology that seems suited to the task of formulating an educational philosophy, though it is not a statement of a philosophy of Christian education as such.

In 1957 the Chancellor of the University of Pittsburgh appointed a Board of Religion for the purpose of studying the needs of the University in the field of religion and directed this board to formulate a statement of general policy and to recommend actions that seemed to be consistent with the policy as stated.

This board consisted of members of the administrative staff, representatives of the student body, and members of the faculties in the divisions of humanities, natural sciences, and social sciences. It worked for several months on its tasks. Papers were prepared by several members of a special committee on policy and objectives; these were reviewed and criticized by members of the board; and the writer, who had served as chairman of the special committee, formulated the final report. The statement of general policy and objectives was adopted by the board and subsequently by the University administration. It is certain that no one person, working independently, could have prepared a statement that so nearly conserves all the interests of the University and places religion so well within a total perspective. The statement was circulated widely in mimeographed form but has not previously appeared in print.

GENERAL POLICY REGARDING THE PROGRAM IN RELIGION AT THE UNIVERSITY

The University of Pittsburgh strives to maintain an environment in which each person may move toward the realization of his maximum potential as a complete human being. While its primary efforts are directed toward intellectual pursuits, it recognizes that intellectual maturity cannot be achieved apart from emotional, moral, social and spiritual growth. Complete intellectual development includes an understanding of religion and its proper relationship to the whole of life.

The University seeks to facilitate the transmission of knowledge, to deepen understanding of modern culture, and to encourage communication between scholars in all the important fields of study and investigation. Religion has been a significant element in every civilization, our own as well as that of other peoples. Knowledge of the formative ideas, the outstanding personalities, the chief writings, and the dominant cultural patterns associated with the world's great religions will enhance appreciation of our own cultural heritage and provide a better basis for cooperation and friendly interchange among those of various cultural orientations.

The University aims not only to impart existing knowledge but also to stimulate the discovery of new knowledge, insights and values. Through search into the problems of dynamic living, critical analysis and synthesis of the results of scholarship in the many fields, and rigorous thought regarding the deeper meanings and richer possibilities of human existence, the University can add to present knowledge and understanding and thus create new dimensions and perspectives for religion in the future.

The University is concerned with the application of knowledge to the problems of every day life. It does not attempt isolation from the world outside but seeks ever closer identification with all its significant and legitimate interests. It therefore provides opportunities for establishing and maintaining association with organized religion, participating in constructive religious activities, and extending appreciation of the meaning and value of religion in daily life and experience.

The University endeavors to combine freedom of intellectual inquiry with respect for personal conviction and commitment. It is non-sectarian in the sense that it officially sponsors no one specific form of religion. This does not mean that it is neutral or negative with respect to the values of religion. Freedom of religious expression is encouraged in richness and variety, and adherents of all faiths are welcomed without discrimination. Participation in any phase of the program in religion is always voluntary.

The University seeks to coordinate and integrate the several elements of its program in religion in ways that will promote unity (not uniformity) and comprehensiveness. It aims to relate the program in religion to other phases of University life so that all elements may make their best contributions toward the adequate performance of the total functions of the University.

OBJECTIVES OF THE PROGRAM IN RELIGION

The University of Pittsburgh through its program in religion seeks:
  (1) To contribute to the development of the highest potentialities

of each individual as a complete human being, with respect for the worth and dignity of his personality;

(2) To provide for the scholarly study of religion so as to enhance knowledge and understanding of the religious heritage of mankind, with accent upon its values for contemporary living;

(3) To stimulate new discoveries, insights, and values in religion and to relate these effectively to other areas of human concern;

(4) To combine integrity of religious conviction, freedom of inquiry, respect for differences, and cooperative search for deeper meanings and richer possibilities for human life both now and in the future;

(5) To provide opportunities for experiences and activities that will enable participants to establish and maintain association with organized religious groups, deepen religious insights and faith, extend appreciation of the values of religion, and increase effectiveness in religious thought and action;

(6) To achieve coordination and comprehensiveness in its program in religion so that all elements may contribute significantly to the better performance of the total functions to which the University is committed.

Workshops in the Christian Education of Adults

This methodology for formulating statements of the philosophy of Christian education may be further illustrated by two workshops in the Christian education of adults at the University of Pittsburgh, one held in the summer of 1958 and another in 1961.

The 1958 workshop brought together the responsible leaders of adult Christian education in the principal Protestant denominational and interdenominational agencies of the United States and Canada: pastors; directors of religious education; executives of denominational boards of Christian education; directors of adult work in the denominations; state, regional, and national executives of church councils; leaders in men's and women's work; Y.M.C.A. and Y.W.C.A. secretaries; and professors of Christian education in theological seminaries. A dozen nationally known specialists in fields other than Christian education acted as consultants. These represented such widely separated fields as economics, political science, psychology, psychiatry, sociology, public education, educational administration, adult education, journalism, the ecumenical movement, and theology.

The consultants presented addresses and papers, in which each sought to summarize the findings and insights gained through study and research in his own field that seem relevant to the task of Christian education, and made such application as he was able to the educational work of the churches. These addresses and papers were followed by panel discussions and symposiums and were analyzed in study and discussion groups from the standpoint of their implications for the Christian education of adults.[54]

The study groups prepared two statements which were adopted by the workshop: "Basic Assumptions of Adult Christian Education" and "A Tentative Statement of Purpose and Objectives of Adult Christian Education."[55] These statements were referred to the denominations and agencies represented for further study and for whatever use they might choose to make of them.

The workshop of 1961 was focused upon the curriculum of Christian education for adults and sought answers to such questions as the following: What are the principal problems that confront producers and users of the curriculum of Christian education for adults? What are the requirements of an adequate curriculum for adults? What is the present status of the curriculum? What changes, improvements, and additions are needed in order to meet the requirements of an adequate curriculum? How can these needed changes be brought about?

At the present writing, two reports have been issued from the workshop of 1961: (1) a volume of addresses and papers presented by the consultants; and (2) another containing the reports of "task groups" which studied the addresses and papers from the standpoint of their implications for the curriculum of Christian education for adults.[56] Both of these volumes contain valuable material for use in the future development of a philosophy of Christian education for adults.

These workshops were made possible by financial aid from Lilly Endowment, Inc., and provide an excellent pattern whereby a foundation, a university, and religious leaders may combine their resources

---

[54] For a selection of the addresses and papers presented in the workshop see Lawrence C. Little (ed.), *The Future Course of Christian Adult Education.*

[55] Lawrence C. Little (ed.), *Formulating the Objectives of Christian Adult Education* (Pittsburgh: The Department of Religious Education, University of Pittsburgh, 1958), pp. 57-60. Mimeographed and out of print.

[56] Lawrence C. Little (ed.). (1) *Selected Addresses and Papers Presented in a Workshop on the Curriculum of Christian Education for Adults;* and (2) *Guidelines for the Development of Christian Education Curricula for Adults.* A revised and expanded edition of the first-named volume is in process of publication by the University of Pittsburgh Press.

in bridging the chasm between secular learning, theology, and the practical aspects of the work of the church.

All such co-operative efforts between leaders of Christian education and competent leaders in other fields of knowledge should enable us to move in the direction of a more adequate philosophy of Christian education for our times.

XIV. WHAT IS
CHRISTIAN EDUCATION?

This study has been concerned with the foundations of the philosophy of Christian education rather than with the formulation of a complete statement of that philosophy. The study began with an analysis of some of the conditions that suggest the need for a more adequate statement of philosophy. Some of the difficulties that stand in the way of formulating such a statement were pointed out. An outline was offered of some of the principal components that should be included, and the importance of integrating these into a coherent whole was insisted upon. The remainder of the study has been devoted to the problem of relating present knowledge regarding the nature of personality and the conditions that affect its development to the basic affirmations of the Christian faith. It is time now to make explicit the meaning of Christian education implied in such considerations.

A Definition of Christian Education

Christian education is the process through which the church seeks to enable persons to understand, accept, and exemplify the Christian faith and way of life. It is the effort to enable them to comprehend the full meaning and latent possibilities of human nature as revealed in Jesus Christ and in the light of modern knowledge, to help them establish and maintain the relationships with God and with other persons that will lead toward the actualization of their highest potentialities, and to engage and sustain them in the continuing endeavor to bring closer to realization the will and purpose of God for themselves and for all mankind.

Some Distinguishing Characteristics

Christian education rests its case upon the validity of Jesus' concept of God and his understanding of what this involves in human relationships. Christian education today is a continuation of his teaching ministry. It is carried on by those who choose to follow him and to share in his proclamation of God's redeeming love and in his efforts to establish a community in which this love may find practical expression in human conduct. Christian education therefore places central emphasis upon the personality, life, and teachings of Jesus. It regards his estimate of human worth and his attitudes and way of life as normative.

Knowledge and understanding of the Bible are regarded as essential elements in Christian education. It is the principal source of information about Jesus. It presents an account of the origin and development of the Hebrew faith which he shared with his people. It records some of the principal events of his life, illustrating how he applied his faith to the practical problems of everyday living. It contains the heart of his teachings. It gives the story of the rise of the early Christian church, which resulted from the impact of his life and teachings upon his contemporaries. It provides a basis for Christian doctrine in the writings of those who were directly influenced by their association with him and with his disciples. It has been an important factor in shaping Christian history in every period since its beginning.

Christian education is person-centered. Like any other education, it is directed at persons and is therefore concerned with the nature of personality and with the conditions that affect its development. But unlike many other types of education, it places primary stress upon the perspective from which Jesus viewed personality. He regarded human beings as of infinite worth because they are created by a personal God whose love is extended to them without limit. He believed that all material things and all human relationships are to be judged on the basis of their effects upon the growth of individual persons toward the realization of their maximum potentialities as children of God and as the subjects of God's love.

Christian education takes place chiefly within the context of the Christian church and the families that constitute its membership. Although Jesus did not establish a church nor set forth any plan of organization, mode of worship, program of service, or creedal statement, all of these seem to be implied in his teachings and actions. The church was founded soon after the conclusion of his ministry and has existed ever since as the chief instrumentality for carrying on his work in the world. It has taken many forms but has always held steadily to the purpose of continuing his ministry. It has borne the burden of reinterpreting his message for each succeeding generation. So that it provides a rich heritage of history, literature, art, music, architecture, and theology. Through Christian education some of the values of this priceless legacy may be acquired.

The Church and Christian Education

The church is an ongoing enterprise and its gaze is not fixed exclusively upon the past. It is composed of persons who today are learning the Christian way. They find in Jesus' attitude and spirit a guide to the proper manner of facing their own situations. He had a profound respect for the values of his heritage, but he sought new insights through prayer, co-operative endeavor with his associates, and continuing communion with God. He followed implicitly what he came to believe was God's will for him in the immediate circumstances of his life. He attained the full stature of his own selfhood not just by familiarizing himself with the past, but as he solved present problems in the light of his understanding of what God requires. Christians today attain increasing maturity as they meet the demands of their own situations in the same manner. And in their efforts they believe that they are guided and sustained by the Holy Spirit.

Jesus did not hesitate to criticize aspects of the institutional religion of his own day when they stood in the way of full self-realization on the part of individuals. Persons were not judged on the basis of their conformity to established patterns of thought and conduct, but in terms of their personal relation to God.

Jesus saw the corruption of the religion of his day and hurled his strength against the wrongs that hurt his contemporaries. This religion had become perverted in the interest of its own survival. The rulers of the temple had made his Father's house "a den of thieves." Hence he could not refrain from his effort to cleanse the temple. He saw that the outward observance of the forms of religion might actually interfere with the cultivation of the inner virtues which are the primary concern of God, and he insisted that "unless your righteousness exceeds that of the scribes and Pharisees, you will never enter the kingdom of heaven." (Matt. 5:20). With many illustrations he pleaded for genuineness and sincerity in religious profession.

Through Christian education the church of today may come to see its faults more clearly and thus be a better instrument for achieving God's purposes. Christian education is a process through which the church evaluates its own work and reshapes itself through an increasing understanding of what is required of it and by enlisting its members in efforts toward continuing reconstruction.

One of the points at which the modern church needs to re-examine itself is in its use of the Bible. In too many situations, teaching the Bible has degenerated into mere repetition of its words and recalling incidents that happened long ago and in a world so different from our own that people today can see little relevance to the problems they are facing. The teachings of Jesus are sometimes presented as having little bearing upon our present needs. After all, *we* cannot be expected to love *our* enemies! No person in his right mind would ever deliberately choose the cross! No wonder we make such little progress in race relations, church comity, and world peace.

It must be remembered that throughout the Bible there are two emphases that recur over and over again like the themes of a symphony: (1) what God has done and what he is seeking to do for his people; and (2) what is required of man if God is to do what he proposes to do. Situations changed in the course of biblical history and man's actions were modified accordingly. But insistence upon the necessity of following the best one knows with complete devotion is never relaxed anywhere in the Bible.

Jesus' approach to the Bible was no different from that of the ancient Jewish prophets, but he gave to his teaching new vitality and challenge because of his insight into the nature of God and what God expects of his creatures and his complete commitment to the way of life that he saw involved in this new understanding. God is a loving Father, Jesus believed, and he desires all his children to recognize their filial relationship and to treat each other accordingly. Suppose Christian education today were based upon a similar use of the Bible!

This approach to Christian education will lead to a new attitude toward the work of the church. The church is the people of God in the world and its business is to help persons to actualize their highest potentialities as members of the "body of Christ." Persons are its chief concern, persons as God desires them to be.

Hence the church always should be engaged in an examination of its work in the humble recognition that better ways may be found of fulfilling its mission as its people listen attentively to the instruction of the Spirit of God. This examination will extend to its forms of worship and service, which may need to be frequently adjusted to new insights into the possibilities of growth. It will extend to theology, since there is continuing need for more effective ways of communicating the Christian witness. It will extend to the content and method of teaching, for in a changing world old content and methods may lose part of their significance and relevance. It will be extended to all relationships between persons within the church and community, because it is in relationships that personality is achieved.

Criteria for the Formulation and Evaluation of the General Objectives of Christian Education

Christian education could be more effective if its leaders were more certain of the goals they are seeking to realize. This has been a matter of major concern on the part of denominational boards and of the Commission on General Christian Education of the National Council of Churches.[1] It has been found difficult to formulate statements of objectives that gain general acceptance, primarily because of incongruity between educational and theological approaches to personality. But it should be possible to agree upon the criteria by which statements of general objectives should be evaluated. The following criteria are suggested as in line with the viewpoint developed in the foregoing sections of this book.

1. Are the objectives *Christian?*

Are they consistent with the tenets of the Christian faith, with the basic doctrines and convictions which have formed the main body of Christian tradition? Do they take into account the biblical view of God, of man, and of nature? Are they in accord with the best informed Christian thinking of the present day? (Full agreement on all particular points of theology can hardly be expected, but most Christians agree that there is recognizable *content* to the Christian faith as distinguished from alternative points of view. The objectives of Christian education must be consistent with the basic Christian viewpoint.)

2. Are they *psychologically valid?*

Are they person-centered? Are they consistent with the best of current insights into the nature of personality and of the learning process? Are they directed to the needs and capacities of human beings as these are understood by leading specialists in the psychologi-

---

[1] Cf., Lawrence C. Little, "The Objectives of Protestant Religious Education," in Marvin J. Taylor (ed.), *Religious Education: A Comprehensive Survey,* Chap. 6.

cal and social sciences? Do they take into account the fact of individual differences? Do they have both an individual and a social reference?

3. Are they *relevant to all levels of development?*

Do they have significance and value at every stage of Christian growth from birth to old age? Are they adaptable to all age groups? Do they combine suggestions for significant experiences at the present time, with "infinite" possibilities for further growth?

4. Are they *dynamic* enough to inspire and motivate definite action *in real life situations?*

Do they allow for the freedom, initiative, and creativity of the individual? Do they suggest and challenge acceptance of responsibility? Can they be related specifically to "practical" situations? Do they suggest the interrelationships of life rather than "atomistic" goals?

5. Are they such that progress toward their achievement is *measurable and subject to evaluation?*

Are they realistic and attainable? Can they be translated into observable behavior? Can a clear idea be formed of what is involved in the objectives at various age levels and in varying types of situations in which individuals may find themselves? Can progress be measured toward their attainment? Can activities be evaluated so that modifications of program can be made in the direction of greater effectiveness in achieving the objectives?

6. Are the objectives *comprehensive* in scope?

Do they suggest either directly or by implication all the areas of concern in Christian growth? Is it possible to subsume all the types of knowledge, attitudes and skills regarded as essential in the development of Christian personality? Are they coherent and internally consistent?

7. Are the statements *clear and understandable* to those who will use them?

Are they couched in nontechnical language so that their meanings are easily communicable? Are they sufficiently simple to be understood by the typical church-school worker and at the same time profound enough to challenge those who are capable of more mature and critical thought? Are they definite and precise enough so that persons of differing backgrounds and responsibilities may share in efforts toward their realization?

Christian Education and Modern Culture

Christian education is not something that takes place in a vacuum. It is concerned with given individuals, members of specific groups who live in the midst of their own peculiar circumstances within a particular period of time. The church must carry on its work in a world that at many points cuts clearly across the values to which the church is committed. It is *in* the world but not *of* the world. Hence Christian education must always take into account the cultural situation in which it seeks to function, and it must understand its position with respect to that situation.

What is to be said about the relation of Christian education to the culture of our day with its strange contrasts and conflicts? Americans possess lavish wealth while millions in other parts of the world are starving. We have means of instantaneous world-wide communication, everybody has radio and television, but we fill the air waves with twaddle. Mechanical slaves do most of our work, but we have little capacity for the constructive use of our increasing leisure time. We progressively conquer disease and lengthen the life span but we have no well considered plans for our exploding population, and we do not know what to do with the growing proportion of our "senior citizens."

We preach democracy abroad, while whole communities are disrupted when our dispossessed minorities demand their proper respect and rights as citizens. Church membership and attendance are on the upswing, but so also are crime and delinquency. We have productive capacities that could enable us to supply all the world with the basic necessities for healthful living but we use these capacities for developing deadlier instruments of destruction. We put forth feverish efforts to conquer outer space but we become panicky and hysterical when our "enemies" get there first.

We have the organizational structure for a world society but we cannot overcome the tragedy of a continuing cold war. Communism, which we hold to be the deadly enemy of Christianity, is winning its way across the world because dispossessed peoples have lost confidence in the so-called "Christian" countries. Diplomats of many nations no longer trust Americans because they are convinced that national supremacy is our prime concern. Need we continue the analysis further? The illustrations could be multiplied a thousandfold.

What should the leaders of Christian education do about modern culture? For one thing, we should take much more seriously Jesus' basic assumptions: that God is working continuously to bring about abundant life to all members of his family and that we can share creatively in his work; that all human beings are infinitely precious in the sight of God and that human values take precedence over material things and all institutional arrangements; that relations with other people should be actuated by the principle of love; that service to others is the supreme obligation to which all other motives should be subordinated; and that self-denial and voluntary assumption of personal responsibility are required if God's purposes are to be realized. And we should strive more earnestly to base our educational program upon such concepts.

We should seek to give Jesus' way of life a fair chance in our modern era. We should apply to ourselves and to the church of which we are a part his searching question, "Why do you call me 'Lord, Lord,' and not do what I tell you?" (Luke 6:46.) Else, why Christian education?

If we start from these premises, we will take an affirmative attitude toward modern culture. We will assume the role of stewards, accepting the advantages in a spirit of deep gratitude and humility and seeking to overcome weaknesses with courage and self-dedication. We will not reject the culture as wholly evil, nor will we accept it as a satisfactory expression of the highest human aspirations. We will not withdraw from it as though we have no responsibility for its future direction. But we will seek to transform it, through continuing effort toward the realization of God's purposes for ourselves and for all mankind. To throw ourselves into such a glorious adventure with complete abandon, to enlist others in it, and to offer them guidance and fellowship in its consummation, is Christian education.

Beginning Where People Are

Christian education must begin with people as they are and must deal with their problems and concerns in the world of today. In the past it has been less potent than it might have been because it has focused attention too exclusively upon the ancient world and not enough upon the present. To say this is not to minimize, of course, the importance of the Christian heritage. But the rich treasures of our legacy, embodied in the record of the Hebrew prophets, of Jesus and his contemporaries, and of leaders in the successive periods of Christian history, may be of greatest value to us when used as a source of wisdom for guiding us toward more abundant living in our own world. We may have confidence in the guidance of the Holy Spirit in the church of today as well as in times that are past.

Persons learn best when they are personally involved in matters of genuine concern to themselves, when they are pursuing goals which seem important at the time, when they can see that what they do is related to larger purposes which are shared by others whom they admire and trust, and when they are given opportunities to make their own decisions and to take responsibility for carrying them out.

The Christian education of children and young people should be related to the interest and needs (the "developmental tasks") which these age groups actually experience in the several periods of their personal growth and in the situations they face. Ways must be found whereby the basic affirmations of the Christian faith may be made to apply more directly to the persons involved in our educational programs. It is true that often the seeds we sow do not result in harvest because they fall on barren soil. But very often also the harvest is small because we do not sow seed that is adapted to the kinds of soil in which we sow.

Christian education for adults will best perform its function if it enables adults to meet the needs they feel: how to develop an adequate philosophy of life; how to choose a mate and start a family; how to manage a home and rear children; how to achieve mature stature in civic, economic, and social life; how to become established in an occupation and maintain satisfactory standards of living; how to find constructive ways of spending leisure time; how to accept and adjust to the inevitable changes in middle life and later maturity, such as declining health and physical strength, retirement and reduced income, the loss of intimate associates, and approaching death. These pressing problems (and the list is merely suggestive) are real concerns of actual adults in every community and therefore constitute a valid starting point for the Christian education of adults. Christian education should provide resources and insights that enable adults who face such problems to deal with them constructively.

Groups that are formed on the basis of immediate personal concerns soon find that the problems of individuals are often directly related to conditions in the family and the community, which in turn may have a basis in the larger life of the nation and the world. Thus there is no limit to the list of problems that may be included in a total program. The program should be flexible enough so that groups may be formed and reformed on the basis of interests and needs.

Those who have accepted Jesus' view of the infinite worth of every individual, who have accepted responsibility for faithful membership in God's great family, will want to do more than analyze their own problems. They will wish to participate in co-operative efforts to improve the conditions that create problems and to enhance the influences and support the agencies that seek to solve them. Usually the experience of deep fellowship in groups whose members know and care about each other, and who are seeking to sustain each other in their common quest for the good life, can do much more to help individuals in solving their personal problems than just repeating Bible stories, hearing talks by "experts," or reading books. Knowledge and understanding, of course, are needed; and experts and books may supply information not otherwise available. But knowledge is most useful when it is directly related to and becomes a part of experience. Perhaps what we need most of all is resolute action in the directions we already know. Knowledge will grow as our faith is increasingly expressed in our deeds.

BIBLIOGRAPHY

A. PSYCHOLOGICAL
AND CULTURAL FOUNDATIONS

Adler, Alfred. *The Pattern of Life.* New York: Cosmopolitan Book Corporation, 1930.

_____. *The Practice and Theory of Individual Psychology.* New York: Harcourt, Brace & Company, 1924.

_____. *Social Interest: A Challenge to Mankind.* London: Faber and Faber, Ltd., 1938.

_____. *Understanding Human Nature.* New York: Greenberg, Publisher, Inc., 1927.

_____. *What Life Should Mean to You.* Boston: Little, Brown & Company, 1931.

Adorno, T. W., *et al. The Authoritarian Personality.* New York: Harper & Brothers, 1950.

Alexander, Franz. *Fundamentals of Psychoanalysis.* New York: W. W. Norton & Company, Inc., 1948.

Allan, D. Maurice. *The Realm of Personality.* New York and Nashville: Abingdon-Cokesbury Press, 1947.

Allport, Gordon W. *Becoming: Basic Considerations for a Psychology of Personality.* New Haven: Yale University Press, 1955.

_____. *The Individual and His Religion.* New York: The Macmillan Co., 1950.

_____. *The Nature of Personality: Selected Papers.* Reading, Mass.: Addison-Wesley Publishing Company, Inc., 1950.

_____. *The Nature of Prejudice.* Reading, Mass.: Addison-Wesley Publishing Company, Inc., 1954.

_____. *Personality: A Psychological Interpretation.* New York: Henry Holt & Company, 1937.

Anderson, Camilla M. *Beyond Freud: A Creative Approach to Mental Health.* New York: Harper & Brothers, 1957.

Anderson, George C. *Man's Right to Be Human.* New York: William Morrow & Co., Inc., 1959.

Angell, James R. *An Introduction to Psychology.* New York: Henry Holt & Company, 1918.

_____. *Psychology: An Introductory Study of the Structure and Function of Human Consciousness.* New York: Henry Holt & Company, 1904.

Angyal, Andras. *Foundations for a Science of Personality.* New York: Commonwealth Fund, 1941.

Anshen, Ruth Nanda (ed.). *Language: An Enquiry into its Meaning and Function.* New York: Harper & Brothers, 1957.

Aristotle. *Basic Works.* New York: Random House, 1941.

Arnold, Magda B., and Gasson, John A. *The Human Person: An Approach to an Integral Theory of Personality.* New York: The Ronald Press Company, 1954.

Bain, Alexander. *Mental Science: A Compendium of Psychology and the History of Philosophy.* New York: Appleton Company, 1868.

Bakan, David. *Sigmund Freud and the Jewish Mystical Tradition.* Princeton, N. J.: D. Van Nostrand Company, Inc., 1958.

Barker, T. G., and Wright, H. F. *Midwest and Its Children.* Evanston, Ill.: Peterson and Company, 1956.

Bauer, Raymond A. *The New Man in Soviet Psychology.* Cambridge, Mass.: Harvard University Press, 1952.

Bell, John E. *Projective Techniques: A Dynamic Approach to the Study of the Personality.* New York: Longmans, Green and Co., Inc., 1948.

Benedict, Ruth. *Patterns of Culture.* Boston: Houghton Mifflin Company, 1934.

Bettelheim, Bruno. *Love Is Not Enough.* Glencoe, Ill.: Free Press, 1950.

Blackwell, Gordon W., et al. *Church and Community in the South.* Richmond, Va.: John Knox Press, 1949.

Blum, Gerald S. *Psychoanalytic Theories of Personality.* New York: McGraw-Hill Book Co., Inc., 1953.

Boring, Edwin G. *A History of Experimental Psychology.* (2nd ed.) New York: Appleton-Century-Crofts, Inc., 1950.

Brameld, Theodore. *Philosophies of Education in Cultural Perspective.* New York: Dryden Press, 1955.

_____. *Toward a Reconstructed Philosophy of Education.* New York: Dryden Press, 1956.

Brand, Howard (ed.). *The Study of Personality: A Book of Readings.* New York: John Wiley & Sons, Inc., 1954.

Brown, Roger W. *Words and Things.* Glencoe, Ill.: Free Press, 1958.

Brubacher, John S. *Eclectic Philosophy of Education.* New York: Prentice-Hall, Inc., 1951.

_____. *Modern Philosophies of Education.* New York: McGraw-Hill Book Co., Inc., 1939.

_____. (ed.). *Modern Philosophies and Education.* (Fifty-fourth Yearbook of the National Society for the Study of Education, Part I.) Chicago: University of Chicago Press, 1955.

Bursk, Edward C. (ed.). *Business and Religion: A New Depth Dimension in Management.* New York: Harper & Brothers, 1959.

Butler, J. Donald. *Four Philosophies and Their Practice in Education and Religion.* (Rev. ed.) New York: Harper & Brothers, 1957.

Butterfield, Herbert. *International Conflict in the Twentieth Century.* New York: Harper & Brothers, 1960.

Cannon, Walter B. *Bodily Changes in Pain, Hunger, Fear and Rage.* New York: D. Appleton and Company, 1929.

_____. *The Wisdom of the Body.* New York: W. W. Norton & Company, Inc., 1932.

Carroll, John B. (ed.). *Language, Thought and Reality.* New York: John Wiley & Sons, Inc., 1956.

Cattell, Raymond B. *Description and Measurement of Personality.* Yonkers-on-Hudson, N. Y.: World Book Company, 1946.

_____. *Personality and Motivation Structure and Measurement.* Yonkers-on-Hudson, N. Y.: World Book Company, 1957.

_____. *Personality: A Systematic, Theoretical and Factual Study.* New York: McGraw-Hill Book Co., Inc., 1950.

Cherry, Colin. *On Human Communication*. Cambridge, Mass.: Technology Press of Massachusetts Institute of Technology, 1957.

Combs, Arthur W., and Snygg, Donald. *Individual Behavior: A Perceptual Approach to Behavior*. New York: Harper & Brothers, 1959.

Darwin, Charles R. *The Expression of the Emotions in Man and Animals*. New York: D. Appleton and Company, 1873.

_____. *The Origin of Species*. New York: P. F. Collier and Son, 1872.

David, Henry P., and Von Bracken, Helmut (eds.). *Perspectives in Personality Theory*. New York: Basic Book, Inc., 1957.

Davis, W. Allison. *Social Class Influences upon Learning*. Cambridge, Mass.: Harvard University Press, 1948.

_____, and Dollard, John. *Children of Bondage: The Personality Development of Negro Youth in the Urban South*. Washington: American Council on Education, 1940.

_____, and Havighurst, Robert J. *Father of the Man: How Your Child Gets His Personality*. Boston: Houghton Mifflin Company, 1947.

Dennis, Wayne (ed.). *Current Trends in Psychological Theory*. Pittsburgh: University of Pittsburgh Press, 1951.

_____, et al. *Current Trends in Psychology*. Pittsburgh: University of Pittsburgh Press, 1947.

_____, et al. *Current Trends in Social Psychology*. Pittsburgh: University of Pittsburgh Press, 1948.

Deutsch, Morton, and Collins, Mary E. *Interracial Housing: A Psychological Evaluation of a Social Experiment*. Minneapolis: University of Minnesota Press, 1951.

Dewey, John. *Democracy and Education*. New York: The Macmillan Co., 1916.

_____. *How We Think*. Boston: D. C. Heath and Company, 1910.

_____. *Human Nature and Conduct*. New York: Henry Holt & Co., Inc., 1922.

Dicks, Russell L. *Toward Health and Wholeness*. New York: The Macmillan Co., 1960.

Dilthey, Wilhelm. *Gesamelte Schriften*. Leipzig: B. G. Teubner, 1914-1927.

Dollard, John. *Caste and Class in a Southern Town*. New Haven: Yale University Press, 1937.

_____, and Miller, Neal E. *Personality and Psychotherapy*. New York: McGraw-Hill Book Co., Inc., 1950.

English, Oliver S., and Pearson, Gerald H. J. *Emotional Problems of Living*. (Rev. ed.) New York: W. W. Norton and Company, Inc., 1955.

Ericksen, Ephraim G. *Urban Behavior*. New York: The Macmillan Co., 1954.

Erickson, Eric H. *Child and Society*. New York: W. W. Norton and Company, Inc., 1950.

Estes, William K., et al. *Modern Learning Theory*. New York: Appleton-Century-Crofts, Inc., 1954.

Eysenck, Hans J. *Dimensions of Personality*. London: Routledge & Kegan Paul, Ltd., 1947.

_____. *The Scientific Study of Personality*. London: Routledge & Kegan Paul, Ltd., 1952.

_____. *The Structure of Human Personality*. New York: John Wiley & Sons, Inc., 1953.

_____. *The Dynamics of Anxiety and Hysteria*. New York: Frederick A.

Praeger, Inc., 1960.

Fagley, Richard M. *The Population Explosion and Christian Responsibility.* New York: Oxford University Press, 1960.

Federn, Paul. *Ego Psychology and the Psychoses.* New York: Basic Books, Inc., 1952.

Fichter, Joseph H. *Dynamics of a City Church.* Chicago: University of Chicago Press, 1951.

_____. *Social Relations in the Urban Parish.* Chicago: University of Chicago Press, 1954.

Foote, Nelson N., and Cottrell, Leonard S., Jr. *Identity and Interpersonal Competence: A New Direction in Family Research.* Chicago: University of Chicago Press, 1955.

Freud, Sigmund. *Beyond the Pleasure Principle.* New York: Boni and Liveright, 1924.

_____. *Civilization and Its Discontents.* New York: J. Cape and H. Smith, 1930.

_____. *The Future of an Illusion.* London: Horace Liveright, 1928.

_____. *A General Introduction to Psychoanalysis.* Garden City, N. Y.: Garden City Publishing Company, 1943.

_____. *The Interpretation of Dreams.* London: George Allen and Unwin, Ltd., 1932.

_____. *Moses and Monotheism.* New York: Alfred A. Knopf, Inc., 1939.

_____. *An Outline of Psychoanalysis.* New York: W. W. Norton and Company, Inc., 1949.

_____. *Psychopathology of Everyday Life.* New York: The Macmillan Co., 1914.

Fromm, Erich. *The Art of Loving.* New York: Harper & Brothers, 1956.

_____. *Escape from Freedom.* New York: Farrar and Rinehart, Inc., 1941.

_____. *Man for Himself.* New York: Rinehart & Co., 1947.

_____. *Psychoanalysis and Religion.* New Haven: Yale University Press, 1950.

_____. *The Sane Society.* New York: Rinehart & Co., 1955.

Garrett, H. E. *Great Experiments in Psychology.* (3rd ed.) New York: Appleton-Century-Crofts, Inc., 1951.

Gesell, Arnold L., *et al. Child Development.* New York: Harper & Brothers, 1949.

_____, *et al. Infant and Child in the Culture of Today.* New York: Harper & Brothers, 1943.

_____, *et al. The First Five Years of Life.* New York: Harper & Brothers, 1940.

_____, *et al. The Child from Five to Ten.* New York: Harper & Brothers, 1946.

_____, *et al. Youth: The Years from Ten to Sixteen.* New York: Harper & Brothers, 1956.

Glueck, Sheldon, and Glueck, Eleanor. *Physique and Delinquency.* New York: Harper & Brothers, 1956.

_____, and Glueck, Eleanor. *Unraveling Juvenile Delinquency.* New York: Commonwealth Fund, 1950.

Goldstein, Kurt. *Human Nature in the Light of Psychopathology.* Cambridge, Mass.: Harvard University Press, 1940.

_____. *The Organism: A Holistic Approach to Biology Derived from Pathological Data in Man.* New York: American Book Company, 1939.

Gordon, Milton M. *Social Class in American Sociology.* Durham, N. C.: Duke University Press, 1958.

Gordon, Thomas. *Group-centered Leadership: A Way of Releasing the Creative Power of Groups*. Boston: Houghton Mifflin Company, 1955.

Guilford, J. P. *Personality*. New York: McGraw-Hill Book Co., Inc., 1959.

Guthrie, Edwin R. *The Psychology of Human Conflict*. New York: Harper & Brothers, 1938.

————. *The Psychology of Learning*. (Rev. ed.) New York: Harper & Brothers, 1952.

Haimowitz, Morris L., and Haimowitz, Natalie R. *Human Development: Selected Readings*. New York: Thomas Y. Crowell Company, 1960.

Hall, Calvin S., and Lindzey, Gardner. *Theories of Personality*. New York: John Wiley & Sons, Inc., 1957.

Hansen, Kenneth H. *Philosophy for American Education*. Englewood Cliffs, N. J.: Prentice-Hall, Inc., 1960.

Harris, Dale B. (ed.). *The Concept of Development: An Issue in the Study of Human Behavior*. Minneapolis: University of Minnesota Press, 1957.

Hartshorne, Hugh, May, Mark A. *et al. Studies in the Nature of Character*. New York: The Macmillan Co., 1928-1930. 3 volumes.

Havighurst, Robert J. *Developmental Tasks and Education*. New York: Longmans, Green & Co., Inc., Second edition, 1952.

————. *Human Development and Education*. New York: Longmans, Green & Co., Inc., 1953.

————, and Ruth Albrecht. *Older People*. New York: Longmans, Green & Co., Inc., 1953.

————, and Bernice L. Neugarten. *Society and Education*. Boston: Allyn and Bacon, Inc., 1957.

————, and Hilda Taba. *Adolescent Character and Personality*. New York: John Wiley and Sons, Inc., 1949.

Healy, William, Bronner, A. F., and Bowers, A. M. *The Structure and Meaning of Psychoanalysis*. New York: Alfred A. Knopf, Inc., 1930.

Hebb, Donald O. *The Organization of Behavior: A Neuropsychological Theory*. New York: John Wiley & Sons, Inc., 1949.

Herbart, Johann F. *Samtliche Werke*. 12 Vols. Langesalza: Hermann Beyer and Sohne, 1887.

Hilgard, Ernest R. *Theories of Learning*. New York: Appleton-Century-Crofts, Inc., 1956.

Hocking, William E. *Human Nature and Its Remaking*. New Haven: Yale University Press, 1918.

Hollingshead, August B. *Elmtown's Youth*. New York: John Wiley & Sons, Inc., 1949.

————, and Redlich, Frederick C. *Social Class and Mental Illness*. New York: John Wiley & Sons, Inc., 1958.

Holt, E. B. *Animal Drive and the Learning Process*. New York: Henry Holt & Co., 1931.

Honigmann, John J. *Culture and Personality*. New York: Harper & Brothers, 1954.

Horney, Karen. *Neurosis and Human Growth*. New York: W. W. Norton & Company, Inc., 1950.

————. *The Neurotic Personality of Our Time*. New York: W. W. Norton & Company, Inc., 1937.

_____. *New Ways in Psychoanalysis.* New York: W. W. Norton & Company, Inc., 1939.

_____. *Our Inner Conflicts.* New York: W. W. Norton & Company, Inc., 1945.

Hoult, William H. *The Sociology of Religion.* New York: Dryden Press, 1958.

Hull, Clark L. *A Behavior System.* New Haven: Yale University Press, 1952.

_____. *Essentials of Behavior.* New Haven: Yale University Press, 1951.

_____. *Principles of Behavior: An Introduction to Behavior Theory.* New York: Appleton-Century-Crofts, Inc., 1943.

Hunter, Floyd. *Community Power Structure.* Chapel Hill: University of North Carolina Press, 1953.

_____. *Top Leadership U. S. A.* Chapel Hill: University of North Carolina Press, 1959.

Hunter, Walter S. *Human Behavior.* Chicago: University of Chicago Press, 1928.

James, William. *Essays in Radical Empiricism.* New York: Longmans, Green & Co. Inc., 1912.

_____. *The Principles of Psychology.* 2 Vols. New York: Henry Holt & Co., 1890.

Janis, Irving L., *et al. Personality and Persuasibility.* New Haven: Yale University Press, 1959.

Jersild, Arthur T. *In Search of Self.* New York: Bureau of Publications, Teachers College, Columbia University, 1952.

Jourard, Sidney M. *Personal Adjustment—An Approach Through the Study of Healthy Personality.* New York: The Macmillan Co., 1958.

Jung, Carl G. *Contributions to Analytical Psychology.* New York: Harcourt, Brace & Co., 1928.

_____. *The Integration of Personality.* New York: Farrar & Rinehart, Inc., 1939.

_____. *Modern Man in Search of a Soul.* New York: Harcourt, Brace & Co., 1933.

_____. *Psychological Types.* New York: Harcourt, Brace & Co., 1923.

_____. *Psychology and Religion.* New Haven: Yale University Press, 1938.

_____. *Psychology and Religion: West and East.* Translated by R. F. C. Hull. New York: Pantheon Books, 1958.

_____. *The Undiscovered Self.* Boston: Little, Brown & Co., 1958.

Kant, Immanuel. *The Critique of Pure Reason.* Translated by F. Max Mueller. New York: The Macmillan Co., 1896.

Kardiner, Abram. *The Individual and His Society.* New York: Columbia University Press, 1939.

_____, *et al. The Psychological Frontiers of Society.* New York: Columbia University Press, 1945.

Katz, Elihu, and Lazarsfeld, Paul F. *Personal Influence: The Part Played by People in the Flow of Mass Communications.* Glencoe, Ill.: Free Press, 1955.

Kelley, Earl C., and Rasey, Marie I. *Education and the Nature of Man.* New York: Harper & Brothers, 1952.

Kingsley, Howard L., and Garry, Ralph. *The Nature and Conditions of Learning.* Englewood Cliffs, N. J.: Prentice-Hall, Inc., 1957.

Klapper, Joseph T. *The Effects of Mass Communication.* Glencoe, Ill.: Free Press, 1960.

Kluckhohn, Clyde, Murray, Henry A., and Schneider, David M. (eds.) *Personality in Nature, Society and Culture.* New York: Alfred A. Knopf, Inc., 1953.

Knowles, Malcolm S., and Knowles, Hulda. *Introduction to Group Dynamics.* New York: Association Press, 1959.

Koch, Sigmund (ed). *Psychology: A Study of a Science.* Study I. 3 Vols. New York: McGraw-Hill Book Co., Inc., 1959.

Koffka, Kurt. *The Growth of the Mind.* New York: Harcourt, Brace & Co., 1928.

————. *Principles of Gestalt Psychology.* New York: Harcourt, Brace & Co., 1935.

Kohler, Wolfgang. *Dynamics in Psychology.* New York: Liveright Publishing Co., 1940.

————. *Gestalt Psychology.* New York: Liveright Publishing Corporation, 1947.

————. *The Mentality of Apes.* New York: Harcourt, Brace & Co., 1926.

Kretschmer, Ernst. *Physique and Character.* New York: Harcourt, Brace & Co., 1925.

Kroeber, Alfred L. *The Nature of Culture.* Chicago: University of Chicago Press, 1952.

————, and Clyde Kluckhohn. *Culture: A Critical Review of Concepts and Definitions.* Cambridge, Mass.: The Museum, 1952.

Krutch, Joseph Wood. *Human Nature and the Human Condition.* New York: Random House, 1959.

Kunkel, Fritz. *In Search of Maturity.* New York: Charles Scribner's Sons, 1943.

Lafitte, Paul. *The Person in Psychology: Reality or Abstraction.* London: Routledge & Kegan Paul, 1957.

Lange, Carl G., and James, William. *The Emotions.* Baltimore: Williams and Wilkins, 1922.

LaPiere, Richard. *The Freudian Ethic.* New York: Duell, Sloan & Pearce, Inc., 1959.

Larrabee, Eric, and Meyersohn, Rolf. *Mass Leisure.* Glencoe, Ill.: Free Press, 1958.

Lashley, Karl S. *Brain Mechanisms and Intelligence.* Chicago: University of Chicago Press, 1929.

Lavater, Johann K. *Essays on Physiognomy: Designed to Promote the Knowledge and the Love of Mankind.* 5th ed. London: Wm. Tegg & Co., 1848.

Leary, Timoth. *Interpersonal Diagnosis of Personality.* New York: The Ronald Press Company, 1957.

Lecky, Prescott. *Self-Consistency.* New York: Island Press, 1945.

Lee, Dorothy. *Freedom and Culture.* Englewood Cliffs, N. J.: Prentice-Hall, Inc., 1959.

Lerner, Daniel (ed.), *The Human Meaning of the Social Sciences.* New York: Meridian Books, Inc., 1959.

Lerner, Max. *America as a Civilization.* New York: Simon and Schuster, Inc., 1957.

Lewin, Kurt. *A Dynamic Theory of Personality.* New York: McGraw-Hill Book Co., Inc., 1935.

————. *Field Theory in Social Science.* New York: Harper & Brothers, 1951.

————. *Principles of Topological Psychology.* New York: McGraw-Hill Book Co., Inc., 1936.

————. *Resolving Social Conflicts: Selected Papers on Group Dynamics.* Edited by Gertrude W. Lewin. New York: Harper & Brothers, 1948.

Ligon, Ernest M. *Dimensions of Character.* New York: The Macmillan Co., 1956.

Linton, Ralph. *The Cultural Background of Personality.* New York: Appleton-Century Company, Inc., 1945.

————. *Culture and Mental Disorder.* Springfield, Ill.: Charles C. Thomas, Publisher, 1956.

————, Fisher, Mary, and Ryan, W. *Culture and Personality.* Washington: American Council on Education, 1941.

Lippitt, Ronald, Watson, Jeanne, and Westley, Bruce. *The Dynamics of Planned Change.* New York: Harcourt, Brace & Company, 1958.

Locke, John. *An Essay Concerning Human Understanding.* London: Basset, 1690.

Loomis, Earl A., Jr. *The Self in Pilgrimage.* New York: Harper & Brothers, 1960.

Macmurray, John. *The Self as Agent.* New York: Harper & Brothers, 1957.

Malinowski, Bronislaw. *The Sexual Life of Savages in Northwestern Melanesia.* New York: Eugenics Publishing Company, 1929.

Manwell, Elizabeth M., and Fahs, Sophia L. Rev. ed. *Consider the Children How They Grow.* Boston: Beacon Press, 1951.

Maslow, Abraham H. *Motivation and Personality.* New York: Harper & Brothers, 1954.

————. *Self-Actualizing People: A Study of Psychological Health.* Personality Symposium No. 1. New York: Grune & Stratton, Inc., 1950.

———— (ed.). *New Knowledge and Human Values.* New York: Harper & Brothers, 1959.

May, Rollo. *Man's Search for Himself.* New York: W. W. Norton & Company, Inc., 1953.

————. *The Meaning of Anxiety.* New York: The Ronald Press Company, 1950.

Mayer, Martin. *Madison Avenue, U.S.A.* New York: Harper & Brothers, 1958.

McCary, James L. (ed.). *Psychology of Personality.* New York: Logos Press, Inc., 1956.

McClelland, D. C. *Personality.* New York: Dryden Press, 1951.

McDougall, William. *Body and Mind: A History and a Defense of Animism.* London: Methuen and Company, 1911.

————. *The Energies of Men.* New York: Charles Scribner's Sons, 1932. . . . .

————. *An Introduction to Social Psychology.* London: Methuen and Company, 1908.

————. *Modern Materialism and Emergent Evolution.* New York: D. Van Nostrand Co., Inc., 1929.

————. *Outline of Abnormal Psychology.* New York: Charles Scribner's Sons, 1926.

————. *Outline of Psychology.* New York: Charles Scribner's Sons, 1923.

————. *Psychoanalysis and Social Psychology.* London: Methuen and Company, 1936.

Mead, George H. *Mind, Self and Society.* Chicago: University of Chicago Press, 1934.

Mead, Margaret. *Male and Female.* New York: William Morrow & Co., Inc., 1949.

————. *Sex and Temperament in Three Primitive Societies.* New York: William Morrow & Co., Inc., 1935.

———— (ed.). *Cooperation and Competition among Primitive Peoples.* New York: McGraw-Hill Book Co., Inc., 1937.

_____ (ed.). *Cultural Patterns and Social Change*. New York: New American Library, 1955.

_____ (ed.). *Cultural Patterns and Technical Change*. Paris: Unesco, 1953.

Miles, Matthew B. *Learning to Work in Groups*. New York: Bureau of Publications, Teachers College, Columbia University, 1959.

Miller, Alexander. *The Man in the Mirror*. Garden City, N. Y.: Doubleday & Company, Inc., 1958.

_____. *The Renewal of Man*. New York: Doubleday & Company, Inc., 1955.

Miller, George A. *Language and Communication*. New York: McGraw-Hill Book Co., Inc., 1951.

Miller, Hugh. *An Historical Introduction to Modern Psychology*. New York: The Macmillan Co., 1947.

Miller, Neal E., and Dollard, John. *Social Learning and Imitation*. New Haven: Yale University Press, 1941.

Mills, Charles Wright. *The Power Elite*. New York: Oxford University Press, Inc., 1956.

_____. *The Sociological Imagination*. New York: Oxford University Press, Inc., 1959.

_____. *White Collar*. New York: Oxford University Press, Inc., 1951.

Missenard, Andra. *In Search of Man*. Translated from the French by Lawrence G. Blockman. New York: Hawthorne Books, Inc., 1957.

Monroe, Ruth L. *Schools of Psychoanalytic Thought*. New York: Dryden Press, 1955.

Montagu, Ashley. *Anthropology and Human Nature*. Boston: Porter Sargent, Publisher, 1957.

Moore, Thomas V. *The Driving Forces of Human Nature and Their Adjustment*. New York: Grune and Stratton, Inc., 1948.

Moustakas, Clark E. (ed.). *The Self: Explorations in Personal Growth*. New York: Harper & Brothers, 1956.

Mowrer, O. Hobart. *The Crisis in Psychiatry and Religion*. Princeton, N. J.: D. Van Nostrand Co., Inc., 1961.

_____. *Learning Theory and Behavior*. New York: John Wiley & Sons, Inc., 1960.

_____. *Learning Theory and Personality Dynamics*. New York: The Ronald Press Company, 1950.

_____. *Learning Theory and the Symbolic Processes*. New York: John Wiley & Sons, Inc., 1960.

Murchison, Carl (ed.). *Psychologies of 1930*. Worcester, Mass.: Clark University Press, 1930.

Murphy, Gardner. *Historical Introduction to Modern Psychology*. New York: Harcourt, Brace & Company, 1949.

_____. *Human Potentialities*. New York: Basic Books, 1958.

_____. *In the Minds of Men: The Study of Human Behavior and Social Tensions in India*. New York: Basic Books, Inc., 1953.

_____. *Personality: A Biosocial Approach to Origins and Structure*. New York: Harper & Brothers, 1947.

_____ (ed.). *Human Nature and Enduring Peace*. Boston: Houghton Mifflin

Company, 1945.

————, and Jensen, F. *Approaches to Personality*. New York: Coward-McCann, Inc., 1932.

————, and Likert, Ronald. *Public Opinion and the Individual*. New York: Harper & Brothers, 1938.

Murphy, Lois B., *et al. Personality in Young Children*. 2 Vols. New York: Basic Books, Inc., 1956.

Murray, Henry A. *Thematic Apperception Test Manual*. Cambridge, Mass.: Harvard University Press, 1943.

————. *Explorations in Personality*. New York: Oxford University Press, Inc., 1938.

National Education Association, Educational Policies Commission. *Moral and Spiritual Values in the Public Schools*. Washington, 1951.

Nef, John U. *Cultural Foundations of Industrial Civilization*. Cambridge: Cambridge University Press, 1958.

Packard, Vance. *The Hidden Persuaders*. New York: David McKay Co., Inc., 1957.

————. *The Status Seekers*. New York: David McKay Co., Inc., 1959.

————. *The Waste Makers*. New York: David McKay Co., Inc., 1960.

Parker, Edward C., Barry, David W., and Smythe, Dallas W. *The Television-Radio Audience and Religion*. New York: Harper & Brothers, 1955.

Parsons, Talcott. *The Social System*. Glencoe, Ill.: Free Press, 1951.

————. *The Structure of Social Action*. Glencoe, Ill.: Free Press, 1949.

————. *Structure and Process in Modern Societies*. Glencoe, Ill.: Free Press, 1960.

————, *et al. Family, Socialization and Interaction Process*. Glencoe, Ill.: Free Press, 1955.

————, Shils, Edward, Naegele, Kasper D., and Pitts, Jesse R. (eds.). *Theories of Society: Foundations of Modern Sociological Theory*. 2 Vols. Glencoe, Ill. The Free Press of Glencoe, Inc., 1961.

Pavlov, Ivan P. *Conditioned Reflexes*. London: Oxford University Press, 1927.

————. *Experimental Psychology and Other Essays*. New York: Philosophical Library, Inc., 1957.

————. *Selected Works*. Moscow: Foreign Languages Publishing House, 1955.

Peck, Robert F., and Havighurst, Robert J., *The Psychology of Character Development*. New York: John Wiley & Sons, Inc., 1960.

Peters, R. S. (ed.). *Brett's History of Psychology*. London: Allen and Unwin, 1953.

Phenix, Philip H. *Philosophy of Education*. New York: Henry Holt and Company, Inc., 1958.

Plant, James S. *The Envelope: A Study of the Impact of the World upon the Child*. New York: Commonwealth Fund, 1950.

————. *Personality and the Cultural Pattern*. New York: Commonwealth Fund, 1937.

Plato. *The Works of Plato*. 6 Vols. London: G. Bell and Sons, 1896-1900.

Prescott, D. A. *Emotion and the Educative Process*. Washington: American Council on Education, 1938.

Pressey, Sidney L., and Kuhlen, Raymond G. *Psychological Development through the Life Span*. New York: Harper & Brothers, 1957.

Progoff, Ira. *The Death and Rebirth of Psychology*. New York: Julian Press, Inc.,

1956.

_____. *Depth Psychology and Modern Man*. New York: Julian Press, Inc., 1959.

Rank, Otto. *Beyond Psychology*. Camden, N. J.: Haddon Craftsman, 1941.

_____. *Psychology and the Soul*. Philadelphia: University of Pennsylvania Press, 1950.

_____. *The Trauma of Birth*. New York: Harcourt, Brace & Company, 1929.

_____. *Truth and Reality*. New York: Alfred A. Knopf, Inc., 1936.

_____. *Will Therapy*. New York: Alfred A. Knopf, Inc., 1936.

Redl, Fritz, and Wineman, David. *Children Who Hate*. Glencoe, Ill.: Free Press, 1951.

Reeves, J. W. *Body and Mind in Western Thought*. Baltimore: Penguin Books, Inc., 1958.

Reissman, Leonard. *Class in American Society*. Glencoe, Ill.: Free Press, 1959.

Remmers, Hermann H., and Radler, D. H. *The American Teenager*. New York: The Bobbs-Merrill Company, Inc., 1957.

Reisman, David, *et al. The Lonely Crowd*. New Haven: Yale University Press, 1950.

Roback, A. A. *History of American Psychology*. New York: Library Publishers, Inc., 1952.

_____. *The Psychology of Character*. New York: Harcourt, Brace & Company, 1928.

_____. *Present-day Psychology*. New York: Philosophical Library, Inc., 1955.

Robinson, Edward S. *Man as Psychology Sees Him*. New York: The Macmillan Co., 1932.

Rogers, Carl R. *Client-Centered Therapy*. Boston: Houghton Mifflin Company, 1951.

_____. *Counseling and Psychotherapy: Newer Concepts in Practice*. Boston: Houghton Mifflin Company, 1942.

_____, and Dymond, Rosalind F. (eds.). *Psychotherapy and Personality Change: Co-ordinated Studies in the Client-Centered Approach*. Chicago: University of Chicago Press, 1954.

Rokeach, Milton. *The Open and Closed Mind*. New York: Basic Books, Inc., 1960.

Ruesch, Jurgen. *Disturbed Communication*. New York: W. W. Norton & Company, Inc., 1957.

Sahlins, Marshall D., and Service, Elman R. (eds.). *Evolution and Culture*. Ann Arbor, Mich.: The University of Michigan Press, 1960.

Sartre, Jean P. *Existential Psychoanalysis*. New York: Philosophical Library, Inc., 1953.

Saul, L. J. *Emotional Maturity: The Development and Dynamics of Personality*. Philadelphia: J. P. Lippincott Co., 1947.

Schachtel, Ernest G. *Metamorphosis*. New York: Basic Books, Inc., 1959.

Schramm, Wilbur. *The Impact of Educational Television*. Urbana: University of Illinois Press, 1960.

_____. *The Process and Effects of Mass Communication*. Urbana: University of Illinois Press, 1954.

_____. *Responsibility in Mass Communication*. New York: Harper & Brothers, 1957.

Sears, Robert R. "Social Behavior and Personality Development." In Talcott Parsons, *et al., Toward a General Theory of Action*. Cambridge, Mass.: Harvard University Press, 1951.

————. "A Theoretical Framework for Personality and Social Behavior." *American Psychologist* 6:476-482 (1951).

————. Maccoby, E. E., and Lewin, H. *Patterns of Child Rearing.* Evanston, Ill.: Row, Peterson & Company, 1957.

Seeley, John R., Sim, Alexander, and Loosley, Elizabeth W. *Crestwood Heights: A Study of the Culture of Suburban Life.* New York: Basic Books, Inc., 1956.

Seward, Georgene. *Psychotherapy and Culture Conflict.* New York: The Ronald Press Company, 1956.

Shapiro, Harry L. (ed.). *Man, Culture and Society.* New York: Oxford University Press, Inc., 1956.

Sheldon, William H. *Atlas of Men: A Guide for Somatotyping the Adult Male at All Ages.* New York: Harper & Brothers, 1954.

————, et al. *Varieties of Delinquent Youth: An Introduction to Constitutional Psychiatry.* New York: Harper & Brothers, 1949.

————, et al. *The Varieties of Human Physique: An Introduction to Constitutional Psychology.* New York: Harper & Brothers, 1940.

————, and Stevens, S. S. *The Varieties of Temperament: A Psychology of Constitutional Differences.* New York: Harper & Brothers, 1942.

Sherif, Muzafer. *The Psychology of Social Norms.* New York: Harper & Brothers, 1936.

————, and Cantril, H. *The Psychology of Ego Involvements.* New York: John Wiley and Sons, Inc., 1947.

Shippey, Frederick A. *Church Work in the City.* Nashville: Abingdon Press, 1952.

Shuster, George N. *Education and Moral Wisdom.* New York: Harper & Brothers, 1960.

Simon, Herbert A. *Models of Man: Social and Rational.* New York: John Wiley and Sons, Inc., 1957.

Simpson, George E., and Yinger, J. Milton. *Racial and Cultural Minorities: An Analysis of Prejudice and Discrimination.* New York: Harper & Brothers, 1958.

Skinner, Burrhus F. *The Behavior of Organisms: An Experimental Analysis.* New York: Appleton-Century-Crofts, Inc., 1938.

————. *Science and Human Behavior.* New York: The Macmillan Co., 1953.

Slotkin, James S. *Personality Development.* New York: Harper & Brothers, 1952.

————. *Social Anthropology.* New York: The Macmillan Co., 1950.

Smuts, Jan C. *Holism and Evolution.* New York: The Macmillan Co., 1926.

Sorokin, Pitirim A. *Social and Cultural Dynamics.* Boston: Extending Horizons Books, 1957.

————. *The Ways and Power of Love.* Boston: Beacon Press, 1954.

Spearman, Charles E. *The Abilities of Man.* New York: The Macmillan Co., 1927.

Spindler, George D. *The Transmission of American Culture.* Cambridge, Mass.: Harvard University Press, 1959.

Spock, Benjamin. *The Common Sense Book of Baby and Child Care.* New York: Duell, Sloan and Pearce, Inc., 1946.

Spranger, Edward. *Types of Men.* Translated by P. J. W. Pigors. Halle: M. Niemeyer, 1928.

Stern, George G., *et al. Methods in Personality Assessment.* Glencoe, Ill.: Free Press, 1956.

Stern, William. *General Psychology from the Personalistic Standpoint.* H. D. Spoerl, trans. New York: The Macmillan Co., 1938.

_____. *Person und Sache: System der Philosophischen Weltanschauung.* Leipzig: J. A. Barth, 1906-1924.

Sternberg, Fritz. *The Military and Industrial Revolution of Our Time.* New York: Frederick A. Praeger, Inc., 1959.

Stinnette, Charles R. *Anxiety and Faith.* Greenwich, Conn.: The Seabury Press, Inc., 1955.

Stock, Dorothy, and Thelen, Herbert A. *Emotional Dynamics and Group Culture.* New York: New York University Press, 1957.

Stratemeyer, Florence B., *et al. Developing a Curriculum for Modern Living.* New York: Bureau of Publications, Teachers College, Columbia University, 1947.

Strong, Edward K., Jr. *Change in Interests with Age.* Stanford, Calif.: Stanford University Press, 1931.

_____. *Vocational Interests of Men and Women.* Stanford, Calif.: Stanford University Press, 1943.

Sullivan, Harry S. *Conceptions of Modern Psychiatry.* Washington: William Alanson White Psychiatric Foundation, 1947.

_____. *The Interpersonal Theory of Psychiatry.* New York: W. W. Norton & Company, Inc., 1953.

Symonds, Percival M. *Diagnosing Personality and Conduct.* New York: Appleton-Century-Crofts, Inc., 1931.

_____. *The Dynamics of Human Adjustment.* New York: Appleton-Century Company, 1946.

_____. *The Dynamics of Parent-Child Relationships.* New York: Bureau of Publications, Teachers College, Columbia University, 1949.

_____. *The Ego and the Self.* New York: Appleton-Century-Crofts, Inc., 1951.

Terman, Lewis M. *Genetic Studies of Genius.* Stanford, Calif.: Stanford University Press, 1925.

_____, Miles, Catherine C. *et al. Sex and Personality: Studies in Masculinity and Femininity.* New York: McGraw-Hill Book Co., Inc., 1936.

Thelen, Herbert A. *Dynamics of Groups at Work.* Chicago: University of Chicago Press, 1954.

_____, *Education and the Human Quest.* New York: Harper & Brothers, 1960.

Thibaut, John W., and Kelly, Harold H. *The Social Psychology of Groups.* New York: John Wiley and Sons, Inc., 1959.

Thorndike, Edward L. *Educational Psychology.* 2 Vols. New York: Bureau of Publications, Teachers College, Columbia University, 1913.

_____. *The Fundamentals of Learning.* New York: Bureau of Publications, Teachers College, Columbia University, 1932.

_____. *Human Nature and the Social Order.* New York: The Macmillan Co., 1940.

_____. *The Psychology of Wants, Interests and Attitudes.* New York: Appleton-Century-Crofts, Inc., 1935.

Thorpe, Louis P., and Schmuller, A. M. *Contemporary Theories of Learning.* New

York: The Ronald Press Company, 1954.

————, and Schmuller, A. M. *Personality: An Interdisciplinary Approach.* Princeton, N. J.: D. Van Nostrand Co., Inc., 1958.

Titchener, Edward B. *Systematic Psychology: Prolegomena.* New York: The Macmillan Company, 1929.

Tolman, Edward C. *Purposive Behavior in Animals and Men.* New York: The Century Company, 1932.

Tournier, Paul. *The Meaning of Persons.* New York: Harper & Brothers, 1957.

Toynbee, Arnold J. *A Study of History.* 6 Vols. London: Oxford University Press, 1935-1939.

Truxall, Andrew G., and Merrill, Francis E. *The Family in American Culture.* Englewood Cliffs, N. J.: Prentice-Hall, Inc., 1947.

Vidich, Arthur J., and Bensman, Joseph. *Small Town in Mass Society.* Princeton, N. J.: Princeton University Press, 1958.

Viola, G. *Le Legge de Correlazione Morfolagia dei tippi Individuali.* Padova, Italy: Prosperini, 1909.

Warner, Wm. Lloyd. *American Life: Dream and Reality.* Chicago: University of Chicago Press, 1953.

————. *Democracy in Jonesville.* New York: Harper & Brothers, 1949.

————. *The Living and the Dead.* New Haven: Yale University Press, 1959.

————, et al. *Social Class in America.* Chicago: Science Research Associates, 1949.

————, and Lunt, Paul S. *The Social Life of a Modern Community.* New Haven: Yale University Press, 1941.

Watson, John B. *Behaviorism.* New York: W. W. Norton & Company, Inc., 1930.

————. *Psychology from the Standpoint of a Behaviorist.* Philadelphia: J. B. Lippincott Co., 1919.

Weiss, Albert P. *A Theoretical Basis of Human Behavior.* Columbus, Ohio: R. G. Adams & Co., 1929.

Wertheimer, Max. *Productive Thinking.* New York: Harper & Brothers, 1945.

Westley, Bruce H., and Barrow, Lionel C. Jr. *Exploring the News: A Comparative Study of the Teaching Effectiveness of Radio and Television.* Madison, Wisc.: University of Wisconsin Television Laboratory, 1959.

Whiting, John W. M., and Child, Irvin L. *Child Training and Personality Development.* New Haven: Yale University Press, 1953.

Whyte, William Foote. *Street Corner Society.* Chicago: University of Chicago Press, 1943.

Whyte, William H., Jr. *The Organization Man.* New York: Simon and Schuster, Inc., 1956.

Wiener, Norbert. *Cybernetics, or Control and Communication in the Animal and the Machine.* New York: John Wiley & Sons, Inc., 1948.

————. *The Human Use of Human Beings.* Garden City, N. Y.: Doubleday Anchor Books, 1956.

Windelband, Wilhelm. *An Introduction to Philosophy.* Translated by Joseph McCabe. London: Unwin, 1921.

Winter, Gibson. *Love and Conflict: New Patterns of Family Life.* Garden City, N. Y.: Doubleday & Company, Inc., 1958.

Wolff, Werner. *The Expression of Personality.* New York: Harper & Brothers, 1943.

_____. *Values and Personality: An Existential Psychology of Crisis.* New York: Grune & Stratton, Inc., 1950.

_____ (ed.). *Psychiatry and Religion.* New York: MD Publications, Inc., 1956.

Wolman, Benjamin B. *Contemporary Theories and Systems in Psychology.* New York: Harper & Brothers, 1960.

Wood, Robert C. *Suburbia: Its People and Their Politics.* Boston: Houghton Mifflin Company, 1959.

Woodward, Luther E. *Relations of Religious Training and Life Patterns to the Adult Religious Life.* New York: Bureau of Publications, Teachers College, Columbia University, 1950.

Woodworth, Robert S. *Contemporary Schools of Psychology.* New York: The Ronald Press Company, 1931.

_____. *Dynamic Psychology.* New York: Columbia University Press, 1918.

_____. *Dynamics of Behavior.* New York: Henry Holt & Company, Inc., 1958.

_____. *Experimental Psychology.* New York: Henry Holt & Company, Inc., 1938.

Wundt, Wilhelm. *Elements of Folk Psychology.* London: Macmillan & Co., Ltd., 1916.

_____. *Outlines of Psychology.* Translated by Charles H. Judd. New York: G. E. Stechert & Co., 1907.

Yinger, J. Milton. *Religion, Society and the Individual.* New York: The Macmillan Co., 1957.

Zorbaugh, Harvey W. *Gold Coast and Slum.* Chicago: University of Chicago Press, 1929.

Zubeck, John P., and Solberg, P. A. *Human Development.* New York: McGraw-Hill Book Co., Inc., 1954.

B. RELIGIOUS
AND THEOLOGICAL FOUNDATIONS

Adams, Hampton. *Vocabulary of Faith.* St. Louis: The Bethany Press, 1956.

Aubrey, Edwin E. *Humanistic Teaching and the Place of Ethical and Religious Values in Higher Education.* Philadelphia: University of Pennsylvania Press, 1959.

_____. *Present Theological Tendencies.* New York: Harper & Brothers, 1936.

Aulen, Gustaf. *The Faith of the Christian Church.* Philadelphia: Muhlenberg Press, 1948.

Baillie, Donald M. *God Was in Christ.* New York: Charles Scribner's Sons, 1948.

Baillie, John. *The Idea of Revelation in Recent Thought.* New York: Columbia University Press, 1956.

Bainton, Roland H. *Christian Attitudes Toward War and Peace.* Nashville: Abingdon Press, 1960.

Baker, Eric. *The Faith of a Methodist.* Nashville: Abingdon Press. 1959.

Baker, Oren H. *Human Nature Under God.* New York: Association Press, 1958.

Barnes, Roswell P. *Under Orders: The Churches and Public Affairs.* Garden City, N. Y.: Doubleday & Company, Inc., 1961.

Barth, Karl. *Church Dogmatics.* Translated by A. C. Cochrane. Philadelphia: The Westminster Press, 1953.

————. *Dogmatics in Outline.* Translated by G. T. Thomson. New York: Philosophical Library, Inc., 1949.

————. *The Knowledge of God.* New York: Charles Scribner's Sons, 1939.

————. *Protestant Thought from Rousseau to Ritschl.* Translated by Barin Cozens. New York: Harper & Brothers, 1959.

Barry, F. R. *Recovery of Man.* New York: Charles Scribner's Sons, 1949.

Beach, Waldo. *Conscience on Campus: An Interpretation of Christian Ethics for College Life.* New York: Association Press, 1958.

Bennett, John C. *Christians and the State.* New York: Charles Scribner's Sons, 1958.

Benson, Purnell H. *Religion in Contemporary Culture.* New York: Harper & Brothers, 1960.

Bentwich, Norman D. *The Religious Foundations of Internationalism.* New York: Bloch Publishing Co., Inc., 1960.

Berdyaev, Nicolas. *The Destiny of Man.* New York: Charles Scribner's Sons, 1937.

Bergevin, Paul, and McKinley, John. *Design for Adult Education in the Church.* Greenwich, Conn.: The Seabury Press, Inc., 1958.

Bertocci, Peter A. *Religion as Creative Insecurity.* Nashville: Abingdon Press, 1958.

Blanshard, Paul. *American Freedom and Catholic Power.* Boston: Beacon Press, 1958.

Bonhoeffer, Dietrich. *The Cost of Discipleship.* New York: The Macmillan Co., 1948.

————. *Life Together.* Translated by J. W. Doberstein. New York: Harper & Brothers, 1954.

Bonthius, Robert. *Christian Paths to Self-Acceptance.* New York: King's Crown Press, 1948.

Bower, William C., and Hayward, Percy R. *Protestantism Faces Its Educational Task Together.* Appleton, Wisc.: C. C. Nelson Publishing Co., 1949.

Boyd, Malcolm. *Christ and Celebrity Gods.* Greenwich, Conn.: The Seabury Press, Inc., 1958.

Brengle, S. L. *Helps to Holiness.* London: Salvationist Publishing and Supplies, 1948.

Brennan, Robert E. *Thomistic Psychology: A Philosophic Analysis of the Nature of Man.* New York: The Macmillan Co., 1941.

Bright, John. *The Kingdom of God.* Nashville: Abingdon Press, 1953.

Brightman, Edgar S. *Personality and Religion.* New York: Abingdon Press, 1934.

————. *Persons and Value.* Boston: Boston University Press, 1952.

Brown, Robert M., and Weigel, Gustave. *An American Dialogue: A Protestant Looks at Catholicism and a Catholic Looks at Protestantism.* Garden City, N. Y.: Doubleday & Company, Inc., 1961.

Brunner, Emil. *The Christian Doctrine of God.* Philadelphia: The Westminster Press, 1950.

————. *Christianity and Civilization.* 2 Vols. New York: Charles Scribner's Sons, 1949.

————. *The Divine-Human Encounter.* Philadelphia: The Westminster Press, 1943.

————. *Man in Revolt: A Christian Anthropology.* Philadelphia: The Westminster Press, 1947.

Buber, Martin. *Between Man and Man.* Traslated by Ronald G. Smith. New York: The Macmillan Co., 1948.

_____. *I and Thou*. Translated by Ronald G. Smith. New York: Charles Scribner's Sons, 1937.

Bultmann, Rudolph K. *Jesus Christ and Mythology*. New York: Charles Scribner's Sons, 1958.

_____. *Theology of the New Testament*. 2 Vols. New York: Charles Scribner's Sons, 1951-1955.

Burr, Nelson R. *A Critical Bibliography of Religion in America*. Smith, James Ward, and Jamison, A. Leland (eds.). Princeton, N. J.: Princeton University Press, 1961.

Burrows, Miller. *An Outline of Biblical Theology*. Philadelphia: The Westminister Press, 1946.

Buttrick, George A. *Biblical Thought and the Secular University*. Baton Rouge: Louisiana State University Press, 1960.

Cailliet, Emile. *The Christian Approach to Culture*. Nashville: Abingdon Press, 1953.

_____. *The Dawn of Personality*. New York: The Bobbs-Merrill Company, Inc., 1955.

Calvin, John. *Calvin's Commentaries*. Grand Rapids, Mich.: Wm. B. Eerdmans Publishing Co., 1938.

_____. *Institutes of the Christian Religion*. Translated by John Allen. Philadelphia: Presbyterian Board of Publication and Sabbath School Work, 1902.

_____. *On the Christian Faith: Selections from the Institutes, Commentaries, and Tracts*. John T. McNeill, ed. New York: The Liberal Arts Press, Inc., 1957.

Carnell, Edward J. *The Case for Orthodox Theology*. Philadelphia: The Westminster Press, 1959.

_____. *Christian Commitment*. New York: The Macmillan Co., 1957.

Casserly, J. V. L. *The Retreat from Christianity in the Modern World*. New York: Longmans, Green & Co., Inc., 1953.

Casteel, John. *Spiritual Renewal Through Personal Groups*. New York: Association Press, 1957.

Chaplin, Dora P. *Children and Religion*. New York: Charles Scribner's Sons, 1948.

Clark, Walter H. *The Psychology of Religion*. New York: The Macmillan Co., 1958.

Clemmons, Robert S. *Dynamics of Christian Adult Education*. Nashville: Abingdon Press, 1958.

Come, Arnold B. *Human Spirit and Holy Spirit*. Philadelphia: The Westminster Press, 1959.

Corson, Fred P. *The Christian Imprint*. Nashville: Abingdon Press, 1955.

Day, Leroy Judson. *Dynamic Christian Fellowship*. Philadelphia: Judson Press, 1960.

De Chardin, Pierre T. *The Phenomenon of Man*. New York: Harper & Brothers, 1959.

Dewar, Lindsay. *The Holy Spirit and Modern Thought*. New York: Harper & Brothers, 1959.

Dewey, John. *A Common Faith*. New Haven: Yale University Press, 1934.

DeWire, Harry A. *The Christian as Communicator*. Philadelphia: The Westminster Press, 1960.

DeWolf, L. Harold. *The Case for Theology in Liberal Perspective*. Philadelphia: The Westminster Press, 1959.

————. *The Religious Revolt Against Reason.* New York: Harper & Brothers, 1959.

————. *A Theology of the Living Church.* New York: Harper & Brothers, 1953.

Dillenberger, John. *Protestant Thought and Natural Science.* Garden City, N. Y.: Doubleday & Company, Inc., 1960.

Dillistone, F. W. *Christianity and Communication.* New York: Charles Scribner's Sons, 1956.

Ditmanson, Harold H., Hong, Howard V., and Quanbeck, Warren A. (eds.). *Christian Faith and the Liberal Arts.* Minneapolis: Augsburg Publishing House, 1960.

Duff, Edward. *The Social Thought of the World Council of Churches.* New York: Association Press, 1956.

Duvall, Evelyn M., and Duvall, Sylvanus M. (eds.). *Sex Ways—In Fact and Faith.* New York: Association Press, 1961.

Eckardt, A. Roy. *The Surge of Piety in America.* New York: Association Press, 1958.

Elmen, Paul. *The Restoration of Meaning to Contemporary Life.* Garden City, N. Y.: Doubleday & Company, Inc., 1958.

Ensley, F. Gerald. *The Marks of Christian Education.* Nashville: Abingdon Press, 1958.

Ernsberger, David J. *A Philosophy of Adult Christian Education.* Philadelphia: The Westminster Press, 1959.

Fairchild, Roy W., and Wynn, John Charles. *Families in the Church: A Protestant Survey.* New York: Association Press, 1961.

Fairfield, Hoxie N. (ed.). *Religious Perspectives in College Teaching.* New York: The Ronald Press Company, 1952.

Ferre, Nels F. S. *Searchlights on Contemporary Theology.* New York: Harper & Brothers, 1961.

Finegan, Jack. *Beginnings in Theology.* New York: Association Press, 1956.

Flew, R. N. (ed.). *The Nature of the Church.* New York: Harper & Brothers, 1952.

Forell, George W. *The Protestant Faith.* Englewood Cliffs, N. J.: Prentice-Hall, Inc., 1960.

Fosdick, Harry E. *On Being a Real Person.* New York: Harper & Brothers, 1943.

————. *What Is Vital in Religion?* New York: Harper & Brothers, 1955.

Frankl, Viktor. *The Doctor and the Soul.* New York: Alfred A. Knopf, Inc., 1955.

Fuller, Edmund (ed.). *The Christian Idea of Education.* New Haven: Yale University Press, 1957.

Gable, Lee J. *Christian Nurture Through the Church.* New York: National Council of the Churches of Christ in the U. S. A., 1955.

————. *Encyclopedia for Church Group Leaders.* New York: Association Press, 1959.

Galdston, Iago. *Ministry and Medicine in Human Relations.* New York: International Universities Press, Inc., 1955.

Geaney, Dennis. *Christians in a Changing World.* Notre Dame, Indiana: Fides Publishers Association, 1959.

Gerstner, John N. *Steps to Salvation: The Evangelistic Message of Jonathan Edwards.* Philadelphia: The Westminster Press, 1960.

Gilkey, Langdon. *Maker of Heaven and Earth.* Garden City, N. Y.: Doubleday & Company, Inc., 1959.

Glen, J. Stanley. *The Recovery of the Teaching Ministry.* Philadelphia: The Westminster Press, 1960.

Goldbrunner, Josef. *Holiness Is Wholeness.* New York: Pantheon Books, Inc., 1955.

Greeley, Andrew M. *The Church and the Suburbs.* New York: Sheed & Ward, 1959.

Green, Bryan. *Christians Alive.* New York: Charles Scribner's Sons, 1959.

Grimes, Howard. *The Church Redemptive.* Nashville: Abingdon Press, 1958.

Grimm, Harold J. (ed.). *Luther's Works.* Translated by W. A. Lambert. Philadelphia: Muhlenberg Press, 1957.

Halverson, Marvin, and Cohen, Arthur A. (eds.). *A Handbook of Christian Theology.* New York: Meridian Books, Inc., 1958.

Handy, Robert T. *Members One of Another: Studies in the Nature of the Church as It Relates to Evangelism.* Philadelphia: Judson Press, 1959.

Harkness, Georgia. *Understanding the Christian Faith.* Nashville: Abingdon Press, 1947.

Harris, Erdman. *God's Image and Man's Imagination.* New York: Charles Scribner's Sons, 1959.

Harrison, Everett F. (ed.). *Baker's Dictionary of Theology.* Grand Rapids, Mich.: Baker Book House, 1960.

Haselden, Kyle. *The Racial Problem in Christian Perspective.* New York: Harper & Brothers, 1959.

Hazelton, Roger. *New Accents in Contemporary Theology.* New York: Harper & Brothers, 1960.

Heim, Karl, *Christian Faith and Natural Science.* New York: Harper & Brothers, 1953.

Henderlite, Rachel. *A Call to Faith.* Richmond, Va.: John Knox Press, 1955.

Henry, Carl F. H. *Revelation and the Bible: Contemporary Evangelical Thought.* Grand Rapids, Mich.: Baker Book House, 1959.

Herberg, Will. *Protestant—Catholic—Jew: An Essay in American Religious Sociology.* New York: Doubleday & Company, Inc., 1955.

Hershberger, Guy F. *The Way of the Cross in Human Relations.* Scottdale, Pa.: Herald Press, 1958.

Hiltner, Seward. *The Christian Shepherd.* Nashville: Abingdon Press, 1959.

_____. *Religion and Health.* New York: The Macmillan Co., 1943.

_____. *Self-Understanding Through Psychology and Religion.* New York: Charles Scribner's Sons, 1951.

Hocking, William E. *The Coming World Civilization.* New York: Harper & Brothers, 1956.

_____. *Living Religions and a World Faith.* New York: The Macmillan Co., 1940.

The Holy Bible. Revised Standard Version. New York: Thomas Nelson & Sons, 1952.

Hordern, William, *A Layman's Guide to Protestant Theology.* New York: The Macmillan Co., 1955.

_____. *The Case for a New Reformation Theology.* Philadelphia: The Westminster Press, 1959.

Horton, Walter M. *Christian Theology: An Ecumenical Approach.* New York:

Harper & Brothers, 1955.

Howe, Reuel L. *The Creative Years*. Greenwich, Conn.: The Seabury Press, Inc., 1959.

————. *Man's Need and God's Action*. Greenwich, Conn.: The Seabury Press, Inc., 1953.

Hunt, George L. *A Guide to Christian Unity*. St. Louis: The Bethany Press, 1958.

————. *Rediscovering the Church*. New York: Association Press, 1956.

Hutchison, John A. (ed.). *Christian Faith and Social Action*. New York: Charles Scribner's Sons, 1953.

James, William. *The Varieties of Religious Experience*. New York: Longmans, Green & Co., Inc., 1902.

Jessup, T. E., *et al*. *The Christian Understanding of Man*. Chicago: Willett, Clark & Co., 1938.

Johnson, E. Ashby. *The Crucial Task of Theology*. Richmond, Va.: John Knox Press, 1958.

Johnson, F. Ernest (ed.). *Patterns of Faith in America Today*. New York: Harper & Brothers, 1957.

Johnson, Paul E. *Christian Love*. Nashville: Abingdon-Cokesbury Press, 1951.

————. *Personality and Religion*. Nashville: Abingdon Press, 1957.

————. *Psychology of Religion*. Rev. ed. Nashville: Abingdon Press, 1959.

Johnson, Robert C. *Authority in Protestant Theology*. Philadelphia: The Westminster Press, 1959.

Kierkegaard, Søren. *Concluding Unscientific Postscript*. Princeton, N. J.: Princeton University Press, 1941.

————. *Philosophical Fragments*. Princeton, N. J.: Princeton University Press, 1936.

————. *The Sickness Unto Death*. Princeton, N. J.: Princeton University Press, 1941.

Kimmel, William, and Clive, Geoffrey (eds.). *Dimensions of Faith*. New York: Twayne Publishers, 1960.

Kimpel, Ben F. *Language and Religion: A Semantic Preface to a Philosophy of Religion*. New York: Philosophical Library, Inc., 1957.

Koenig, Robert E. *The Use of the Bible with Adults*. Philadelphia: Christian Education Press, 1959.

Kraemer, Hendrik. *A Theology of the Laity*. London: Lutterworth Press, 1958.

————. *The Communication of the Christian Faith*. Philadelphia: The Westminster Press, 1956.

Krumm, John M. *Modern Heresies: A Guide to Straight Thinking about Religion*. Greenwich, Conn.: The Seabury Press, Inc., 1961.

Leach, Max. *Christianity and Mental Health*. Dubuque, Iowa: William C. Brown Company, Publishers, 1957.

Leavenworth, Lynn (ed.). *Great Themes in Theology*. Philadelphia: Judson Press, 1958.

LeFevre, Perry D. *The Christian Teacher*. Nashville: Abingdon Press, 1958.

Leibrecht, Walter (ed.). *Religion and Culture: Essays in Honor of Paul Tillich*. New York: Harper & Brothers, 1959.

Littell, Franklin H. *The German Phoenix*. Garden City, N. Y.: Doubleday & Company, Inc., 1960.

Little, Sara. *Learning Together in the Christian Fellowship*. Richmond, Va.: John Knox Press, 1956.

_____. *The Role of the Bible in Contemporary Christian Education*. Richmond, Va.: John Knox Press, 1961.

Loos, A. William (ed.). *Religious Faith and World Culture*. New York: Prentice-Hall, Inc., 1951.

McCann, Richard V. *Delinquency: Sickness or Sin?* New York: Harper & Brothers, 1957.

McGavran, Donald A. *The Bridges of God*. London: World Dominion Press, 1955.

Machen, J. Gresham. *The Christian View of Man*. Grand Rapids, Mich.: Wm. B. Eerdsmans Publishing Co., 1947.

Maritain, Jacques. *Approaches to God*. New York: Harper & Brothers, 1954

Martin, Bernard. *The Healing Ministry in the Church*. Richmond, Va.: John Knox Press, 1960.

Marty, Martin E. *The New Shape of American Religion*. New York: Harper & Brothers, 1959.

Mascall, E. L. *Christian Theology and Natural Science*. New York: The Ronald Press Company, 1957.

Maves, Paul B. (ed.). *The Church and Mental Health*. New York: Charles Scribner's Sons, 1953.

_____, and Cedarleaf, J. Lennart. *Older People and the Church*. Nashville: Abingdon Press, 1949.

Meehl, Paul, *et al. What, Then, Is Man? A Symposium of Theology, Psychology, and Psychiatry*. St. Louis: Concordia Publishing House, 1958.

Meland, Bernard E. *Faith and Culture*. New York: Oxford University Press, Inc., 1953.

Michalson, Carl. *Faith for Personal Crises*. New York: Charles Scribner's Sons, 1958.

Miller, Allen. *Invitation to Theology: Resources for Christian Nurture and Discipline*. Philadelphia: Christian Education Press, 1958.

Miller, Donald G. *The Nature and Mission of the Church*. Richmond, Va.: John Knox Press, 1957.

Minear, Paul S. *Horizons of Christian Community*. St. Louis: The Bethany Press, 1959.

_____ (ed.). *The Nature of the Unity We Seek*. St. Louis: The Bethany Press, 1958.

Mohan, Robert P. (ed.). *Technology and Christian Culture*. Washington: The Catholic University of America Press, 1960.

Monsma, John C. (ed.). *The Evidence of God in an Expanding Universe*. New York: G. P. Putnam's Sons, 1958.

Moreau, Jules L. *Language and Religious Language*. Philadelphia: The Westminster Press, 1960.

Mould, Elmer W. K. *The World-View of Jesus*. New York: Harper & Brothers, 1941.

Mounier, Emmanuel. *The Character of Man*. New York: Harper & Brothers, 1959.

Muehl, William. *Politics for Christians*. New York: Association Press, 1956.

Muelder, Walter G. *Foundations of the Responsible Society: A Comprehensive Survey of Christian Social Ethics*. Nashville: Abingdon Press, 1959.

————. *Religion and Economic Responsibility*. New York: Charles Scribner's Sons, 1953.

Musselman, G. Paul. *The Church on the Urban Frontier*. Greenwich, Conn.: The Seabury Press, Inc., 1960.

Nash, Arnold (ed.). *Protestant Thought in the Twentieth Century*. New York: The Macmillan Co., 1951.

Neill, Stephen. *A Genuinely Human Existence*. Garden City, N. Y.: Doubleday & Company, Inc., 1959.

————. *The Christian Character*. New York: Association Press, 1955.

————. *Christian Faith Today*. Baltimore: Penguin Books, Inc., 1955.

————. *Christian Holiness*. New York: Harper & Brothers, 1960.

Nelson, J. Robert (ed.). *Christian Unity in North America*. St. Louis: The Bethany Press, 1958.

Niblett, William R. *Christian Education in a Secular Society*. New York: Oxford University Press, Inc., 1960.

Nichols, Roy F. *Religion and American Democracy*. Baton Rouge: Louisiana State University Press, 1959.

Nida, Eugene A. *Customs and Cultures*. New York: Harper & Brothers, 1954.

————. *God's Word in Man's Language*. New York: Harper & Brothers, 1952.

————. *Message and Mission: The Communication of the Christian Faith*. New York: Harper & Brothers, 1960.

Niebuhr, H. Richard. *Christ and Culture*. New York: Harper & Brothers, 1951.

————. *The Kingdom of God in America*. Chicago: Willett, Clark and Company, 1937.

————. *Radical Monotheism and Western Culture*. New York: Harper & Brothers, 1960.

Niebuhr, Reinhold. *Moral Man and Immoral Society*. New York: Charles Scribner's Sons, 1932.

————. *The Nature and Destiny of Man*. 2 Vols. New York: Charles Scribner's Sons, 1941-1943.

————. *Pious and Secular America*. New York: Charles Scribner's Sons, 1958.

————. *The Self and the Dramas of History*. New York: Charles Scribner's Sons, 1955.

Nygren, Anders. *Agape and Eros*. Philadelphia: The Westminster Press, 1953.

Oates, Wayne E. *Religious Dimensions of Personality*. New York: Association Press, 1957.

Obenhaus, Victor. *The Responsible Christian*. Chicago: University of Chicago Press, 1957.

Outler, Albert. *Psychotherapy and the Christian Message*. New York: Harper & Brothers, 1954.

Painter, L. V. N. *Luther on Education*. St. Louis: Concordia Publishing House, 1928.

Pelikan, Jaroslav. *The Riddle of Roman Catholicism*. Nashville: Abingdon Press, 1959.

Phenix, P. H. *Religious Concerns in Contemporary Education*. New York: Bureau of Publications, Teachers College, Columbia University, 1959.

Phillips, J. B. *The Gospels Translated into Modern English*. New York: The Macmillan Co., 1953.

_____. *Letters to Young Churches*. New York: The Macmillan Co., 1952.

Pittenger, W. Norman. *The Historic Faith and a Changing World*. New York: Oxford University Press, Inc., 1950.

_____. *Rethinking the Christian Message*. Greenwich, Conn.: The Seabury Press, Inc., 1956.

_____. *Theology and Reality*. Greenwich, Conn.: The Seabury Press, Inc., 1955.

Poteat, Edwin M. *Jesus' Belief in Man*. Nashville: Abingdon Press, 1956.

Pratt, James B. *Eternal Values in Religion*. New York: The Macmillan Co., 1950.

_____. *The Religious Consciousness*. New York: The Macmillan Co., 1930.

Rall, Harris F. *Religion as Salvation*. Nashville: Abingdon Press, 1953.

Ramsdell, Edward T. *The Christian Perspective*. Nashville: Abingdon Press, 1950.

Rasmussen, Albert T. *Christian Social Ethics*. Englewood Cliffs, N. J.: Prentice-Hall, Inc., 1956.

Rauschenbusch, Walter. *Christianizing the Social Order*. New York: The Macmillan Co., 1912.

_____. *Rauschenbusch Reader*, ed. Benson Y. Landis. New York: Harper & Brothers, 1957.

Raven, Charles E. *Natural Religion and Christian Theology*. Cambridge, England: Cambridge University Press, 1953.

Read, David H. C. *The Communication of the Gospel*. London: S. C. M. Press, 1956.

Religious Education Association. *What Is the Nature of Man: Images of Man in Our American Culture*. Philadelphia: Christian Education Press, 1959.

Rhodes, Arnold B. (ed.). *The Church Faces the Isms*. Nashville: Abingdon Press, 1958.

Richardson, Alan, and Wolfgang Schweitzer (eds.). *Biblical Authority for Today*. Philadelphia: The Westminster Press, 1951.

Roberts, David E. *The Grandeur and Misery of Man*. New York: Oxford University Press, Inc., 1955.

_____. *Psychotherapy and the Christian View of Man*. New York: Charles Scribner's Sons, 1954.

Robertson, E. H. *Man's Estimate of Man*. Richmond, Va.: John Knox Press, 1958.

Ross, Floyd H. *Addressed to Christians: Isolationism vs. World Community*. New York: Harper & Brothers, 1950.

Rutenber, Culbert G. *The Reconciling Gospel*. Philadelphia: Judson Press, 1960.

Schilling, S. Paul. *Methodism and Society in Theological Perspective*. Nashville: Abingdon Press, 1960.

Schweitzer, Albert. *The Philosophy of Civilization: Civilization and Ethics*. London: A. and C. Black, 1929.

Scott, Nathan A. (ed.). *The Tragic Vision and the Christian Faith*. New York: Association Press, 1957.

Shinn, Roger L. *The Existentialist Posture*. New York: Association Press, 1959.

Sinnott, Edmund W. *Two Roads to Truth*. New York: The Viking Press, Inc., 1953.

Sisemore, John T. *The Sunday School Ministry to Adults*. Nashville: Convention Press, 1959.

Sloyan, Gerard S. (ed.). *Shaping the Christian Message*. New York: The Macmillan Co., 1958.

Smethurst, Arthur F. *Modern Science and Christian Belief*. Nashville: Abingdon Press, 1955.

Smith, Huston. *The Purposes of Higher Education.* New York: Harper & Brothers, 1955.

Smith, James Ward, and Jamison, A. Leland (eds.). *Religious Perspectives in American Culture.* Princeton, N. J.: Princeton University Press, 1961.

——————, and Jamison, A. Leland (eds.). *The Shaping of American Religion.* Princeton, N. J.: Princeton University Press, 1961.

Snyder, Alton G. *Teaching Adults.* Philadelphia: Judson Press, 1959.

Soper, David W. *Major Voices in American Theology.* Philadelphia: The Westminster Press, 1953.

Spike, Robert W. *In But Not of the World.* New York: Association Press, 1957.

Spurrier, William A. *Guide to the Christian Faith.* New York: Charles Scribner's Sons, 1952.

Stinnette, Charles R., Jr. *Faith, Freedom and Selfhood.* Greenwich, Conn.: The Seabury Press, Inc., 1959.

Strunk, Orlo, Jr. (ed.). *Readings in the Psychology of Religion.* Nashville: Abingdon Press, 1959.

Tavard, H. G. *The Church, the Layman and the Modern World.* New York: The Macmillan Co., 1959.

Taylor, Marvin J. (ed.). *Religious Education: A Comprehensive Survey.* Nashville: Abingdon Press, 1960.

Temple, William. *Nature, Man and God.* London: Macmillan & Company, Ltd., 1934.

Thompson, Kenneth W. *Christian Ethics and the Dilemmas of Foreign Policy.* Durham, N. C.: Duke University Press, 1959.

Thouless, Robert H. *Authority and Freedom: Some Psychological Problems of Religious Belief.* Greenwich, Conn.: The Seabury Press, Inc., 1954.

Tillich, Paul. *Biblical Religion and the Search for Ultimate Reality.* Chicago: University of Chicago Press, 1955.

——————. *The Courage to Be.* New Haven: Yale University Press, 1952.

——————. *Dynamics of Faith.* New York: Harper & Brothers, 1957.

——————. *Systematic Theology.* Chicago: University of Chicago Press, 1952.

——————. *Theology of Culture.* New York: Oxford University Press, 1959.

Torrance, T. F. *Conflict and Agreement in the Church.* London: Lutterworth Press, 1959.

Toynbee, Arnold J. *An Historian's Approach to Religion.* New York: Oxford University Press, Inc., 1956.

——————. *Christianity Among the Religions of the World.* New York: Charles Scribner's Sons, 1957.

Trueblood, D. Elton. *Philosophy of Religion.* New York: Harper & Brothers, 1957.

Underwood, Kenneth W. *Protestant and Catholic: Religious and Social Interaction in an Industrial Community.* Boston: Beacon Press, 1957.

Van der Veldt, James H., and Odenwald, Robert P. *Psychiatry and Catholicism.* New York: McGraw-Hill Book Co., Inc., 1952.

Van Deusen, Dayton G. *Redemptive Counseling.* Richmond, Va.: John Knox Press, 1960.

Van Dusen, Henry P. *Spirit, Son and Father.* New York: Charles Scribner's Sons, 1958.

Vidler, Alex R. *Christian Belief and This World*. Greenwich, Conn.: The Seabury Press, Inc., 1957.

Viner, Jacob. *Religious Thought and Economic Society: The European Background*. Smith, James Ward, and Jamison, A. Leland, eds. Princeton, N. J.: Princeton University Press, 1961.

Wach, Joachim. *Sociology of Religion*. Chicago: University of Chicago Press, 1944.

Ward, Leo R. *Catholic Life, U. S. A.* St. Louis: B. Herder Book Co., 1959.

Webber, George W. *God's Colony in Man's World*. Nashville: Abingdon Press, 1960.

White, Ernest. *Christian Life and the Unconscious*. New York: Harper & Brothers, 1956.

Whittemore, Lewis B. *The Church and Secular Education*. Greenwich, Conn.: The Seabury Press, Inc., 1960.

Wieman, Henry Nelson, and Wieman, Regina Westcott. *Normative Psychology of Religion*. New York: Thomas Y. Crowell Company, 1935.

Williams, Colin W. *John Wesley's Theology Today*. Nashville: Abingdon Press, 1960.

Williams, Daniel Day. *God's Grace and Man's Hope*. New York: Harper & Brothers, 1949.

_____. *What Present-Day Theologians Are Thinking*. Rev. ed. New York: Harper & Brothers, 1959.

Williams, J. Paul. *What Americans Believe and How They Worship*. New York: Harper & Brothers, 1952.

Winter, Gibson. *The Suburban Captivity of the Churches*. Garden City, N. Y.: Doubleday & Company, Inc., 1961.

Wise, Carroll A. *Psychiatry and the Bible*. New York: Harper & Brothers, 1956.

_____. *Religion in Illness and Health*. New York: Harper & Brothers, 1942.

Witherington, H. C. *Psychology of Religion: A Christian Interpretation*. Grand Rapids, Mich.: Wm. B. Eerdmans Publishing Co., 1955.

World Council of Churches. *Man's Disorder and God's Design*. New York: Harper & Brothers, 1948.

Wright, G. Ernest. *God Who Acts: Biblical Theology as Recital*. Chicago: Henry Regnery Co., 1952.

Wynn, J. C. *How Christian Parents Face Family Problems*. Philadelphia: The Westminster Press, 1955.

Yarnold, Greville D. *The Spiritual Crisis of the Scientific Age*. New York: The Macmillan Co., 1959.

Ziegler, Earl F. *Christian Education of Adults*. Philadelphia: The Westminster Press, 1958.

C. SELECTED WRITINGS IN THE PHILOSOPHY OF CHRISTIAN EDUCATION

Bower, William C. *Character Through Creative Experience*. Chicago: University of Chicago Press, 1930.

_____. *Christ and Christian Education*. New York and Nashville: Abingdon-Cokesbury Press, 1943.

_____. *Church and State in Education.* Chicago: University of Chicago Press, 1944.

_____. *The Curriculum of Religious Education.* New York: Charles Scribner's Sons, 1925.

_____. *The Living Bible.* New York: Harper & Brothers, 1946.

_____. *Moral and Spiritual Values in Education.* Lexington: University of Kentucky Press, 1952.

Bushnell, Horace. *Christian Nurture.* New Haven: Yale University Press, Reprinted 1947.

Byrne, Herbert W. *A Christian Approach to Education: A Bibliocentric View.* Grand Rapids, Mich.: Zondervan Publishing House, 1961.

Chamberlin, J. Gordon. *Parents and Religion: A Preface to Christian Education.* Philadelphia: The Westminster Press, 1961.

Chave, Ernest J. *A Functional Approach to Religious Education.* Chicago: University of Chicago Press, 1947.

_____. *Personality Development in Children.* Chicago: University of Chicago Press, 1937.

Clark, Gordon H. *A Christian Philosophy of Education.* Grand Rapids, Mich.: Wm. B. Eerdmans Publishing Co., 1946.

_____. *A Christian View of Men and Things.* Grand Rapids, Mich.: Wm. B. Eerdmans Publishing Co., 1952.

Coe, George A. *Education for Citizenship.* New York: Charles Scribner's Sons, 1932.

_____. *Education in Religion and Morals.* New York: Fleming H. Revell Company, 1904.

_____. *Law and Freedom in the School.* Chicago: University of Chicago Press, 1924.

_____. *The Motives of Men.* New York: Charles Scribner's Sons, 1928.

_____. *The Religion of a Mature Mind.* New York: Fleming H. Revell Co., 1902.

_____. *A Social Theory of Religious Education.* New York: Charles Scribner's Sons, 1917.

_____. *The Spiritual Life.* New York: Eaton and Mains, 1900.

_____. *What Ails Our Youth?* New York: Charles Scribner's Sons, 1924.

_____. *What Is Christian Education?* New York: Charles Scribner's Sons, 1929.

_____. *What Is Religion Doing to our Consciences?* New York: Charles Scribner's Sons, 1943.

Cully, Iris V. *The Dynamics of Christian Education.* Philadelphia: The Westminster Press, 1958.

Elliott, Harrison S. *The Bearing of Psychology upon Religion.* New York: Association Press, 1927.

_____. *Can Religious Education Be Christian?* New York: The Macmillan Co., 1940.

_____. *The Process of Group Thinking.* New York: Association Press, 1928.

_____, and Elliott, Grace L. *Solving Personal Problems.* New York: Henry Holt & Co., Inc., 1936.

Fahs, Sophia L. *Today's Children and Yesterday's Heritage.* Boston: Beacon Press,

1952.

Fallaw, Wesner. *Church Education for Tomorrow.* Philadelphia: The Westminster Press, 1960.

_____. *The Modern Parent and the Teaching Church.* New York: The Macmillan Co., 1946.

_____. *Toward Spiritual Security.* Philadelphia: The Westminster Press, 1952.

Gaebelein, Frank E. *Christian Education in a Democracy.* New York: Oxford University Press, Inc., 1951.

_____. *The Pattern of God's Truth.* New York: Oxford University Press, Inc., 1954.

Hartshorne, Hugh. *Character in Human Relations.* New York: Charles Scribner's Sons, 1932.

_____. *Childhood and Character.* Boston: Beacon Press, 1919.

Horne, Herman H. *The Democratic Philosophy of Education.* New York: The Macmillan Co., 1932.

_____. *Jesus, the Master Teacher.* New York: Association Press, 1920.

_____. *The Philosophy of Christian Education.* New York: Fleming H. Revell Co., 1937.

_____. *The Philosophy of Education.* New York: The Macmillan Co., 1904.

_____. *This New Education.* New York: The Abingdon Press, 1931.

_____. *The Teacher as Artist.* Boston: Houghton Mifflin Company, 1917.

Hunter, Edith F. *The Questioning Child and Religion.* Boston: The Starr King Press, 1956.

International Council of Religious Education. *Christian Education Today.* Chicago, 1940.

Jaarsma, Cornelius R. (ed.). *Fundamentals in Christian Education.* Grand Rapids, Mich.: Wm. B. Eerdmans Publishing Co., 1953.

Le Bar, Lois E. *Children in the Bible School.* Westwood, N. J.: Fleming H. Revell Co., 1952.

_____. *Education That Is Christian.* Westwood, N. J.: Fleming H. Revell Co., 1958.

Ligon, Ernest M. *A Greater Generation.* New York: The Macmillan Co., 1948.

_____. *Dimensions of Character.* New York: The Macmillan Co., 1956.

_____. *The Psychology of Christian Personality.* New York: The Macmillan Co., 1935.

_____. *Their Future Is Now.* New York: The Macmillan Co., 1939.

Little, Lawrence C. (ed.). *Formulating the Objectives of Christian Adult Education.* Pittsburgh: The Department of Religious Education, University of Pittsburgh, 1958.

_____ (ed.). *Guidelines for the Development of Christian Education Curricula for Adults.* Pittsburgh: The Department of Religious Education, University of Pittsburgh, 1961.

_____ (ed.). *The Future Course of Christian Adult Education.* Pittsburgh: University of Pittsburgh Press, 1959.

_____, (ed.). *Religion and Education for Professional Responsibility.* Pittsburgh: The Department of Religious Education, University of Pittsburgh, 1956.

————— (ed.). *Selected Addresses and Papers Presented in a Workshop on the Curriculum of Christian Education for Adults.* Pittsburgh: The Department of Religious Education, University of Pittsburgh, 1961.

Mason, Harold C. *Abiding Values in Christian Education.* Westwood, N. J.: Fleming H. Revell Co., 1955.

The Methodist Church, Curriculum Committee of the General Board of Education. *Foundations of Christian Teaching in Methodist Churches.* The Committee, 1960.

Miller, Randolph C. *Be Not Anxious.* Greenwich, Conn.: The Seabury Press, Inc., 1957.

—————. *Biblical Theology and Christian Education.* New York: Charles Scribner's Sons, 1956.

—————. *The Clue to Christian Education.* New York: Charles Scribner's Sons, 1950.

—————. *Christian Nurture and the Church.* New York: Charles Scribner's Sons, 1961.

—————. *Education for Christian Living.* Englewood Cliffs, N. J.: Prentice-Hall, Inc., 1956.

Munro, Harry C. *Protestant Nurture.* Englewood Cliffs, N. J.: Prentice-Hall, Inc., 1956.

Murch, James D. *Christian Education and the Local Church.* Cincinnati: Standard Publishing Foundation, 1943.

Murray, A. Victor. *Education into Religion.* New York: Harper & Brothers, 1954.

—————. *Natural Religion and Christian Theology.* New York: Harper & Brothers, 1955.

—————. *Personal Experience and the Historic Faith.* New York: Harper & Brothers, 1955.

National Council of the Churches of Christ in the U. S. A., Division of Christian Education. *A Guide for the Curriculum in Christian Education.* Chicago, 1955.

Pope Pius XI. *Christian Education of Youth.* New York: The America Press, 1936.

Redden, John D., and Ryan, Francis A. *A Catholic Philosophy of Education.* Milwaukee: The Bruce Publishing Co., 1942.

Richardson, Norman E. *The Christ of the Classroom.* New York: The Macmillan Co., 1931.

Schreyer, George M. *Christian Education in Action.* New York: Comet Press, 1957.

Sherrill, Lewis J. *The Gift of Power.* New York: The Macmillan Co., 1955.

—————. *Guilt and Redemption.* Richmond, Va.: John Knox Press, 1945.

—————. *Lift Up Your Eyes.* Richmond, Va.: John Knox Press, 1949.

—————. *The Opening Doors of Childhood.* New York: The Macmillan Co., 1939.

—————. *The Rise of Christian Education.* New York: The Macmillan Co., 1944.

—————. *The Struggle of the Soul.* New York: The Macmillan Co., 1951.

Smart, James D. *The Teaching Ministry of the Church.* Philadelphia: The Westminster Press, 1954.

Smith, H. Shelton. *Changing Conceptions of Original Sin: A Study in American Theology Since 1750.* New York: Charles Scribner's Sons, 1955.

—————. *Faith and Nurture.* New York: Charles Scribner's Sons, 1941.

Soares, Theodore G. *Religious Education*. Chicago: University of Chicago Press, 1928.

————. *The Social Institutions and Ideals of the Bible*. New York: The Abingdon Press, 1915.

Vieth, Paul H. *The Church School*. Philadelphia: The Westminster Press, 1957.

————. *How to Teach in the Church School*. Philadelphia: The Westminster Press, 1935.

————. *Improving Your Sunday School*. Philadelphia: The Westminster Press, 1930.

————. *Objectives in Religious Education*. New York: Harper & Brothers, 1930.

————. *Teaching for Christian Living*. St. Louis: The Bethany Press, 1929.

————, (ed.). *The Church and Christian Education*. St. Louis: The Bethany Press, 1947.

Waterink, Jan. *Basic Concepts in Christian Pedagogy*. Grand Rapids, Mich.: Wm. B. Eerdmans Publishing Co., 1954.

Weigle, Luther A. *American Idealism*. New Haven: Yale University Press, 1928.

————. *Jesus and the Educational Method*. New York and Nashville: Abingdon-Cokesbury Press, 1939.

————. *Talks to Sunday-school Teachers*. New York: George H. Doran Company, 1920.

————. *The Training of Children in the Christian Family*. Boston: Pilgrim Press, 1922.

Wyckoff, D. Campbell. *The Gospel and Christian Education*. Philadelphia: The Westminster Press, 1959.

————. *The Task of Christian Education*. Philadelphia: The Westminster Press, 1955.

————. *Theory and Design in Christian Education Curriculum*. Philadelphia: The Westminster Press, 1961.

Index